The Making of the Modern Mediterranean

The Making of the Modern Mediterranean

Views from the South

Edited by Judith E. Tucker

UNIVERSITY OF CALIFORNIA PRESS

University of California Press, one of the most distinguished university presses in the United States, enriches lives around the world by advancing scholarship in the humanities, social sciences, and natural sciences. Its activities are supported by the UC Press Foundation and by philanthropic contributions from individuals and institutions. For more information, visit www.ucpress.edu.

University of California Press
Oakland, California

Library of Congress Cataloging-in-Publication Data

Names: Tucker, Judith E., editor, contributor. | Abi-Mershed, Osama, contributor. | Burke, Edmund, 1940– contributor. | Clancy-Smith, Julia Ann, contributor. | Granara, William, contributor. | Matar, N. I. (Nabil I.), 1949– contributor. | White, Joshua M., 1981– contributor.
Title: The making of the modern Mediterranean : views from the south / edited by Judith Tucker.
Description: Oakland, California : University of California Press, [2019] | Includes bibliographical references and index. |
Identifiers: LCCN 2019001399 (print) | LCCN 2019005108 (ebook) | ISBN 9780520973206 (ebook and ePDF) | ISBN 9780520304598 (cloth : alk. paper) | ISBN 9780520304604 (pbk. : alk. paper)
Subjects: LCSH: Mediterranean Region—History.
Classification: LCC DE83 (ebook) | LCC DE83 .M34 2019 (print) | DDC 909/.09822—dc23
LC record available at https://lccn.loc.gov/2019001399

Manufactured in the United States of America

26 25 24 23 22 21 20 19
10 9 8 7 6 5 4 3 2 1

In memory of Faruk Tabak (1954–2008),
our friend and colleague, man of the Mediterranean

CONTENTS

ILLUSTRATIONS

ACKNOWLEDGMENTS

The idea for this volume arose from a conference, "The Mediterranean Re-imagined," held at Georgetown University in March 2013, under the auspices of the Georgetown University Center for Contemporary Arab Studies (CCAS) and chaired by Professor Osama Abi-Mershed, then director of CCAS. The conference was held, in part, to commemorate the work of our late colleague Faruk Tabak (1954–2008), in particular his magisterial *The Waning of the Mediterranean, 1550–1870: A Geohistorical Approach* (Johns Hopkins University Press, 2008). All of the chapters in this volume emerged from papers delivered at this conference, although they have undergone substantial revision in the interim.

I would like to thank Osama for encouraging us to rethink the Mediterranean from the southern shores. A number of individuals from the CCAS staff assisted with the planning and running of the conference, including, in particular, Marina Krekorian and Elisabeth Sexton. Vicki Valosik from CCAS also provided valuable assistance in the early stages of the editing.

We benefited from the generosity of colleagues, who devoted precious time and attention to reviewing the manuscript and offered many helpful suggestions that greatly improved the coherence and analytical reach of the volume. I am truly indebted to them. Ilham Khuri-Makdisi and Konstantina Zanou read the entire manuscript and drew on their extensive knowledge of the history of the Mediterranean to guide us in our revisions. Sharif Elmusa gave the introduction a close reading and provided valuable guidance on the relevant literature of space and place.

Niels Hooper, from the University of California Press, supported this project from the beginning and employed his editor's eye in ways that greatly enhanced the substance and the look of the book. Robin Manley and Kate Hoffman, also from the press, gave critical attention and assistance during the production process and in the preparation of the final manuscript. Ann Donahue was a superb copyeditor, whose broad knowledge, high standards, and attention to detail whipped the book into its final and, I hope you will agree, very fine shape.

I want to thank, last but not least, my colleagues who contributed chapters to this book. It is an honor for me to have edited a volume that contains the work of scholars I so admire. And the long years of correspondence with contributors, during which I dunned them repeatedly for one thing or another, were very pleasant ones thanks to the graciousness and collegiality of all.

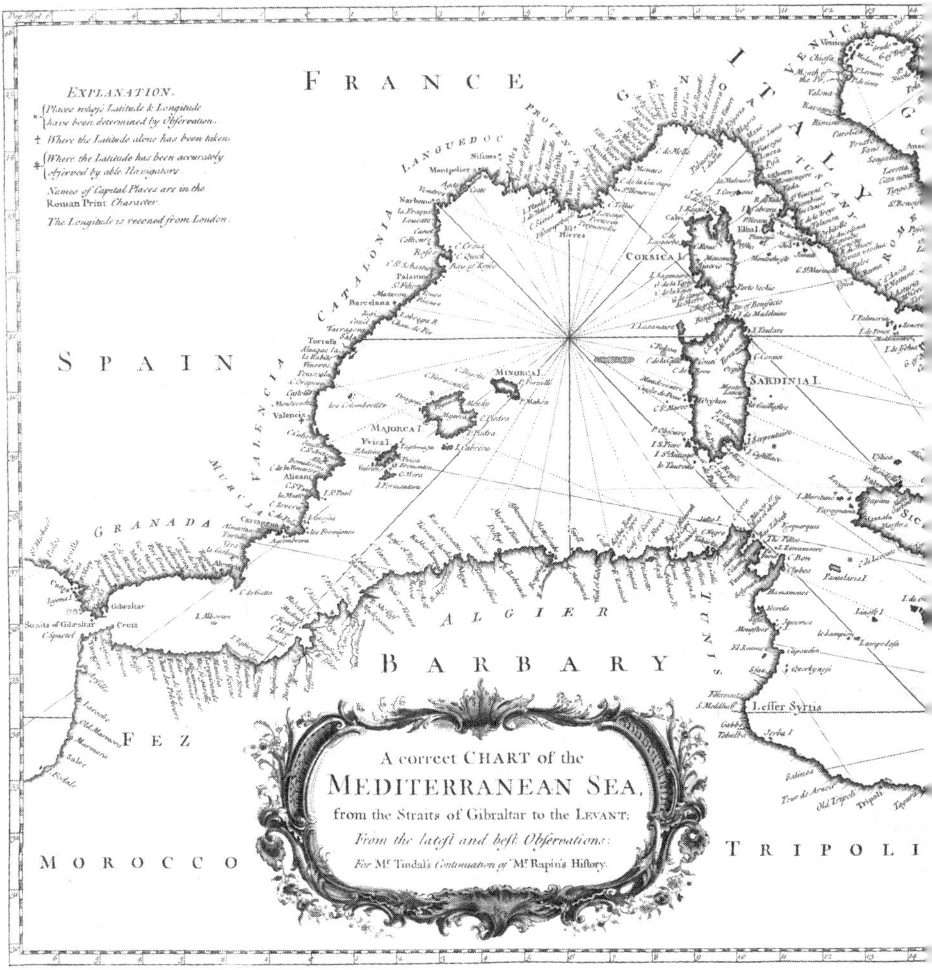

Richard William Seale, chart of the Mediterranean Sea, 1745. Courtesy of Wikimedia Commons.

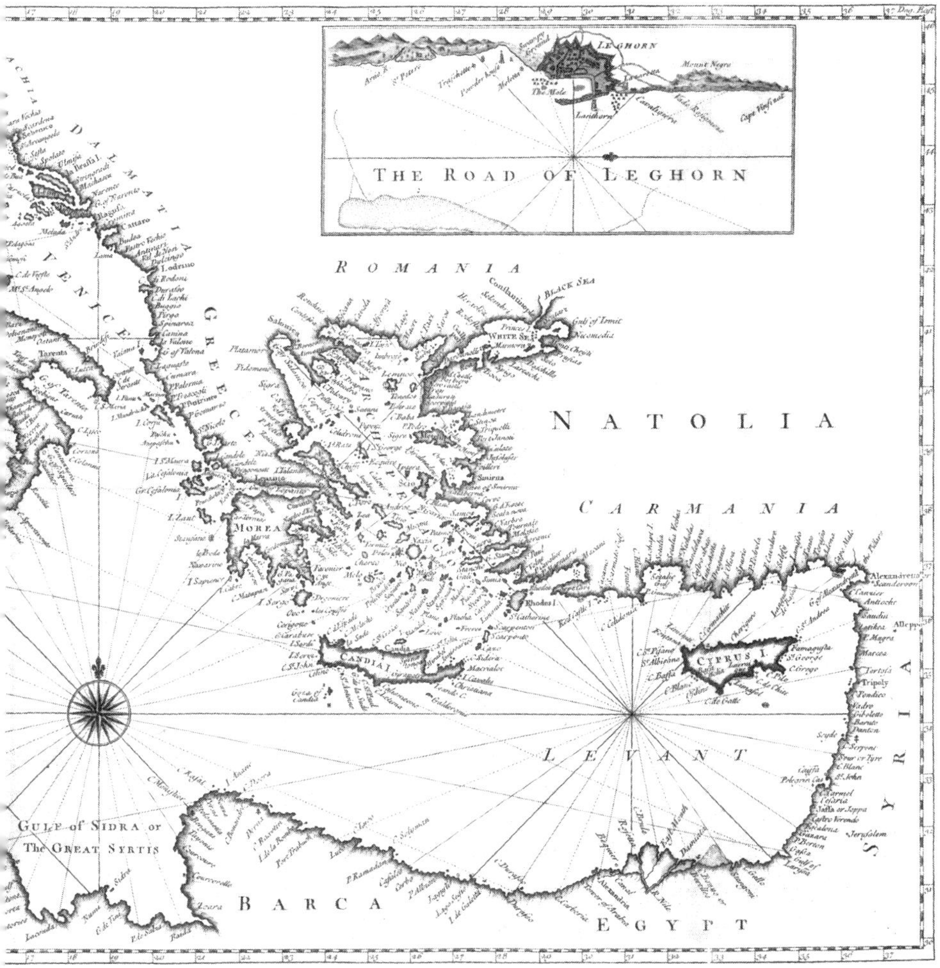
THE ROAD OF LEGHORN
LEGHORN
Mount Negro
The Mole
ROMANIA
BLACK SEA
NATOLIA
CARMANIA
MOREA
CANDIA I.
Rhodes I.
CYPRUS I.
LEVANT
GULF of SIDRA or
The GREAT SYRTIS
BARCA
EGYPT
SYRIA
Alexandretta
Scanderoon
Aleppo
Tripoly
Jerusalem

Introduction

Judith E. Tucker

THINKING ABOUT THE MEDITERRANEAN

What is the Mediterranean? What are its borders, its defining characteristics? Is it a space of connection or an arena of conflict? Does it make sense as a unit of historical analysis? What forces of nature or politics or culture or economics have made the Mediterranean, and how long have they endured, or how long will they endure? How can we most productively think about the Mediterranean as a place? And, most germane to this collection, what happens when we rethink the Mediterranean from its southern or eastern shores? These questions and tensions linger in the field of Mediterranean studies, despite its embrace of the general concept of coherence.

At the outset, there is the issue of geography. John Agnew, in his essay on space and place, draws our attention to the different ways of thinking about places: as "nodes in space" that are acted on by external economic, social, or physical processes, on the one hand, or as "milieus" that play a role in shaping these processes, on the other—or, as he terms it, a "geometric conception of place as a mere part of space," as opposed to "place as a distinctive coming together in space."[1] One of the best illustrations of these different ways of thinking about place, for Agnew, comes directly out of the study of the Mediterranean:

> If the classic work of Fernand Braudel (1949) tends to view the Mediterranean over the long term as a grand space or spatial crossroads in exchange, trade, diffusion and connectivity between a set of grand source areas to the south, north and east, the recent revisionist account of Peregrine Horden and Nicholas Purcell (2000) views the Mediterranean region as a congeries of micro-ecologies or places separated by distinctive agricultural and social practices in which connectivity and mobility

> within the region is more a response to the management of environmental and social risks than the simple outcome of extra-regional initiatives.[2]

The difference between Braudel's vision of the Mediterranean as a watery space of economic and cultural connections, forged by forces emanating from an evolving world economic system, and Horden and Purcell's vision of the Mediterranean as a site of multiple distinct places linked by mutual needs is more than a matter of emphasis. Braudel asserts a claim to physical Mediterranean unity on the basis of shared environment and climate, but his work pivots in the main around the Mediterranean as a "human unit" of "collective destinies" arising from the movement of peoples and goods on the sea, as a result of the economics of trade and the politics of empire in the early modern period. It was these seaborne movements in time and space that produced striking similarities and overlaps in patterns of civilization and conflict.[3] For Horden and Purcell, on the other hand, the point of departure is the land around the shores: "The distinctiveness of Mediterranean history results (we propose) from the paradoxical coexistence of a milieu of relatively easy seaborne communications with a quite unusually fragmented topography of microregions in the sea's coastlands and islands."[4]

There is no geographic unity as such to the Mediterranean but rather a set of places or microecologies that share an environmental precariousness and are driven, as a result, to seek out connections with each other to protect against their vulnerabilities. The Mediterranean as a body of water seems to play a secondary role—important for the facilitation of such connections, while the most significant action has moved to the coasts and the islands. While neither Braudel nor Horden and Purcell doubt the significance or connectivity of the Mediterranean, they handle the issue of the Mediterranean as a place very differently: the former draws our attention to the sea and its ties to a world beyond, whereas the latter look to the shore and the variety of its human settlements.[5]

The physical boundaries of the Mediterranean have been called into broader question. When we talk of the Mediterranean as a region, we usually think of the sea, its islands, and its littoral. David Abulafia, for instance, locates its boundaries, "where first nature and then man set them," at the Straits of Gibraltar in the west and the Dardanelles in the east. He includes the islands and port cities of the shores, "particularly those where cultures met and mixed."[6] Horden and Purcell suggest that the physical Mediterranean has been delimited within two distinct frames of reference: an *interactionist* approach, which looks to a history of commercial and cultural ties and therefore confines its gaze to the water, islands, and ports, and a more expansive *ecologizing* approach, which looks to physical geography—climate and soil in particular—and therefore expands into the hinterlands.[7] W. V. Harris points to a number of unresolved issues concerning the boundaries of the Mediterranean. What of its rivers, its hinterlands, and its inland mountains?

Should we include the valleys and basins of the rivers that flow into the Mediterranean? If the Mediterranean ends in the south at the edge of the desert, what is the comparable northern border? Is it a zone delimited by climate, or by patterns of agricultural production—the zone of the grape and the olive for example?[8] Or perhaps we should look to history, rather than simply to physical features, and draw the boundaries of the Mediterranean according to its economic and cultural connections.

Some recent historians have argued for an expansive spatial conception of the Mediterranean in connection with the movement of goods, people, cultures, and ideas. In their discussion of the Mediterranean in the nineteenth century as a space of fluid borders and mass migration, Maurizio Isabella and Konstantina Zanou describe a place where there was a "flux of peoples, cultures, and ideas" and "the ties created between the Mediterranean and its surrounding lands, from Portugal, to Russia and Anatolia, would at times leave observers with the sense that the basin bordered on regions beyond itself."[9] Patricia Lorcin further suggests, in a special issue of the *Journal of North African Studies*, that attention to the southern shores cannot but heighten our awareness of the deep hinterland of the Mediterranean and the role these shores played "in creating commercial, social and intellectual links far beyond the territories along its coastlines."[10]

The focus on connections leads to a second major debate, over issues of unity and conflict, in the discussion of the Mediterranean as a place: was the Mediterranean connected or fractured by its environmental features, trade patterns, cultural practices, religious identities, and political developments? Before Braudel's contribution, the work of Henri Pirenne had established a powerful paradigm of the Mediterranean as a theater of conflict, arising with the expansion of Islam into the region and its confrontation with Christian Europe. This vision of the Mediterranean as a "battlefield," in the words of Eric Dursteler, had and still has some purchase among subscribers to the "clash of civilizations" theory, although, as he notes, the contributions of Braudel, and more recently Horden and Purcell, make the case for the Mediterranean as a lively "bazaar." It is this interpretation that now dominates in the academy and has inspired a wave of new research and revisionist scholarship exploring the human activities that wove the many connecting strands.[11]

How scholars weigh in on the debate over unity and conflict seems to be strongly influenced by where they fix their attention. Environmental historians—arguably Braudel himself, as well as John McNeill and Faruk Tabak—embrace themes of unity and coherence, basing their arguments on the region as an ecological unit, as a single ecosystem or series of ecosystems that share ecological features. As McNeill observes, ecologists may differ on the details, but "all recognize its distinctiveness."[12] For Braudel, there is a signature Mediterranean climate, "which has imposed its uniformity on both landscape and ways of life" and is "the source of that even light which shines at the heart of the Mediterranean."[13] Tabak, in his study of the Mediterranean during the "waning" years from 1550 to 1870, contests the idea that the region was losing its coherence in the period, stressing instead a shared geohistory of climate change and vegetal migrations that transformed virtually all Mediterranean shores in similar ways.[14] And McNeill, concerned with Mediterranean mountain life and its decline in the nineteenth and early twentieth centuries, argues for a pervasive "ecological frailty" that unites the region in its time of growing marginalization.[15] The environmental approach weighs in on the side of unity, then, on the basis of shared climate, topography, and cropping patterns, all of which influenced both how the people of the region lived in relation to the natural world and how that relationship in turn shaped their social worlds.

Historians of the economy, and of trade in particular, also tend to find unity in the many interactions produced by the movement of people and goods between and among shores. Merchants, smugglers, pirates, and economic migrants of all stripes pursued economic interests along routes that crisscrossed the Mediterranean and fostered contact for the purposes of survival, if not profit. Biray Kolluoğlu and Meltem Toksöz, in the introduction to their edited volume on the cities of the Mediterranean, attribute the recent wave of interest in the region's port cities to current fascinations with "networks of flows of capital, commodities, peoples, information and knowledge," in which these cities played a starring role.[16] Horden and Purcell seek to integrate such an "interactionist" approach into their analysis by attending to "the normal rhythms of Mediterranean exchange. . . . Whether they take the form of *cabotage,* slave-raiding, piracy or pilgrimage, they act to bind the microecologies together."[17] And Julia Clancy-Smith develops this line of thought further in the context of the nineteenth century, with her attention to migration and the burgeoning hybridities of Mediterranean port cities, where laws and practices of locals and migrants were interacting and melding.[18] Although none of these analyses deny the history of conflict—the Mediterranean has certainly been the site of many disputes over trade routes, to say nothing of imperial adventures driven by bids for economic dominance—the doing of business and the seeking of employment seem to help shine a Braudelian "even light" on the region.

Study of the political sphere produces more ambivalence around the theme of Mediterranean unity. Much of the political history of the region has been written as narratives of empire and nation, a frame that privileges themes of expansion, conflict, resistance, and boundaries. Molly Greene points out that many historians of the Ottoman Empire embrace the image of the Mediterranean as a borderland, a space of conflict and confrontation rather than connection. A case in point is the critique of Braudel in Andrew Hess's *The Forgotten Frontier: A History of the Sixteenth Century Ibero-African Frontier.* Hess accuses Braudel of focusing on the cultural zone of Latin Christendom and therefore overplaying unity and connection; on the Ibero-African frontier, according to Hess, it was another world of cultural difference and conflict.[19] Nationalist scholarship in the modern period in both North Africa and Spain has followed in this vein, engrossed as it has been in the teleological task of tracing the path to the modern nation. In North Africa, historians have prioritized resistance to colonialism and the emergence of the state, downplaying European connections and influences. The writing of national history in Spain has swung between a paradigm of civilizational confrontation and, more recently, one of peaceful coexistence, with very little engagement between the two. In both cases, scant attention has been given to developments or connections beyond territorial Spain.[20] Perhaps it should not surprise us, given the fascination with conflicts and boundaries that characterizes the writing of political history in general, that the themes of connection recede when politics and the state are the loci of interest.

Ambivalence persists as well in the arena of culture and religion. Although few today would subscribe wholeheartedly to Pirenne's vision of the Mediterranean as the field of a pitched and prolonged battle between Christendom and Islam, the question of how to weigh the role played by religious difference endures. Greene elsewhere examines the argument that the arrival of northern Europeans in the seventeenth century ushered in a new era, in which economic competition replaced religious competition, and calls for more nuance on the grounds that the Mediterranean in the period was both a collection of sovereign states and a religious borderland. On the basis of her study of Orthodox Greeks who were Ottoman subjects, she traces tensions between religious solidarities and state sovereignties while noting the many business and security arrangements that crossed both national and religious boundaries.[21] Adnan A. Husain notes a parallel tension in looking at the Mediterranean in the medieval and early modern periods as a zone of interaction among the three monotheistic traditions. All three made universal claims about history and identity, but these "conflicting universalisms . . . nevertheless patterned and shaped one another in particular social and theological encounter."[22] Although there was religiously inspired conflict to be sure, Husain comes down squarely on the side of unity in the sense of shared patterns of hybridity, syncretism, and heterogeneity.

Others have turned their attention to the role of people on the move. Many individuals crossed religious and cultural borders, voluntarily or not: Dursteler points to his own work and that of E. Natalie Rothman on transimperial subjects in Venice and Istanbul and Robert Davis's research on abducted Christian slaves as tangible illustration of how cultural intermediaries acted to circulate religious and cultural knowledge.[23] Most authors eschew generalization: these kinds of cultural connections were far from static in their patterns and intensity but were influenced over time by developments in the economics and politics of the region.

This aspect of temporality, the ways in which Mediterranean studies has periodized the region and the implications for how we think about its coherence and connectivity, constitutes a third area where differences emerge. Most scholarship on the Mediterranean is anchored within one of four periods: the ancient, medieval, early modern, or modern. Concerns and premises often differ by period. The unity imposed by the Roman Empire on mare nostrum, for example, is a point of departure for those studying the ancient period, whereas the fragmentations and confrontations of the Arab conquests and the Crusades deeply concern medievalists. The scholarship on the early modern period has been among the most engaged with issues of connectivity in recent revisionist scholarship, while work on the nineteenth and twentieth centuries displays more ambivalence about a Mediterranean dominated by imperial designs and nationalist challenges.

Horden and Purcell capture the shifts in the ways historians have thought about the Mediterranean in their discussion of the contributions of "four men in a boat," the four historians in the twentieth century who had the biggest impact on the field, and who might be recast as four blind men confronting the Mediterranean elephant. Mikhail Rostovtzeff, a historian of the Roman and Hellenistic periods, was captured by the "grandly interactionist" ancient Mediterranean world of a connected urban vitality, whereas Henri Pirenne, focusing on the early medieval period, argued for the persistence of the unity of the Mediterranean until the seventh century, after which the disruptions of the Arab expansion severed many of the key connections. Shlomo Dov Goitein, with his attention to the later medieval period, brought connection back in with his detailed study of mobile Jewish merchants and their Mediterranean networks, and the last of the quartet, Braudel, made the case, as we well know, for a Mediterranean coherence in early modern times.[24] Extending Horden and Purcell's insights about the waxing and waning of the scholarly embrace of the Mediterranean as a unit to those who work on the nineteenth and twentieth centuries, we find that many historians of the modern period are resigned to the idea that connectivity was a casualty of the quickening and uneven pace of political and social change in colonial and postcolonial times.[25] Tabak places this turn away from notions of coherence among historians who work on even earlier periods, and notes that,

> This volte-face in the historiography of the Inner Sea away from holistic accounts to singular and sectional histories can therefore be attributed to the underlying assumptions that the forces that had fostered unity along the Mediterranean had, in its autumn, lost their coherence and that the destiny shared by polities in the basin at the zenith of its power had consequently ceased to be common.[26]

Others take the view that the conceptual unity imposed on the nineteenth- and twentieth-century Mediterranean is, in any case, a unity of European imperial design anchored in a hegemonic goal of control of sea and shore, a concept to be resisted by the southern shores.[27] The Mediterranean is not the same place across time, neither in its power relations nor even in terms of its climate, flora, and fauna, as historians of the environment have been quick to tell us; it should not come as a surprise, then, that different periods have elicited different approaches and themes despite powerful arguments for continuities.

Finally, the study of the Mediterranean has been inflected by a variety of intellectual and political agendas. On the intellectual side, Braudel's work, while relatively neglected in the early years after publication, came to cast a long shadow on later attempts to come to terms with the Mediterranean. The Annaliste project of integrating geography with history in a *histoire totale* infused later scholarship, as did the emerging world-systems paradigm, the effects of which are strikingly present in Anglophone historiography, according to Maria Fusaro. Although she also suggests that the turn in Anglo-American historiography toward "Atlantic history" over the last forty years drew attention away from the Mediterranean, the region had never receded as a focus of many European historiographical traditions, particularly those with Mediterranean shores. Braudel's world vision did not preclude attention to the microlevel of analysis they favored, which tilted toward writing history *in* rather than *of* the Mediterranean. Over the past decade or so, inspired in part by Horden and Purcell's contribution, historians of all stripes have more fully engaged the post–sixteenth-century Mediterranean at both micro- and macrolevels and made it into the lively field it is today.[28]

Writing about the Mediterranean has also responded to broader intellectual fashions, many of which Dursteler mentions, including the interest in borderlands; representations of the other; religious and cultural syncretism; and people living on the margins, including smugglers, pirates, and slaves.[29] As we saw above, environmental history found a home in the Mediterranean early on, and urban history, particularly that of port cities, has undergone a renaissance. More notable for its relative absence, however, is women's and gender history, with the exception of some recent interest in female captives and slaves.[30] This is a puzzling lacuna, related perhaps to the fact that many of the topics most commonly addressed in the study of the Mediterranean, notably the environment, trade, cities, and security, have yet to integrate women and gender fully into their analytical frameworks.

Finally, political agendas have also made their mark on the field. The imperial dreams of modern Europe could take a Mediterranean form, most famously in the case of France and its territorial expansion into the lands of North Africa. After its invasion of Algeria, France began to trumpet itself as the heir of Rome, a destiny that would reestablish and improve on Roman glory in the Mediterranean by restoring the physical integrity of the region. Such ambitions could not but influence scholarly production, and a French colonial environmental history arose that shaped this imaginary, as well as related policies.[31] To be sure, it was no accident that Braudel's sojourn as a high school teacher in Algeria for nine years in the 1920s drew his attention to the Mediterranean world and helped incubate his ideas about Mediterranean connections in an earlier period—and that French scholarship has maintained a record of continuous engagement with Mediterranean studies ever since. In the Mediterranean of much European scholarship, however, beginning in the late nineteenth century, Arabs and Muslims were shadowy presences, marginalized or even excluded from membership in a Mediterranean identity.[32]

Anticolonial and postcolonial nationalism eschewed this Mediterranean of imperial imagination in any case, and the national narratives of most states on the southern and eastern shores have had little to say about a Mediterranean identity. Looking east to other Arab lands, south to African connections, and above all within territorial boundaries, nationalist historians of North Africa, for example, wrote the history of the state without much reference to a Mediterranean past or to a connection to Europe outside of resistance to colonialism. In Kenneth Perkins's essay on historiography in North Africa, which appeared in a volume focused primarily on indigenous historians and the decolonizing of history, the Mediterranean as a meaningful site or concept does not make an appearance.[33] The same holds true for most of the other essays that discuss North African historiography. The impression that the Mediterranean as a historical frame is treated by those from the southern and eastern shores with a certain amount of reticence is reinforced by the fact that the lion's share of academic journals focused on the Mediterranean World are European publications, and there is no comparable journal published in Arabic.[34]

The Mediterranean enjoyed another upsurge in Europe as a concept and a theater of action in the 1990s, when European policy makers came to embrace it as a delineated place that made sense for the political agendas of the time. The Euro-Mediterranean Partnership or "Barcelona Process" initiated in 1995 envisioned new forms of cooperation in the realms of politics, security, and economics as well as social and cultural affairs among the Mediterranean countries of the northern, southern, and eastern shores, and interest in these cooperative projects gained new momentum after 9/11. Isabel Schäfer argues that such initiatives were a direct response to European concerns about what it saw as a variety of threats to its security coming from the south and east: migration, radical Islam, and economic crisis drew attention to the Mediterranean as a zone of instability in need of guidance and reform, fostering the notion of cultural unity to legitimize European pursuit of its interests in the region.[35] The theme of an inclusive cultural heritage did not originate in the 1990s; rather, it drew on an existing strand of scholarship, as well as on French utopian thought about a "Mediterranean dream" of concord and harmony. The Saint-Simonians of the late nineteenth century; French intellectuals such as Albert Camus in the 1930s; and more recently Jacques Berque, with his formulation of the "Mediterranean of two shores," all spoke to the richness of a shared Mediterranean identity. French political discourse has, on occasion, continued to incorporate this theme: the minister of foreign affairs, Dominique de Villepin, gave a speech in 2002 in Rabat titled, "The Dream of Two Shores."[36]

Ideas about Mediterranean cultural commonalities developed in uneasy tension with impulses to differentiate and confront. Schäfer portrays European Union policy as wavering between a "Mediterraneanism" that promotes a shared Euro-Mediterranean identity and a "delimitation" that constructs the south and east as dependent "antechambers to Europe" in need of protection.[37] Ambivalence and ambiguity haunt the European approach to the Mediterranean: "the common cultural heritage continued to be invoked while firm policies on security, migration and enlargement are pursued, which draw a clear frontier in the middle of the Mediterranean."[38] Fabre notes the ongoing purchase of "paradigms of discord," à la Pirenne and Huntington, alongside the more utopian visions, and characterizes Euro-Mediterranean relations as a "hegemonic peace" of inherent instability.[39] At this writing, as a mood of anti-Muslim sentiment appears to be escalating in Europe, and the refugee crisis calls into question claims of a shared Mediterranean fate, European political agendas seem to be swinging hard toward policies of difference and the solidification of borders—this Mediterranean dream is in retreat.

The Mediterranean has proved elusive as a place. Scholars and policy makers alike have disagreed about almost everything of importance—its physical boundaries, its primary characteristics, its unity, its connectivity, and the value of its past and future as a space for political projects, economic ties, cultural connections, and meaningful identities. We have seen that angles of vision make a difference. The Mediterranean has been viewed from environmental, economic, political, and cultural perspectives, with a resulting variety of outcomes and judgments on its utility as a unit of analysis for intellectual or political projects. The Mediterranean has lent itself equally to the development of different themes in various historical contexts; those who study ancient, medieval, early modern, or modern periods are preoccupied with distinct topics, some of which may or may not travel well over time. And as with all academic fields, Mediterranean studies is located in a broader context of political and economic power imbalances and struggles. Few would quarrel with the notion that the intellectual center of gravity has been located in Europe, and studies of the Mediterranean have privileged the European experience of the place. In this book, the hope is to contribute to a growing body of scholarship that is fostering a more inclusive study of the Mediterranean by taking the experiences of the southern and eastern shores into account.

LOOKING FROM SOUTH AND EAST

What is the rationale for yet another volume on the Mediterranean? When Harris posed the same question over ten years ago as the editor of *Rethinking the Mediterranean,* he found himself unsure. Why should the topic engage us today? Is the Mediterranean as a unit of analysis a "romantic delusion," a "piece of Eurocentric cultural imperialism," or just plain overworked and "boring"?[40] In part, this collection confronts these questions in the context of a compensatory project: the experiences of, and perspectives on, the Mediterranean from the southern and eastern shores, which have been neglected by scholars. Braudel's study was based almost exclusively on European sources, and four years after the publication of *The Corrupting Sea,* Horden and Purcell regretted that they "did not have the time, even after too many years work, to get to grips with the evidence for the Ottoman Mediterranean world."[41] Even in the case of the post–Horden and Purcell revisionist scholarship, the European experience is still receiving the lion's share of attention, especially in the lively areas of cultural encounter and exchange.[42] Arguably, the Arab and Turkish voices are still rather faint, and the significance of the Mediterranean frame is far from established on the southern and eastern shores.

There are signs, however, of a growing desire to take a more inclusive approach, one that may help us rethink the region. Several of the edited volumes on the Mediterranean mentioned above feature contributions from multiple shores. In Kolluoğlu and Toksöz's *Cities of the Mediterranean* (2010), many of the contributors study the eastern port cities. They draw on Ottoman and Arab sources and provide, as a result, a fuller picture of the networks and connections that made the Mediterranean a meaningful place for the history of the eastern shores. Because historians of Ottoman and Arab lands are well represented in Fusaro, Omri, and Heywood's *Trade and Cultural Exchange in the Early Modern Mediterranean* (2010), we are able to better understand how the lives of residents of the southern and eastern shores were intricately connected to the sea—to the commerce as well as the attacks and diseases it facilitated—and how they thought about the Mediterranean as a result. Several historians of the region have authored monographs that frame their study of Arab or Turkish shores as *of* instead of *in* the Mediterranean. Molly Greene's *A Shared World* is a powerful example of how to rethink cultural intersections in the Mediterranean from the east, and Julia Clancy-Smith's *Mediterraneans* reveals the importance of the Maghrib for understanding the interplay of mobilities and modernities in the nineteenth-century Mediterranean. Ilham Khuri-Makdisi's study of the eastern Mediterranean, by examining the flows of radical ideas and projects, rewrites the history of radicalism as a phenomenon in the Mediterranean and beyond.[43] Although far from an exhaustive list, these books suggest the extent to which research anchored on the eastern and southern shores can stir the still waves of Mediterranean studies.

This book aspires to further the conversation by bringing together a number of contributions that speak to some of the central issues of the Mediterranean in fresh ways, made possible by taking the Arab and Turkish lands as points of departure. The topics are familiar ones: the making of space and place in the Mediterranean, the patterns and modalities of connectivity among its peoples and shores, and the ways in which it has been imagined and reimagined over time. The approaches are diverse, coming from and often combining a variety of fields, including conceptual, social, environmental, economic, legal, intellectual, and cultural history. Such eclecticism has been a hallmark of scholarship on the Mediterranean, and we follow here in that tradition. The time frame of the volume is a capacious one, extending from the seventeenth century into the twentieth, which allows the reader to follow shifts in how the people of the Mediterranean have conceived of and experienced the sea over time. Most importantly, by attending principally to the east and south, these pieces make a number of intriguing suggestions.

First, there is a rethinking of the tensions between space and place, and in particular how ways of perceiving and living in the physical Mediterranean were influenced by local, regional, and global contexts. Nabil Matar, in his exploration of Arab views of the Mediterranean in the seventeenth and eighteenth centuries, questions the extent to which it was a meaningful place, or even a coherent space, for Arab thinkers. Matar points to the discursive construction of the sea as a highly fragmented environment, riven by physical divisions and the actions of enemies. His vantage point provides a sobering reminder that perceptions of Mediterranean space were points of view incubated in local environments and experiences, and that we need to be open to the variety of perspectives on the Mediterranean that can be found on different shores. Clancy-Smith follows with another invitation to view the Mediterranean from the Maghrib, with a particular focus on movements on the margins, on persons and things, such as the kidnapped and the shipwrecked, that went missing in Mediterranean space. These marginal people and things have much to tell us about this space in the eighteenth and nineteenth centuries. In her account, the Mediterranean as seen from the southern shores is often a space of fragmentation and threat, but it is counterbalanced by a vigorous complexity of movement on the part of actual seafarers, who made it a place of business and travel. Those who moved on the sea experienced the Mediterranean in ways quite distinct from those who remained on the shore. The many arrangements and mediations that facilitated their voyages, as well as their misadventures, delineated a connected space that reached far beyond their places of origin. Edmund Burke III takes a different perspective as he addresses the Mediterranean during the long nineteenth century by inserting it into a larger and more comparative frame. Similar to Matar and Clancy-Smith, he argues for looking elsewhere, to the southern shores and even to Eurasia, in order to understand Mediterranean space. He finds Mediterranean coherence and unity emerging in the nineteenth century in the form of a convergence of similar tastes, identities, aspirations, and patterns of movement that characterize the modernities of the time. The Mediterranean is a place that partakes in the new rhythms of modernity, not simply as a recipient of European models, but more importantly as a participant in broader Eurasian trajectories. In Burke's analysis, the "placeness" of the Mediterranean is produced by the modern lifestyles, identities, and ideologies that circulate within and through the region. These three chapters challenge us, in brief, to rethink issues of space and place in the Mediterranean by making the south and the east our ports of embarkation.

The second pair of chapters engages the issue of connectivity by drawing attention to the semilicit world of piracy in the south and east, which, ironically enough, played a major role in promoting communication and connection in the Mediterranean. Joshua White examines a late sixteenth- and seventeenth-century practice of "slave laundering," a method of illegal enslavement and forced migration that has, until now, gone virtually unremarked on. The personnel and networks that were called into the service of these illicit operations illustrate the strength and complexity of the many ties among officials and pirates, as well as eastern and southern shores, ties essential to the business of slave laundering. Although there was much connection and cooperation among these networks, White also paints a nuanced picture in which tensions over the practice could arise between the Ottoman center and its periphery. Slave laundering illustrates fissures and conflicts in Mediterranean space, as well as connectivity. Judith Tucker discusses Mediterranean piracy in the eighteenth century in relation to the development of shared laws and legal practices, arguing that the Mediterranean was a site for the convergence of understandings about the appropriate ways to regulate piracy. Despite the intractability of many of the pirates and black marketeers involved, laws, practices, and formal agreements evolved to create a shared Mediterranean in which pirates and officials alike knew and generally followed the rules. At the same time, there were always occasions when rule-breaking was the more attractive option. These two chapters point us to the ways in which Mediterranean connections were being made by piracy, while simultaneously commenting on the irregularity and instability of some of these linkages.

The last two chapters directly address the third issue of imagining the Mediterranean from the vantage point of the southern shores. Osama Abi-Mershed discusses the utopian vision of a prominent St. Simonian based in French Algeria, Michel Chevalier, who foresaw a Mediterranean place of peace, economic cooperation, and social reform, to be facilitated by the workings of modern technologies of communication and transportation. Abi-Mershed situates this Mediterranean utopia of reconciliation of Orient and Occident squarely on the colonized Maghribi shore, and reflects on how it subsequently inspired a group of practices that buttressed the cultural and historical claims of the colonial power. William Granara moves this discussion into postcolonial times with his exploration of a developing Mediterranean historical consciousness in twentieth-century Tunisian literature. He argues that Arab writers of the southern shores were moving to take back Mediterranean space, to understand its place in the more dominant Arab-Islamic literary imagination of the colonial and postcolonial periods. It was a complex process for these writers, who struggled to balance the continuities and confrontations of the Mediterranean as lived experience, particularly in the era of

European hegemony. Together, the two chapters underscore the extent to which the representation of the Mediterranean as an integrated space has been a highly critical and contested project in the Maghrib, and one very much caught up in the colonial experience.

Concepts of the Mediterranean meet with new challenges on the southern and eastern shores. All the authors in this volume problematize comfortable notions of blended identities, smooth connections, and consistent images of the Mediterranean, and challenge views of Mediterranean space as shaped by European trajectories. They rethink centers and margins in ways that focus on the fluidity and instability of the Mediterranean space over time and the shifts in power relations that redefined and redesigned the Mediterranean as a place in the early modern and modern periods. They do not tell a simple story of European takeover, however, but rather look to how the ideas and experiences on the southern and eastern shores tell a different tale, one of a Mediterranean that continued to be a contested site of meaning and action well into the twentieth century and beyond. There is little agreement about the extent to which views from the south and east destabilize the Mediterranean as a meaningful place altogether. As these scholars of the Arab and Turkish lands attend to the Mediterranean, however, they converge on the diversity, richness, and many tensions of its history that complicate previous narratives of how the modern Mediterranean was made.

NOTES

1. John A. Agnew, "Space and Place," in *The SAGE Handbook of Geographical Knowledge,* ed. John Agnew and David N. Livingston (Los Angeles: SAGE, 2011), 317.

2. Agnew, "Space and Place," 317.

3. See, in particular, part 2 of vol. 1 of Fernand Braudel, *The Mediterranean and the Mediterranean World in the Age of Philip II,* trans. Siân Reynolds, 2 vols. (New York: Harper and Row, 1972).

4. Peregrine Horden and Nicholas Purcell, *The Corrupting Sea: A Study of Mediterranean History* (Oxford: Blackwell, 2000), 5.

5. For an enlightening comparison of the Mediterranean visions of Braudel and of Horden and Purcell, see Monique O'Connell and Eric R. Dursteler, *The Mediterranean World: From the Fall of Rome to the Rise of Napoleon* (Baltimore: John Hopkins University Press, 2016), 3–10.

6. David Abulafia, *The Great Sea: A Human History of the Mediterranean* (London: Penguin Books, 2011), xxiii–iv.

7. Horden and Purcell, *Corrupting Sea,* 10–15.

8. See W. V. Harris, "The Mediterranean and Ancient History," in *Rethinking the Mediterranean,* ed. W. V. Harris (Oxford: Oxford University Press, 2005), 11–12, for a brief discussion of the problem of fixing the physical boundaries of the Mediterranean.

9. Maurizio Isabella and Konstantina Zanou, eds. *Mediterranean Diasporas: Politics and Ideas in the Long 19th Century* (London: Bloomsbury Academic, 2016).

10. Patricia M. E. Lorcin, introduction to "The Southern Shores of the Mediterranean and Its Networks: Knowledge, Trade, Culture and People," ed. Patricia M. E. Lorcin, special issue, *Journal of North African Studies* 20, no. 1 (January 2015): 4.

11. See Eric Dursteler, "Bazaars and Battlefields: Recent Scholarship on Mediterranean Cultural Contacts," *Journal of Early Modern History* 15, no. 5 (2011): 413–18, for a discussion of this bifurcation in Mediterranean studies and a review of new scholarship that pursues the revisionist line of connection.

12. J. R. McNeill, *The Mountains of the Mediterranean World: An Environmental History* (Cambridge: Cambridge University Press, 1992), 12.

13. Braudel, *Mediterranean,* 1:231.

14. Faruk Tabak, *The Waning of the Mediterranean, 1550–1870: A Geohistorical Approach* (Baltimore: Johns Hopkins University Press, 2008), 15–24.

15. McNeill, *Mountains of the Mediterranean,* 6–12.

16. Biray Kolluoğlu and Meltem Toksöz, eds. *Cities of the Mediterranean: From the Ottomans to the Present Day* (London: I. B. Tauris, 2010), 3.

17. Horden and Purcell, *Corrupting Sea,* 172.

18. Julia A. Clancy-Smith, *Mediterraneans: North Africa and Europe in an Age of Migration, c. 1800–1900* (Berkeley: University of California Press, 2011), 13–15, 333–34.

19. Molly Greene, *A Shared World: Christians and Muslims in the Early Modern Mediterranean* (Princeton, NJ: Princeton University Press, 2000), 3–4.

20. A point made by the founders of the Spain-North Africa Project. For further discussion, see Yuen-Gen Liang, Abigail Krasner Balbale, Andrew Devereux, and Camilla Gómez-Rivas, eds. *Spanning the Strait: Studies in Unity in the Western Mediterranean* (Leiden: Brill 2013), 7–18.

21. Molly Greene, "Beyond the Northern Invasion: The Mediterranean in the Seventeenth Century," *Past and Present,* no. 174 (February 2002): 43–46, 58–62.

22. Adnan A. Husain, "Introduction: Approaching Islam and the Religious Cultures of the Medieval and Early Modern Mediterranean," in *A Faithful Sea: The Religious Cultures of the Mediterranean, 1200–1700,* ed. Adnan A. Husain and K. E. Fleming (Oxford: Oneworld, 2007), 23.

23. See Dursteler, "Bazaars and Battlefields," 428–32.

24. Horden and Purcell, *Corrupting Sea,* 31–39.

25. See, for example, Kolluoğlu and Toksöz, *Cities of the Mediterranean,* 1–2.

26. Tabak, *Waning of the Mediterranean,* 2.

27. See, for example, Patricia M. E. Lorcin and Todd Shepard, eds. introduction to *French Mediterraneans: Transnational and Imperial Histories* (Lincoln: University of Nebraska Press, 2016), 1–18.

28. See Maria Fusaro, "After Braudel: A Reassessment of Mediterranean History between the Northern Invasion and the *Caravane Maritime,*" in *Trade and Cultural Exchange in the Early Modern Mediterranean: Braudel's Maritime Legacy,* ed. Maria Fusaro, Colin Heywood, and Mohamed-Saleh Omri (London: I. B. Tauris, 2010), 1–5, for a useful discussion of these historiographical trends.

29. See Dursteler, "Bazaars and Battlefields," 419–32.

30. See, for example, Khalid Bekkaoui, *White Women Captives in North Africa: Narratives of Enslavement, 1735–1830* (London: Palgrave Macmillan, 2011); Linda Colley, *Captives: Britain, Empire and the World, 1600–1800* (Westminster: Knopf, 2004), 43–44; and Eric R. Dursteler, *Renegade Women: Gender, Identity, and Boundaries in the Early Modern Mediterranean* (Baltimore: Johns Hopkins University Press, 2011).

31. See Diana K. Davis, "Restoring Roman Nature: French Identity and North African Environmental History," in *Environmental Imaginaries of the Middle East and North Africa,* ed. Diana K. Davis and Edmund Burke III (Athens: Ohio University Press, 2011), 60–86.

32. Clancy-Smith, *Mediterraneans,* 10.

33. Kenneth Perkins, "Recent Historiography of the Colonial Period in North Africa: The 'Copernican Revolution' and Beyond," in *The Maghrib in Question: Essays in History and Historiography,* ed. Michel Le Gall and Kenneth Perkins (Austin: University of Texas Press, 1997), 121–35.

34. Susan E. Alcock, "Alphabet Soup in the Mediterranean Basin: The Emergence of the Mediterranean Serial," in *Rethinking the Mediterranean,* ed. M. V. Harris (Oxford: Oxford University Press, 2005), 334.

35. Isabel Schäfer, "The Cultural Dimension of the Euro-Mediterranean Partnership: A Critical Review of the First Decade of Intercultural Cooperation," *History and Anthropology* 18, no. 3 (September 2007): 337–38.

36. See Thierry Fabre, "Face to Face, Side by Side: Between Europe and the Mediterranean," *History and Anthropology* 18, no. 3 (September 2007): 356–59.

37. Schäfer, "Cultural Dimension," 337.

38. Schäfer, "Cultural Dimension," 342.

39. Fabre, "Face to Face," 354–56, 363.

40. Harris, "Mediterranean and Ancient History," 1–2.

41. Horden and Purcell, "Four Years of Corruption: A Response to Critics," in *Rethinking the Mediterranean,* ed. W. V. Harris (Oxford: Oxford University Press, 2005), 361.

42. As noted by Dursteler, in "Bazaars and Battlefields," 420–26.

43. Greene, *A Shared World;* Clancy-Smith, *Mediterraneans;* Ilham Khuri-Makdisi, *The Eastern Mediterranean and the Making of Global Radicalism, 1860–1914* (Berkeley: University of California Press, 2010).

1

The "Mediterranean" through Arab Eyes in the Early Modern Period

From Rūmī to "White In-Between Sea"

Nabil Matar

The Sea of Andalus, the Sea of Maghrib, the Sea of Alexandria, the Sea of Syria, the Sea of Constantinople, the Sea of the Franks, and the Sea of the Rūm [Europeans/Byzantines] . . . are one sea.

—YĀQŪT AL-ḤAMAWĪ (D. 1229), *MUʿJAM AL-BULDĀN*

The sea belongs to Christians—as it is said, the sea belongs to the Rūm.

—THE MOROCCAN AMBASSADOR ʿABDALLAH IBN ʿAISHA TO HIS FRENCH HOST IN PARIS, JEAN JOURDAN, 1699

This essay will examine Arabic writings about the Mediterranean Sea in the period after Fernand Braudel's *terminus ad quem* (1598) until Napoleon's invasion of Egypt in 1798—the period in which European naval powers, chiefly Britain and France, came to dominate the Mediterranean basin. It focuses on the writings of the Arabic-speaking peoples who inhabited the Arab mainland (*Barr al-ʿArab*), extending from Iskanderun on the southeastern border of Turkey to Tangier, situated at the intersection of the Mediterranean and the Atlantic. Accordingly, it does not take into account the Turkish mainland (Anatolia; *Barr al-Turk*) or the Euro-Christian shores.[1] The reason for this Arabic focus is that, even though the Ottomans ruled the eastern and southern Mediterranean basins (excluding Morocco), Arabs and Arabic speakers constituted the largest population at sea: merchants, scholars, jurists, travelers, fishermen, pilgrims, princes, ambassadors, migrants, and families. And these Arabs held entirely different views regarding the name and significance of the sea than the Ottoman Turks. At the same time, they differed markedly from their European counterparts.

THE MEDITERRANEAN OF EUROPE

After the end of World War I, and as soon as European powers gained control of the Arab countries around the Mediterranean basin, Henry Pirenne wrote in *Muhammad and Charlemagne* that the expansion of Islam from the seventh century on had partitioned what had been a unified sea under the Roman emperors Constantine and Justinian (fourth–sixth centuries CE) into a religious space of confrontation between Christianity and Islam. Disagreeing with Pirenne, his pupil Fernand Braudel showed in *The Mediterranean and the Mediterranean World in the Age of Philip II* (1949) that trade, negotiation, travel, and diplomacy had brought Ottomans together with Frenchmen, Britons with Algerians, and Dutchmen with Aleppans in a manner that turned the sixteenth-century Mediterranean into an interactive geographic unit.[2] Braudel explained that "the movement of boats, pack animals, vehicles and people themselves made the Mediterranean a unit and gave it a certain uniformity in spite of local resistance."[3] Such Braudelian unity was possible only because by 1949, the sea and its shores had been turned into a European lake, with all the Arab countries around the basin under European or European-sponsored mandate/colonization: Morocco (France and Spain), Algeria and Tunisia (France), Libya (Italy), Egypt and Palestine (Britain and Israel), and Lebanon and Syria (France). Looking back, Braudel projected twentieth-century European navigational and commercial hegemony over the Mediterranean onto the sixteenth century, when the "northern invaders" (chiefly British and French, with the Dutch playing some role) had begun to consolidate their control over the sea.[4]

At the end of his book, however, Braudel admitted that the evidence he had used to build his case for a "unifying" Mediterranean had been limited. He had not consulted sources in Arabic or Ottoman—the languages of the southern, of the eastern, and of part of the northern shores of the Mediterranean basin—and he urged scholars to do that. One of his students, Ömer Lutfi Barkan, began studying the Mediterranean through Ottoman population and taxation records to test Braudel's theory of the unity of the Mediterranean,[5] yet half a century after Braudel, Peregrine Horden and Nicholas Purcell in *The Corrupting Sea* (2000) paid no attention to the non-European sources, dealing with the history of the sea in a synchronic manner.[6] Faruk Tabak's extensive study of trade, ecology, and geography in *The Waning of the Mediterranean 1550–1870* (2008) also reflected an exclusively European epistemology of the sea, with a special focus on Venice and Genoa and on the food production (grains, wine, olives) in the hillsides and mountains beyond the Euro-Mediterranean basin. And much as David Abulafia in *The Great Sea* (2011) aimed to study both the sea itself and those who sailed its waters, what he called the "human history of the sea . . . those who dipped their toes into the sea" (more so than Braudel's people's history), he too ignored Turkish and Arabic cartography and geography.[7]

The view of the Mediterranean as a single unity and the interest in its *connectivities* (Horden and Purcell's term) has not been confined to academe. The 1995 Barcelona Process of Euro-Mediterranean partnership made the Mediterranean part of European/Western political strategy, and in 2005, the European Union "defined the Mediterranean as a strategic priority;"[8] two years later, the French President, Nicolas Sarkozy, proclaimed the "unity of the Mediterranean" (later changed to the "unity for the Mediterranean" as a result of German insistence). This "unity" served to resolve historical dilemmas, as well as to confirm European hegemony:[9] it retroactively justified the European colonization of the Arab-Islamic coast in the first half of the twentieth century. At that time, Mussolini and other leaders replaced Arabic place names in North Africa with their Latin precedents, while, since their conquest of Algeria in 1830, the French had appealed to the classical past to turn Algeria into France.[10] The unity established the Mediterranean basin as a European "middle sea" of geographical and commercial connectivities, recapitulating thereby the mare nostrum of Roman imperial memory. That is how Braudel (and for that matter Albert Camus before him) could present the sea as a "humanistic Mediterranean" shared by all the peoples of the basin, from the French to the Syrians and Moroccans.[11]

Ironically, crises in the Arab-Islamic Mediterranean have begun to cast their shadow over Europe in recent years. As refugees and migrants from the Mediterranean countries have flooded into western Europe, the Mediterranean has changed in recent discourse into "an area of permanent conflict faced with immigration, inequality, racism and impassable frontiers," as the brochure for "Between Myth and Fright: The Mediterranean as Conflict," a 2016 exhibition at the Institut Valencià d'Art Modern, demonstrates. It seems that the idea of a "unified" Mediterranean no longer serves the ideological goals of European governments, which now would prefer that it serve as a *ḥājiz* (barrier) between them and the desperate refugees in their ships of death.[12]

THE ARABS AND THE "MEDITERRANEAN"

The European construction of a Mediterranean of connectivities was made possible by the fact that the European colonial conceptualization of the Mediterranean completely ignored Arabic writings and Arab voices—even though over half the Mediterranean basin in the early modern period was populated by Arabic speakers with their own histories, chronicles, travelogues, and nomenclatures of the sea. Had Arabic sources been examined, they would have shown that the conceptualization of the Mediterranean as a unifying basin not only was not present but was also widely contested, which is why Arab writers used different names for the sea but never the "In-Between Sea" of Roman Latin derivation. The name *al-Mutawassiṭ*, or In-Between, does not appear on any of the medieval maps that have survived,[13] and as Tarek Kahlaoui has shown, *al-Mutawassiṭ* was rarely used in chronicles or geographical texts.[14] Rather, names such as *Rūmī* (Byzantine Sea),[15] *Shāmī* (Syrian Sea), *Akhḍar* (Green Sea), *Māliḥ* (Salty Sea), and others dominate the cartographic and historical nomenclature (along with *Qubṭī* [Coptic Sea] on fifteenth- and sixteenth-century Ottoman maps).[16]

Actually, as far back as the tenth century, al-Mas'ūdī (d. CE 956), one of the greatest Arab travelers and historiographers, showed in his *Murūj al-dhahab* and *al-Tanbīh wa-l-ishrāf* that the name most frequently associated with the Mediterranean Sea was *Rūmī*. The sea belonged and was named after the adversarial "other." The Mediterranean as a sea unifying the peoples and civilizations around it did not appear in Arabic because the sea was many seas with many names reflecting many and different peoples. It was also a sea of danger because, as Arabs moved their boats and pack animals (in the words of Braudel), they saw a Rūmī/European mare nostrum, which brought on them naval attacks and invasions. The "Mediterranean" Sea made up of an "immense network of regular and casual connections," as Braudel imagined it, did not exist.[17] Arab geographers also did not recognize the sea as "part of *Mamlakat al-Islam*"/the dominion of Islam. Rather, it was a "disappearing Muslim space that was being challenged by the *Rūm*,"[18] a multiplicity of regional seas with the Rūm assuming control over it.[19] Actually, as historian Shams al-Dīn al-Kīlanī has noted, it was the Indian Ocean and the Red Sea that were viewed by Muslim Arabs as extensions of the Islamic *barr* (region), and not the Rūmī Sea.[20] After all, the only sea associated with the Arabs is the Arabian Sea near the Indian Ocean.

In addition, the medieval Arabic view of the sea was that of a space separating, rather than connecting, two adversarial shores:[21] a *ḥājiz* (barrier) between *bilād al-Rūm* and *bilād Miṣr*, or a defensive space between the lands of the Europeans and of the Egyptians, as the thirteenth-century Yaqūt al-Ḥamawī put it.[22] Clearly, after Genoese and Venetian ships started carrying crusader armies to the East, al-Ḥamawī could not but hope that the sea would serve as a defense against the invaders. The atlas of the Tunisian al-Sharafī al-Ṣifāqī produced two centuries later in 1551, along with its subsequent renditions, has no name for the sea, even though the maps were intended as a "reconstruction of political landscape."[23] It is possible that as Spain and the Ottoman Empire were vying for control of the Mediterranean, the Ṣifāqī cartographers used neither a Spanish nor a Turkish designation for the sea because they did not know how to name it. After Yūsuf ibn ʿĀbid al-Fāsī traveled in 1587 along the Atlantic coast of Morocco, he launched eastward on his journey to Yemen, using the coastal road near what he called simply *al-Baḥr al-Māliḥ* (the Salty Sea), a name that dates as far back as al-Idrīsī (d. 1161) and Ibn al-Athīr (ca. 1234).[24] His compatriots warned him, however, to stay inland, since the Rūm came from the sea to hunt for Muslims (*yataṣayyadū li-l-muslimīn*) on land.[25] Common to him and to other Muslims was the image of the sea as terrifying, not because Arabs and Muslims had a religiously engrained or an instinctive hostility to the sea,[26] but because they feared attacks from European fleets and pirates.

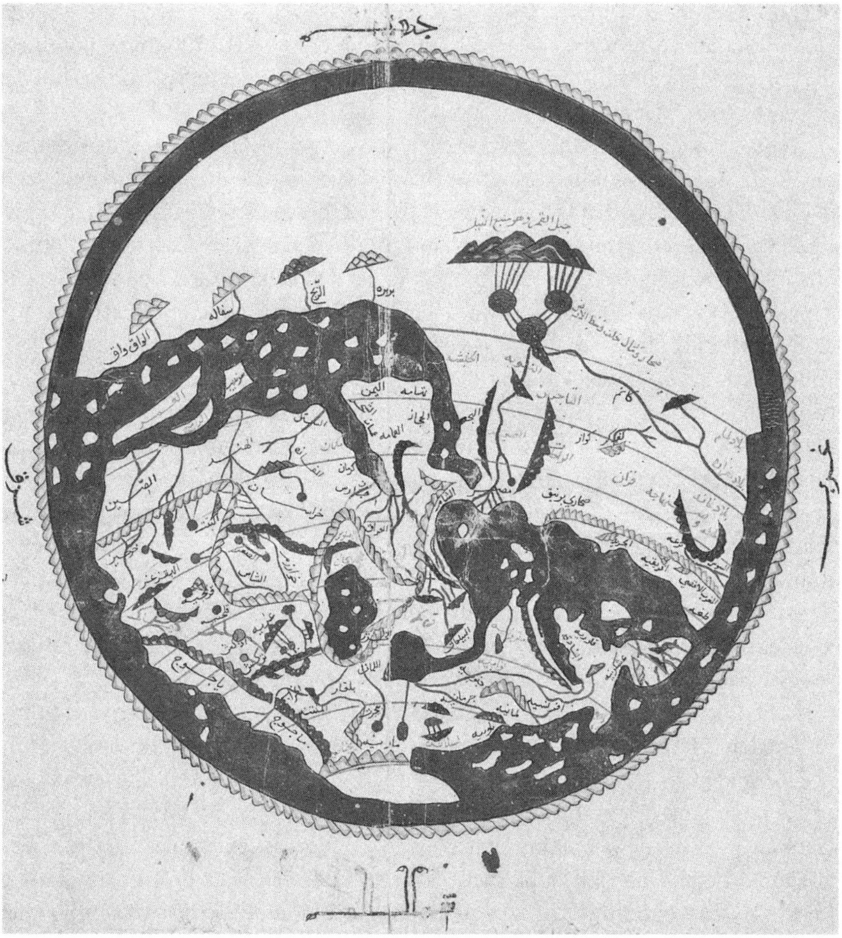

FIGURE 1. *Al-Idrisi's World Map.* Courtesy of Wikimedia Commons.

The attacks had been relentless. From 1415 on, North African port cities had been conquered and occupied by Europeans: Ceuta (1415) and Melilla (1497), both of which remain in Spanish hands today; Asila and Tangier (1471), occupied by the Portuguese, with the latter in British hands until 1684; Santa Cruz/Agadir (1505–41), occupied by the Portuguese; Tripoli (1510), attacked first by the Spanish and then by the Knights of Malta (1530); Mazagan/El Jadida (1502–1769), occupied by the Portuguese; Azemmour (1513–41), occupied by the Portuguese; Tunis (1535), attacked and occupied by Spain until 1574; Algiers (1661), attacked by the British; Jijel, Algeria (1664), attacked by the French; Tripoli, attacked by the British (Libya,

1675); and Algiers, bombarded by the French (1682, 1683, 1688). From July 1 to 16, 1688, the French navy, according to a report by an Englishman, blasted the city of Algiers with 10,420 bombs.[27] Europeans not only conquered these outposts but also Christianized them, holding processions with the Virgin Mary (in Catholic outposts) that marked physical and spiritual possession.[28] Throughout the period, pirates and colonists of all European nationalities seized North African men, women, and children for domestic and transatlantic slavery. ʿAli ibn Muḥammad al-Tamjrūtī sailed from Tetuan to Istanbul in 1590 and, as did his contemporaries, worried about danger at sea. His account is the only pre–late eighteenth-century travelogue that has survived in Arabic of such a journey from one end of the Mediterranean to the other, but in it he has neither a conception of a larger, or unified, "Mediterranean" nor indeed even a name for the sea. Although he had access to a map/*ṣūra* "of the sea, [drawn] on animal skin with names on both sides of the sea," he did not pick up from this portolan map the name of the sea but focused instead on coastal names.[29] Al-Tamjrūtī mentioned *al-Baḥr al-Aswad*/the Black Sea and *Baḥr al-Muḥīṭ*/the Atlantic, and consistent with other Arab writers who gave the sea a local name, he referred to *Baḥr Tanja*/the Sea of Tangier.[30] Sailing from Tetuan, al-Tamjrūtī made numerous references to Christian pirates, whose nationalities he did not know.[31] In this context of sea fear, al-Tamjrūtī told the story of a man from Darʿa in Morocco, who so feared European pirates that he decided to migrate inland to a region where its people did not even know what a sea was.[32]

British and French naval attacks so frightened the North Africans that they moved away from the sea coast. After British admiral Robert Blake bombarded Tunis in April 1655, the bey wrote that Muslims had their subsistence from the land and did not expect help from the sea.[33] English diplomat Sir William Temple (d. 1699) confirmed that "for many Years they [North Africans] hardly pretend to any Successes on that Element [sea], but commonly say [that] *God has given the Earth to the Mussulmans, and the Sea to the Christians.*"[34] In 1699, Mulay Ismāʿīl of Morocco (r. 1672–1727) wrote a letter to James II, the exiled king of England in Paris, saying that had he not been an "an Arab" belonging to "a people who knew nothing of the sea," he would have sent him a fleet to help invade Britain and regain his throne.[35] Although Morocco had a long coastline, and although in the first half of the seventeenth century Saletian pirates had caused havoc on European shipping, neither Morocco nor, for that matter, any of the Ottoman regencies were able to advance their naval and maritime technology to repel the attacks by the *inglīz, ʿajam,* and *franṣīṣ* (English, Spanish, and French).[36]

North African pirates and privateers spread fear among European travelers and coastal inhabitants, from Italy to England and from Ireland to Iceland.[37] But what was different between the Europeans and the North Africans in their maritime aggressions was that the latter confined themselves to the abduction of captives and to hit-and-run raids, as opposed to the former, who permanently enslaved

Muslims (sometimes sending them off to North and South America) at the same time that they were establishing what they hoped would be permanent colonies on North African soil. Furthermore, their fleets bombarded port cities with weapons that were unmatched by their North African counterparts. No fleet in North Africa developed the high-powered naval projectiles or guns that could bomb European coastal cities in the manner that the British and the French fleets bombed Muslim ports, destroyed their shipping, burnt their food supplies, and sank their fishing vessels.

The North African failure at sea was a result of a steady decline in navigation, ship-building, and cartography.[38] Such decline helps to explain the absence of any uniformity in the Arabic conceptualization of the sea. Aḥmad ibn Qāsim, an Andalusian who fled to Morocco at the end of the sixteenth century, served as translator and emissary in the Saʿdian court in the first quarter of the seventeenth century. Although he was exposed to European maps and atlases, as he mentions in his memoir, he still described the sea that surrounded Africa from the north as the "Small" Sea and the Rūmī Sea.[39] Muḥammad ibn ʿabd al-Rafīʿ al-Andalusī, another Andalusian who fled to Tunisia, viewed all the sea coast as belonging to the *Rūm: sāḥil al-baḥr kulluhu li-l-Rūm.*[40] Although the seventeenth-century chronicler of al-Andalus al-Maqqarī (d. 1631) is the only writer in the period under study to use the designation *mutawassiṭ,*[41] he most frequently referred to *al-Baḥr al-Shāmī (*the Syrian Sea)—having traveled to and lived in Syria. A quarter of a century later, in 1663, the Moroccan traveler Abū Sālim alʿAyyāshī recounted how he and his companions arrived in Damietta by way of *Baḥr al-Rūm*. There they rented a ship to take them across a *buḥayra* (lake) but were terrified when they saw some Naṣārā (Christians) on board the ship. Fortunately these Christians were peaceful, and they all parted "amicably."[42] For him, the sea was the Salty (*Māliḥ*) Sea,[43] as it was for his contemporary, Ibrahīm ibn ʿAbd al-Raḥmān al-Khiyārī, who wrote of the Salty Sea that led not only to Alexandria but, more ominously, to the "lands of the infidels."[44] In his compendium of seventeenth-century biographies, Muḥammad Amīn ibn Faḍlallah al-Muḥibbī (d. 1699) gave no name to the sea. The approximately fourteen hundred biographies he included range in length from a few lines to multiple pages and describe a huge amount of travel and mobility. Interestingly, cities on the sea's coastline appear very infrequently: Gaza in *al-diyār al-muqaddasa* (the Holy Lands),[45] and Tripoli in Lebanon (and even less so Tripoli in Libya). But in all his account, al-Muḥibbī never names the sea, mentioning only the danger of captivity in Malta.[46] Others gave the sea different names. The historian of Tunis Ibn Abī Dīnar (d. ca. 1698) called the sea between Tunis and Sicily *Baḥr Ifrīqiya* (Sea of Tunis), seemingly dissociating it from the other seas,[47] and in the next century, the chronicler Aḥmad al-Damurdāshī (ca. 1755) mentioned that a certain Jarkas Muḥammad Bayk had fled from the Egyptian delta toward the Libyan city of Derna on the coast of *al-Baḥr al-Māliḥ* (Salty Sea), after which he boarded a Russian ship to *Mosco.*[48] The Tunisian Ḥammūdah ibn Muḥammad Ibn ʿAbd al-ʿAzīz (d. 1788), wrote of *Baḥr al-Shām,* the sea in which *mālik al-Mosco* (the king of the Russians) raided British and French ships and captured Tunisians on board them.[49] In the nineteenth–century Būlāq edition of the *Arabian Nights,*[50] *al-Baḥr al-Māliḥ* and *Baḥr al-ʿAjam* (non-Arabs) appear together in the stories about Muslim captivity in Italy.[51] From the sea, came the danger of abduction and forcible conversion to Christianity.[52]

Muslim fear of European sea attacks was also felt in the Mashriq. The Druze prince Fakhr al-Dīn, fleeing from Mount Lebanon to Italy in 1613, encountered the *qurṣān,* an Arabic transliteration of "corsairs," as he and his retinue sailed aboard one French ship and two Flemish ones. Later, his secretary wrote an account describing "their travel by sea" from Sidon to Livorno, a journey that took fifty-three days, but at no point did he record the name of the sea.[53] By the time the prince was sailing, the eastern Mediterranean was no longer as effectively protected by the Ottoman fleet as it had been in the previous century. European pirates, from Malta all the way to England, roamed the shipping zone between Alexandria and Izmir, at the same time that they attacked the Syrian, Lebanese, and Palestinian coasts. The autobiography of the Spanish Maltese pirate Alosno de Contrera describes the havoc that he and his ships wrought in all parts of the Mediterranean in the early seventeenth century, while the hundreds of Arabic documents about European piracy in the Egyptian archives describe the plight of Muslim captives seized by European marauders and record the failure of the Ottoman navy to provide adequate protection to commercial and pilgrimage shipping.[54]

Meanwhile, Arab writers and sailors continued to debate the name of the sea. The Syrian chronicler Aḥmad ibn Yūsuf al-Qaramānī (d. 1610) mentioned that the Palestinian cities of ʿAsqalān and ʿAkkā were located on *al-Baḥr al-Shāmī,*[55] and while traveling from Mecca to Istanbul in 1629, Muḥammad ibn ʿAbdallah al-Ḥusaynī explained that *al-Baḥr al-Rūmī* was really *Baḥr al-Shām wa-l-Qustantīniyya; Baḥr al-Shām,* he added, was the sea near Iskandarūn.[56] In his chronicle about Egypt and its Ottoman rulers, Muḥammad ʿAbd al-Muʿṭī al-Isḥāqī (d. 1649) described how the Nile poured into *al-Baḥr al-Rūmī,* near the city of Rashīd, where the sea was known as *Baḥr al-Gharb* (Western Sea).[57] An anonymous manuscript copied in 1655 (and edited thirty years later) showed the Nile starting in Jabal al-Qamar and ending in *al-Baḥr al-Māliḥ.*[58] The Sufi traveler Muṣṭafa Asʿad al-Luqaymī (d. 1764) knew every shrine and holy site in *al-arḍ al-muqadassa* (holy land), at the west of which was the "Sea of the Rūm, which is the Salty Sea."[59]

Although there was little Turkish intellectual influence on Arabic geographical writings, a few authors used the Turkish designation *Aq Denizi* (White Sea),[60] as in the case of the Syrian cartographer Abū Bakr al-Dimashqī, who translated Willem Blaeu's atlas for the Ottoman court in Istanbul in the second half of the seventeenth century.[61] The Tunisian vizier Muḥammad ibn Muḥammad al-Andalusī al-Wazīr al-Sarrāj writing in early eighteenth-century Tunis, used the term *al-Baḥr al-Abyaḍ* (White Sea), which, as he explained, was adjacent to *al-Baḥr al-Aswad* (Black Sea).[62] The name *Baḥr Safīd* appears prominently on Ibrahīm Mutafarriqa's 1731 map (the first printed map in the Ottoman Empire), which depicts Egypt and Palestine. A (Catholic) Christian translator of a Turkish ambassador's account of a visit to France in 1720 used the name *al-Baḥr al-Abyaḍ*, as did the Greek Orthodox author and translator of an account about Russia in 1758.[63] But another Christian author borrowed from a 1629 travelogue by the Moroccan Muḥammad ibn ʿAbdallah al-Ḥusaynī that Alexandria was located near *al-Baḥr al-Shāmī*.[64] The Iraqi Catholic priest Ḥanna al-Mūṣallī, sailing from Iskanderun to Venice on board an English ship, made no mention of the sea at all. Later, when he sailed to the Spanish port of San Sebastian from France, he said that he crossed *al-Baḥr al-Gharbī* (Western Sea); and, after continuing by land to Barcelona, he commented that the city was located on *al-Baḥr al-Sharqī* (Eastern Sea).[65] Surprisingly, he did not seem to have picked up the term *Mediterranean* from his European hosts but rather used names that had been common in Arabic for centuries. Writing to an Arabic-speaking readership, he may have felt that the names that were familiar to them would be much more recognizable than European names.[66] Patriarch Mīkhāʾīl Brayk, writing from Aleppo in the second half of the eighteenth century, initially mentioned only *Baḥr Qasbiyān* (Caspian Sea), but when writing closer to his Syrian home, he described how *qurṣān al-baḥr* (sea pirates) attacked the Palestinian port of Jaffa and committed many deeds (*ʿamilū aʿmālan*), including the seizure of two small ships. That the local populace then attacked and looted *Dayr al-Ifranj* (Monastery of the Franks) indicates that these pirates were Christian.[67]

Muḥammad ibn ʿAbd al-Wahāb al-Miknāsī, the most traveled of early modern Arabic writers, wrote detailed accounts about his three journeys across the Mediterranean Sea and into the lands of the Christians and the Muslims. On his 1779 crossing from Ceuta to Cadiz, the only name he had for the sea was *al-Baḥr al-Saghīr* (Small Sea), which poured into *al-Baḥr al-Kabīr* (Great Sea, or the Atlantic).[68] Even after he visited Malta, Sicily, and the kingdom of Naples between 1781 and 1782, and after his third journey, by way of Sicily, to the Ottoman court in 1785, he had not picked up the name "Mediterranean" from his European hosts. Always sailing on board European ships into European ports, and fearing European pirates, al-Miknāsī could not but call the sea *Baḥr al-Rūm*.[69] A few years later, circa 1796, the Moroccan historian Abū al-Qāsim al-Zayānī—a friend and rival of al-Miknāsī's—wrote *al-Tarjumāna al-kubrā*, in which he viewed the sea as threefold: *Baḥr al-Maghrib*, *Baḥr al-Shām*, and *Baḥr al-Rūm*.

> [It] begins in the fourth *iqlīm* [climate zone] and is called *Baḥr al-Zuqāq* [Sea of the Strait] because it is eighteen miles wide. It then proceeds east in the direction of *arḍ al-Barbar* [land of the Berbers] and the north of *al-Maghrib al-Aqsa* [the farthest

> Maghrib] until it reaches *al-Maghrib al-Awsaṭ* [middle Maghrib] and connects with *arḍ Ifrīqiya* [Tunisia] and *Wadī al-Raml* [Valley of Sand]. It continues to *arḍ Barqā* [Libya] and *arḍ Lūqā wa Marāqiya* [Malta?]—to *al-Iskandarīyya* [Alexandria] and the northern part of *arḍ al-Tīh* [Sinai] and from there to *Filasṭīn* [Palestine] and the rest of the coasts of *Shām* until it reaches *Suwaydiyya* [in Syria?]. There it turns back toward *al-Maghrib.* It links up with the Constantinian Gulf, and the island of *Bilonch* [Mount Bilonch?] and *Kashmīl,* continuing to *Ardant*[?]. From there, it continues to the Gulf of Venice and links up with the Sicilian *majāz* [corridor/strait] unto *Bilād Rūmiyya* [land of the Rūm] and *Bilād Seqobyā* [land of the Slavs] and *Aryonā* [?]. It passes by the mountains of *Yūnān* [Greece] and East Andalusia where in the south it reaches the two islands where it had started.[70]

Such multiplicity of seas recalls the seas on the globe that Gerhard Mercator constructed in 1541. But Mercator could "see" a unified sea on the globe in his hands in a manner that the Moroccan did not, even though al-Zayānī was an experienced and knowledgeable traveler, who was able to read maps (*al-karīta*) and determine the location of his ship.[71] He knew French (and possibly Spanish)[72] and had read the major travelogues by Arab writers (although nothing by Europeans). He traveled with his books, which he constantly consulted. He knew the ports from Tetuan to Izmir and seemed familiar, if in a limited manner, with Marseille and some other European ports. Throughout his travels, al-Zayānī tried to verify information, so he corrected whatever errors he encountered. Yet as he described his travel by sea, or mentioned episodes that occurred at sea, the two names he used most frequently for the sea were "Green" and "Syrian." Al-Zayānī picked up some Turkish terms after spending time in the Ottoman east, but, oddly, he never used the Turkish designation of "White Sea" in all his account, which spans half a century.

Neither did al-Zayānī describe the sea as a unifier or a connector but rather as a barrier, positing that the sea had been dug purposely to serve as a *ḥājiz* between North Africa and the Iberian mainland. Originally, he stated, drawing on al-Idrīsī's *Nuzhat al-mushtāq,* there had been no sea between these two landmasses; instead, they had been contiguous.[73] As a result, North African Berbers (and al-Zayānī was proud of his Berber background) frequently attacked Iberia. To prevent the Berbers from defeating the Iberians, Alexander the Great brought his army and carved a watery separation between the two regions, so that the Western Sea (Atlantic) opened onto the Green Sea. By doing so, Alexander created a sea of separation.

Neither al-Zayānī nor any other early modern Arabic writers used the European nomenclature of the "In-Between" Mediterranean Sea, because they had no sense of possessing it (in Stephen Greenblatt's use of the term) in the manner that Europeans did.[74] In this respect, they were much unlike the British, who, early in the seventeenth century, decided to name (or to agree on a name for) the sea the "Mediterranean Sea"; the British gave it a name because their ships and fleets had already roamed that sea. Thus, in March 1620, Trinity House merchants declared that "The Mediterranean Sea . . . [begins] at the Strait of Gibraltar or Morocco and extends to Malaga, Alicante, the Isles of Majorca, Minorca, Zante, Candy, Cyprus, Sacndarowne, Tripoli and Alexandria, and is called the Levant Sea, and has ever been so known to navigators of those countries."[75] Power over the sea empowered the naming of the sea as a single unit—so writers from William Shakespeare to John Donne began to use "Mediterranean," even if they were not fully aware of its geographic location. Only those with power could impose unity on the sea and name it, and only those with sturdy ships could make connectivities across that sea.

The Arabs had neither power nor European-like ships, and, therefore, they could not furnish a uniform name or conceive of a uniform sea. Thus, travelers and geographers from the Arabic-speaking lands gave many names to the sea, or, very often, no name at all. This absence of both conceptualization and naming, and the fact that Arab authors viewed the Mediterranean as a sea of separation (and feared it as a zone of Rūmī dangers), should not obscure the fact that there were constant contacts among Muslims, eastern Christians, Jews, and western Christians around the shores of that sea. Indeed, the sea (or seas) was commercially and economically important to the peoples of *Barr al-ʿArab*. There may also have been some cultural borrowings—after all, the story told by al-Tamjrūtī about the man and the sea oar was long before told about Odysseus.[76] And in the world of trade and commerce, there was a significant jurisprudence aimed directly at the seas: *fiqh al-biḥ ār*.[77] Moreover, one Arabic text shows that the sea was being studied, as well as sailed: in 1747, the Algerian navigator Ibn Ḥamadūsh wrote that he had gathered "all that I have learned [about sea routes] from the science of *al-bulūt* (portolan)." He added that he examined a *carta* of sea winds, in which he used a *qūnās* (compass) with which to draw a circle.[78] Yet as much as he was adopting foreign words instead of Arabic (*carta* instead of *ṣūra*, the common term in Arabic cartography), and much as he was reliant on non-Arabic sources, he still did not have a name for the sea.

If there were any connectivities for the Arabs around the Mediterranean basin, they were connectivities made possible by European shipping. France, Britain, Spain, and other European countries relied on the Mediterranean Sea for trade and diplomacy because they were constantly at war with each other and therefore could not rely on the land routes in the European mainland for mobility. The Mediterranean became not only the safest route but also the only one, and while there was the danger of the "Barbary corsairs," once European fleets attained military superiority over the corsairs from the second half of the seventeenth century on, they assumed dominance over the sea. Meanwhile, the Arabs found themselves either relying on European ships for their travel and trade or using land routes that avoided the sea. On land, and while there was always the danger of Bedouin robbers, Arab travelers did not face physical or political obstacles (such as different national authorities) in the manner of an English merchant traveling overland from Amsterdam to Genoa. In contrast, at no time in the period under study could a Moroccan or an Egyptian pilgrim, merchant, scholar, or ambassador cross from Tangier to Beirut, or from Istanbul to London, or from Marseille to Alexandria, in a ship built by his own countrymen and manned by his coreligionists. Only a Frenchman, Dutchman, or Englishman could sail from the English Channel through the Straits of Gibraltar to Marmara, Jaffa, or Alexandria on board his own people's ship; and only they could hold a physical globe of the world in their hands, trace their fingers over the Mediterranean, and actually "see" the coastlines and harbors and regions. While it may have been a humdrum experience for an Arab to journey from Spain to Egypt during medieval times (according to Goitein's analysis of the Geniza documents, cited by Horden and Purcell),[79] it was no longer so by the seventeenth and eighteenth centuries. No globes showing Arabic names for the seas or for other parts of the world were made in that period: no Arab could "see" the sea unless he had access to European globes. And while Palmira Brummett is correct in stating that the Mediterranean was a "sea that one could sail all the way around, sometimes facing west and sometimes facing east,"[80] only a European could have done that.

For the Arabic-speaking peoples, the sea remained a plurality of seas plagued by European dangers and, therefore, not "their" sea "in-between" their lands. By the end of the period under study, their commercial and naval fleets had deteriorated, and they could no longer confront the growing power of France and Britain. Furthermore, and while the Arabic-speaking peoples from Tangier to Iskenderun traveled and traded in the Mediterranean, their knowledge of the sea and its Rūmī people remained sporadic, unsystematic, and episodic. It never rivaled the European records of reconnaissance and intelligence that were printed in the centers of imperial power, the studies of tides and navigation routes in the Mediterranean basin, the travelers' accounts of fauna and flora from Algeria to Palestine, the ambassadors' insights about political rivalries and social fissures from Meknas to Istanbul, or captives' accounts about the hinterlands—from the Atlas Mountains to the Arabian deserts, and even to Mecca and Medina, as was the case in the account by the English convert Joseph Pitts (1704). As a result, Arabs in the Mashriq and in the Maghrib turned their attention toward the Islamic regions that they could reach by land: a Moroccan from the Maghrib could travel from Tangier to Jerusalem, Mosul, or Mecca without ever crossing a sea. That is why there is no early modern text or map in Arabic that designates the Mediterranean Sea as *mutawassiṭ*, with a network of "connectivity" tying the three continents around the basin together and making it "a shared Mediterranean political sphere." Small-scale contacts between "short distances and definite places" do not produce a large-scale unity or a conceptualization of the Mediterranean as a contiguous basin—at least not in the Arabic sources.[81]

If the Mediterranean was a "frontier," as Linda T. Darling has argued, it was a frontier that the Europeans, not the inhabitants of *Barr al-ʿArab*, were pushing and controlling.[82] With their naval superiority and advanced military capability, the Rūm not only imposed their hegemony over the sea but also confirmed its Latin name as their in-between sea. By the time al-Zayānī was writing, French and British naval powers had overcome all their North African rivals and had assumed Mediterranean dominance. For him, the Mediterranean became a dangerous waterway that brought and continued to bring European fleets and colonizers to *Barr al-ʿArab*: he was still alive when France invaded Algeria in 1830 (he died in 1833). The Mediterranean was not, and therefore was not described as, a sea of connectivities or an in-between sea. Rather, it was a sea of the invading Rūm.

AL-BAḤR AL-ABYAḌ AL-MUTAWASSIṬ, THE WHITE IN-BETWEEN SEA

The nineteenth century witnessed a significant shift in Arabic terminology of the sea, as both Ottoman and European nomenclature began to find currency in Arabic, especially after the French invention of the Mediterranean in the wake of Napoleon's invasion of Egypt.[83] In 1802, a geographical treatise by Chrysanthus Notaras, originally published in Paris in 1715, was translated into Arabic. The translator wrote that the sea was known as the "Middle [sea]/*wasīṭ*, that is the White Sea"—the two names used in European and Turkish cartographies, respectively.[84] This reference is the first that combines the two names—those names that will become the official name of the Mediterranean in modern Arabic geography.

Describing his journey to Paris between 1826 and 1831, Rifāʿa Rāfiʿ al- Ṭahṭāwī recalled crossing "the Sea of the *Rūm*, which is known as the *al-Baḥr al-Mutawassiṭ*/ In-Between Sea or *al-Baḥr al-Abyaḍ*/ the White Sea."[85] Al-Ṭahṭāwī was the first Arab writer (not translator) from the Mashriq to use the two names—"white" and "in-between"—that Arabs eventually came to accept. A few years later, in 1835, an anonymous Maronite chronicler from Lebanon used the designation *abyaḍ* for the sea,[86] but about two decades later, a writer from the Maghrib used *al-Mutawassiṭ*. Traveling to Marseille on board a French ship, Muḥammad al-Saffār started by writing about the "*al-Baḥr al-Ṣaghīr*/Small Sea, since it faced the ocean, which they call big." Later, when he thought of his French destination, he explained that the sea was "*al-Baḥr al-Rūmī* because of the many *Rūmī* countries on its shores." What was Rūmī in his side of the basin, he continued, became "*al-Baḥr al-Shāmī* when it reached the shores of *bilād al-Shām*. And thus it was known as *al-Baḥr al-Mutawassiṭ*," the In-Between Sea, because it separated the Rūm from Bilād al-Shām.[87]

A few years later, in 1850, an ambassador from Algeria visited France, and notwithstanding twenty years of French occupation of his country, he wrote of *al-Baḥr al-Māliḥ*.[88] In 1860, the Moroccan Muḥammad Ibn ʿAbd al-Raḥmān al-Fāsi sailed to England at a time when the seas were completely controlled by Europeans. As he boarded the steamship, he realized that Muslims no longer had anything to do with the sea. Puzzling over this imbalance of power, he rationalized that since these Europeans, who were infidels, would never make it to paradise, God in his infinite mercy had compensated them by giving them paradise on earth: "a garden that extends from *al-Baḥr al-Muhīṭ* in al-Andalus to the bay of Constantinople." The only conception he had of the Mediterranean, then, was that it was a reward given by God to the Europeans.[89] In 1873, the Beirut-based *al-Jinān* journal mentioned *Baḥr Safīd* and *Baḥr al-Rūm;* five years later,[90] the widely traveled Muhammad Bayram al-Tūnisī wrote a description of the world, but for him the sea (Tunis being under Ottoman rule) was still the "White Sea."[91] In 1899, and writing in New York, Yūsuf Naʿmān Maʿlūf used the phrase *al-Baḥr al-Mutawasiṭ al-Rūmī,*[92]and in 1905, the Anglican-trained Palestinian minister Asʿad Manṣūr wrote the first Arabic dictionary of the Bible, in which he located the Holy Land east of *Baḥr al-Rūm.* Two years later, ʿIsā Iskandar al-Maʿlūf wrote from Lebanon a biographical dictionary of the Maʿlūf family, in which he also used *Baḥr al-Rūm.*[93] At the same time, Najīb ʿAbdou, who wrote from the United States, used the same term—even though the English-language map he reproduced from Thomas Cook used "the Mediterranean, Egypt, the Nile and Palestine."[94] Another Lebanese emigrant, Amīn Rīḥānī, also used *Baḥr al-Rūm,*[95] but on February 2, 1908, the Palestinian author Khalīl Sakākīnī, writing in New York, used *al-Baḥr al-Mutawassiṭ.*[96] In 1913, the priest Basil Kherbawi, also in New York, wrote about "*Baḥr al-Rūm* **or** *Baḥr al-Mutawassiṭ*" (emphasis added).[97] In 1923, the Egyptian ʿAbd al-Raḥmān al-Barqūqī wrote "*al-Baḥr al-Rūmī ʿal-Baḥr al-Abyaḍ al-Mutawassiṭ,*"[98] and, a year later, Manṣūr used *al-Baḥr al-Mutawassiṭ.*[99]

If the "historiography of the twentieth century . . . created the idea of the Mediterranean as a space of continuity,"[100] as Claudia Esposito maintains, then it was the imperial European powers that gave currency to its name in Arabic: Mediterranean/*al-Mutawassiṭ.* Only in the first part of the twentieth century did the "unity" of the Mediterranean Sea begin to take shape in Arabic nomenclature—after the completion of European domination of *Barr-al- ʿArab.* Only then did the In-Between/ Mediterranean/Mutawassiṭ name of the sea become geographically established after centuries of confusion, uncertainty, and contestation. And since the Ottoman Empire had ruled Barr al-ʿArab for hundreds of years, it too inserted its own designation. Thus was born of those two imperial parents that Siamese twin: "The White In-Between Sea"/*al-Baḥr al-Abyaḍ al-Mutawassiṭ.*[101]

NOTES

Epigraphs: Yāqūt al-Ḥamawī, "Baḥr al-Andalus wa Baḥr al-Maghrib wa Baḥr al-Iskandariyya wa Baḥr al-Shām wa Baḥr al-Qusṭanṭīniyya wa Baḥr al-Ifranj wa Baḥr al-Rūm . . . jamīʿuha baḥr wāḥid," in ʿAbdallah Ibrahīm, *ʿĀlam al-qurūn al-wusṭā fī aʿyun al-muslimīn* [The world of the middle centuries in the eyes of the Muslims] (Beirut: Al-mu'assassa al-ʿArabiyya li-l-dirāsat wa-l-nashr, 2007), 89; and "Inna al-Naṣāra qāṭibatan al-baḥr lahum—kama qīl, al-baḥr li-l-Rūm," Marine B7/223/111, August 1, 1699, Archives nationales, Paris.

1. For the division by the sea of Christian from Muslim lands, see Ibn Mājid (ca. 1500), who used the terms *Barr al-Islām* and *Barr al-Ifranj* (Franks) or *Barr Naṣārā al-Ifranj* in *Kitāb al-fawā 'id fī uṣūl ʿilm al-baḥr wa-l-qawā 'id* [The book of information about the principles of the science and law of the sea), ed. Ibrāhīm Khūrī and ʿAzza Ḥasan (Damascus: Al-maṭbaʿa al-ṭaʿāwuniyya, 1971), 147, 275.

2. Henry Pirenne, *Mohammed and Charlemagne,* trans. Bernard Miall (1939; repr. New York: Meridian Books, 1957). The thesis was originally presented in an article published in *Revue belge de Philologie et d'Histoire* 1 (1922): 77–86; Fernand Braudel, *The Mediterranean and the Mediterranean World in the Age of Philip II,* trans. Siân Reynolds, 2 vols. (1949; repr. New York: Harper and Row, 1972).

3. Braudel, *Mediterranean,* 2:277.

4. See Molly Greene, who contests this "northern invasion": "Beyond the Northern Invasion: The Mediterranean in the Seventeenth Century," *Past and Present* 174, no. 1 (2002): 42–71.

5. I am grateful to Professor Giancarlo Casale of the University of Minnesota for discussing the work of Barkan with me on August 22, 2012.

6. Without citing any author writing in Arabic, Horden and Purcell state that "the Arab tradition portrayed the sea as poor, alien and uninviting, but by and large as a unity—a single sea, full of islands, whose integrity was maintained by its geographers despite obvious pressures to divide it between Islam and the rest of the world." Then they quote A. Miquel, *La géographie humaine du monde musulman jusqu'au milieu de XIe siècle,* vol. 2 (Paris, 1967–88), 377: "Nos auteurs [the Arab authors] considèrent la Méditerranée comme une ensemble, et comme un sous-ensemble les iles de cette mer, qu'elles soient d'est ou d'ouest" (Our authors view the Mediterranean as a unity and its islands, both in the east and the west, as a sub-unity), *The Corrupting Sea: A Study of Mediterranean History* (Oxford: Blackwell, 2000), 12.

7. David Abulafia, however, is alone in referring to the sea by its Turkish name. See *The Great Sea: A Human History of the Mediterranean* (Oxford: Oxford University Press, 2011), part 4, chaps. 4–7. *A Companion to Mediterranean History,* ed. Peregrine Horden and Sharon Kinoshita (Oxford: Wiley-Blackwell, 2014), also excludes the Arabic tradition.

8. John Tolan, Giles Beinstein, and Henry Laurens, *Europe and the Islamic World,* trans. Jane Marie Todd (Princeton, NJ: Princeton University Press, 2013), 401.

9. As Michael Herzfeld noted, "Mediterraneanism" is "enmeshed in political and ideological processes": "Practical Mediterraneanism: Excuses for Everything from Epistemology to Eating," in *Rethinking the Mediterranean,* ed. W. V. Harris (Oxford: Oxford University Press, 2005), 63.

10. See Patricia M. Lorcin, "Rome and France in Africa: Recovering Colonial Algeria's Latin Past," *French Historical Studies* 25 (2002): 295–329. See also the essays in Patricia M. E. Lorcin and Todd Shepard, ed., *French Mediterraneans: Transnational and Imperial Histories* (Lincoln: University of Nebraska Press, 2016).

11. See the discussion in the introduction and chapter 1 of Claudia Esposito, *The Narrative Mediterranean: Beyond France and the Maghreb* (Lanham, MD: Roman and Littlefield, 2014).

12. But doubts about the "connectivities" of the Mediterranean had started earlier—and, interestingly, by scholars from the Arab Mediterranean: see Charles Issawi, "The Christian-Muslim Frontier in the Mediterranean," *Political Science Quarterly* 76 (1961): 544–54, especially section C; and Tāriq Ziādeh, "Al-Mutawassiṭ: Baḥr li-ḥiwār al-ḥaḍārāt am buḥayra li-gharqā al-hijra al-bā'isa?" [The Mediterranean: a sea for the dialogue of civilizations or a lake for the drowning victims of migration?], *al-Nahār,* Beirut, Lebanon, August 25, 2015.

13. See the monumental volumes of maps, selections, and translations by Youssouf Kamal, *Monumenta cartographica Africae et Aegypti,* 5 vols. (Cairo: n.p., 1926–51).

14. "Depiction of the Mediterranean in Islamic Cartography (11th–16th Centuries): The Suras (Images) of the Mediterranean from the Bureaucrats to the Sea Captains" (PhD diss., University of Pennsylvania, 2008), 38.

15. See for the meaning of *Rūmi,* André Miquel, "Rome chez les géographes arabes" *Académie des Inscriptions et Belles-Lettres: Comptes Rendus des Séances* 12, no. 151 (January–March 1975), 281–91.

16. While frequent in prophetic hadith about Muʿāwiya's conquest of Cyprus (in the seventh century), *al-Baḥr al-Akhḍar* (the Green Sea), which is the Phoenician name of the sea, was rare but continued to be used well into the nineteenth century. Abū Hāmid al-Ghirnāṭī (d. 1170) mentioned only two seas in his travelogue: *al-Baḥr al-Aswad* (the Black Sea) and the sea that feeds into it, *Baḥr al-Rūm,* which is also *al-Baḥr al-Akhḍar.* As he explained, the water of the Black Sea is very salty, but when it pours into *Baḥr al-Rūm,* it turns green like *zanjibār* (verdigris): *Riḥlat al-Ghirnāṭī,* ed. Qāsim Wahb (Abu Dhabi, 2003), 84. The name also appears in the Jewish convert to Islam, al-Samaw'al ibn Yaḥyā al-Maghribī (d. CE 1174?): *Ifḥām al-Yahūd* [Defeat of the Jews], ed. Muḥammad ʿAbdallah al-Sharqāwī (Nasr City, Egypt, 1986), 67. It can also be found on Ibn Ḥawqal's circa 1200 map, in Kamal, *Monumenta cartographica,* vol. 3, fac. III (1933), 805, 809 (Aya Sofia Library MS 2934, as cited by Kamal); and in his circa 1300 map, also in Kamal, vol. 3, fac. III, 810. I am grateful to Professor Wadad Kadi for consulting the database of Arabic sources about the Green Sea. *Al-Baḥr al-Qubṭī* (the Coptic Sea) appears on Turkish maps from the reign of Bajazet II (1481–1512), sometimes interchangeably with *al-Baḥr al-Lūnī*: Kamal, *Monumenta cartographica,* vol. 2, fac. I (1928), 156, 157 (Aya Sofia Library MS 2610). *Al-Baḥr al-Suryānī* (the Syriac Sea) and *al-Baḥr al-Ifrīqī* (the African Sea) also appear in MS 2610, 161.

17. Braudel, *Mediterranean,* 1:276–77.

18. This was during the time of Ibn Ḥawqal. See Kahlaoui, "Depiction of the Mediterranean," 79; see also 75.

19. See Muḥammad ibn Aḥmad al-Muqaddasī, *Aḥsan at-taqāsīm fī ma'rifat al-aqālīm* [The best divisions for learning about regions], trans. and annotated André Miquel (Damascus: Institut Français de Damas, 1963), 52n77.

20. Shams al-Dīn al-Kīlanī, *Ṣūrat Urubbā ʿinda al-ʿArab fī-l-ʿaṣr al-wasīṭ* [The image of Europe among the Arabs in the medieval period] (Damascus: Wizārat al-thaqāfa, 2004), 297.

21. Andrew Hess had presented this view against Braudel with reference to the Christian-Muslim/Ibero-African frontier: *The Forgotten Frontier: A History of the Sixteenth Century Ibero-African Frontier* (Chicago: University of Chicago Press, 1978).

22. Ibrahīm, *ʿĀlam al-qurūn al-wusṭā,* 89.

23. MS Arabe 2278, fol. 6 v, Bibliothèque nationale de France. See also fol. 3 r for the world map; another manuscript of this atlas is at the Bodleian Library, Oxford, MS Marsh 294, fols. 5 v and 6 r. See Carlo Alfonso Nallino, "Un mappamondo arabo disegnato nel 1578 da ʿAli ibn Ahmad al-Sharafi di Sfax," *Bollettino della Reale Società Geografica Italiana* 53 (1916): 721–36; and the extensive study in Kahlaoui, "Depiction of the Mediterranean," 252–92, esp. 290.

24. See al-Idrīsī, *Nuzhat al-mushtāq fī ikhtirāq al-āfāq,* 2 vols. (Beirut: Dār Ṣadir, 1989), 1:246, who sometimes uses the name *al-Baḥr al-Maliḥ;* Kamal, *Monumenta cartographica,* vol. 3, fac. 4 (1934), 940.

25. *Riḥlat Ibn ʿĀbid al-Fāsī, min al-Maghrib ilā Ḥaḍramūt* [Travels of Ibn ʿĀbid al-Fāsī from the (Muslim) West to *Ḥaḍramūt* (in Yemen)], ed. Ibrahīm al-Samarrāʾi and ʿAbdallah al-Ḥabshī (Beirut: Dār al-Gharb al-Islāmī, 1993), 74.

26. See *L'Islam et la mer: la mosquée et le matelot, VIIe-XXe siècle* (Paris, 2000); and the review by Lawrence I. Conrad, "Islam and the Sea: Paradigms and Problematics," *Al-Qantara* 23 (2002): 123–54. See also the earlier statement by Louis Brunot: the Arabs "n'ont parlé de la mer que comme une source des merveilles extraordinaires et de dangeurs innombrables" (The sea in the local traditions and trade of Rabat-Salé), in *La mer dans les traditions et industries indigènes à Rabat-Salé* (Paris, 1920), 1. It is unfortunate that Planhol did not consult Hassan S. Khalilieh, *Islamic Maritime Law: An Introduction* (Leiden: Brill, 1998); Safāʾ ʿAbd al-Fattāh, *al-Mawāniʾ wa-l-thughūr al-Miṣriyya min al-fatḥ al-Islāmī ilā nihāyat*

al-ʿaṣr al-Fāṭimī [Egyptian harbors and ports from the Islamic conquest until the end of Fatimid rule] (Cairo: Dār al-fikr al-ʿArabi, 1986); and Aḥmad Mukhtār al-ʿAbbadī and ʿAbd al-ʿAzīz Sālim, *Tārīkh al-baḥriyya al-Islāmiyya fī ḥawḍ al-Baḥr al-Abyaḍ al-Mutawassiṭ* [History of the Islamic navy in the White Mediterranean Sea] (Alexandria: Muʾassassat shabāb al-jāmiʿa, 1981). Planhol also did not read carefully the editions by Ibrāhīm Khūrī of early modern Arabic texts about the sea (which, surprisingly, are mentioned in his bibliography).

27. *Correspondance des deys d'Alger avec la cour de France,* vol. 1, ed. Eugène Plantet (Paris: Felix Alcan, 1889), 158 n1. See also the firsthand description by the English captive Joseph Pitts: "The city was so much beaten down that you could not distinguish one street or lane from another." In *A True and Faithful Account of the Religion and Manners of the Mahommetans, with an Account of the Author's Being Taken Captive* (Exeter, 1704), in *Piracy, Slavery, and Redemption: Barbary Captivity Narratives from Early Modern England,* ed. Daniel Vitkus, with an introduction by Nabil Matar (New York: Columbia University Press, 2001), 320.

28. Henk Driessen, *On the Spanish-Moroccan Frontier* (New York: Berg, 1992), 22–23.

29. *Al-Nafḥa al-miskiyya* [The fragrant scent], ed. ʿAbd al-Laṭīf al-Shādhlī (Rabat: al-Maṭbaʿa al-malakiyya, 2002), 139.

30. Al-Tamjrūtī, *Al-Nafḥa al-miskiyya,* 86, 141.

31. See Ahmad Chtioui, "Al-Tamgrûti et la Navigation Maritime d'après sa relation de voyage (XVIème siècle)," *IBLA: revue de l'Institut des belles lettres arabes* 146 (1980–82): 293–307.

32. He took a ship's oar and traveled around villages asking people what it was. He settled in Darʿa because the villagers did not associate it with the sea but thought it the plank that bakers used to scoop bread from the oven. See al-Tamjrūtī, *al-Nafḥa al-miskiyya,* 140.

33. *The Letters of Robert Blake, Together with Supplementary Documents,* ed. J. R. Powell (London: Naval Records Office, 1937), 319.

34. William Temple, *The Works of Sir William Temple* (London, 1740), 226.

35. For the text and study of the letter, see Comte Henry de Castries, *Moulay Ismaïl et Jacques II* (Paris: E. Leroux, 1903).

36. See Nabil Matar, "The Maghariba and the Sea: Maritime Decline in North Africa in the Early Modern Period," in *Trade and Cultural Exchange in the Early Modern Mediterranean: Braudel's Maritime Legacy,* ed. Maria Fusaro, Colin Heywood, and Mohamed-Salah Omri (London: I. B. Tauris, 2010), 117–37.

37. Bruce Taylor discusses the "deepening climate of fear" on the Spanish coasts, without, however, addressing the concurrent fear on the North African coast: "The Enemy Within and Without: An Anatomy of Fear on the Spanish Mediterranean Littoral," in *Fear in Early Modern Society,* ed. William Naphy and Penny Roberts (Manchester: Manchester University Press, 1997): 78–99.

38. See the discussion of the decline of Turkish navigation in chapter 11 of Carlo M. Cipolla, *Guns, Sails and Empires: Technological Innovation and the Early Phases of European Expansion 1400–1700* (New York: Sunflower University Press, 1965). As the author notes, the " 'Moors' of the North African coast put together a considerable fleet of sailing vessels . . . . [but] Western naval technology kept moving ahead faster and the Turks lagged hopelessly behind" (103).

39. Nabil Matar, *Europe through Arab Eyes, 1578–1727* (New York: Columbia University Press, 2009), 201, 202.

40. Abd al-Majīd al-Turkī, "Wathāʾiq ʿan al-hijra al-Andalūsiyya al-akhīra ilā Tūnis," *Ḥawliyyāt al-Jāmiʿa al-Tūnisiyya* 4 (1967): 42.

41. *Nafḥ al-ṭīb,* ed. Maryam Qāsim Ṭāwīl and Yūsuf ʿAlī Ṭawīl, vol. 1 (Beirut: Dar al-kutub al-ʿilmiyya, 1995), 40. See also www.alwaraq.com for other references.

42. Abū Sālim ʿAbdalla ibn Muḥammad al-ʿAyyāshī, *al-Riḥla al-ʿAyyāshiyya* [The Ayyashi journey], ed. Saʿīd al-Fadlī and Sulaymān al-Qurashī, 2 vols. (Abu Dhabi: Dār al-Suwaydī, 2006), 1:274–75.

43. Al-ʿAyyāshī, *al-Riḥla al-ʿAyyāshiyya,* 2:470–71.

44. *Tuḥfat al-udabā' wa salwat al-ghurabā'* [The litterateurs' gift and the strangers' solace], ed. Raja Maḥmūd al-Samarrāi (Baghdad: Wizārat al-thaqāfa wa-l-a'lām, 1969), 193.

45. "Gaza the End of the Holy Land," al-Muḥibbī, *Khulāṣāt al-āthār* [Summaries of antiquities], 4 vols. (Beirut, 1966), 2:230.

46. Al-Muḥibbī, *Khulāṣāt al-āthār,* 1:314; 2:348. Muslims told numerous stories of being hauled off to slave markets during sea travels; by the second half of the eighteenth century, there were by far more Muslim slaves held in Malta or Livorno or Cadiz than Christians in Libyan Tripoli or Salé. See the numbers cited by Thomas Freller, "'The Shining of the Moon'—The Mediterranean Tour of Muhammad ibn Uthman, Envoy of Morocco, in 1782," *Journal of Mediterranean Studies* 12 (2002): 309.

47. *Al-Mu'nis fī akhbār Ifrīqiya wa Tūnis* [A companion to news about Tunis and Africa] (Beirut: Dār al-Masīra, 1993), 24. Tunis had been initially called Ifrīqya (Africa) by the Arab conquerors.

48. Aḥmad al-Damurdāshī, *Kitāb al-durrā al-muṣāna fī akhbār al-kinānah* [The book of the valuable pearl] (Cairo: al-Ma'had al-'ilmī al-Faransī li-l-āthār al-sharqīyya bi-l-Qāhira, 1989), 179.

49. Ḥammūdah ibn Muḥammad ibn 'Abd al-'Azīz, *Al-Kitāb al-Bāshī,* ed. Muḥammad Mādūr, 2 vols. (Tunis: Al-Dār al-Tūnisīyah li-l-nashr, 1970), 1:369.

50. *Alf layla wa layla* [One thousand and one nights], ed. Muḥammad Qaṭṭa al-'Adawī, 2 vols. (Būlāq, 1252 AH), 2:445. This edition was the first version printed in the Arab world.

51. See the stories on pp. 249–69 and 863–94. There are no titles in the Būlāq edition.

52. See my study of these stories in "Christians in the *Arabian Nights,*" in *The Arabian Nights in Historical Context: Between East and West,* ed. Saree Makdisi and Felicity Nussbaum (Oxford: Oxford University Press, 2008), 131–53.

53. *Riḥlat al-Amīr Fakhr al-Dīn ilā Iṭalyā (1613–1618)* [The journey of Prince Fakhr al-Din to Italy], ed. Wisām Wahb (Beirut: Dār al-Suwaydī, 2007), 36.

54. *The Adventures of Captain Alonso de Contreras,* trans. and annotated Philip Dallas (New York: Paragon House, 1989); Jamāl Kamāl Maḥmoud, *al-Qarāṣina fī-l-Baḥr al-Mutawassiṭ fī-l-'Aṣr al-'Uthmānī* [The pirates of the Mediterranean Sea during the Ottoman Period] (Cairo: al-Hay'a al-Miṣriyya al-'āmma li-l-kitāb, 2015); Maḥmoud Aḥmad 'Alī Hadiyya, *Qarāṣinat Gharb al-Baḥr al-Mutawassit* (Pirates of the western Mediterranean) (Dubai: Markaz Jum'a al-Mājid, 2017).

55. *Akhbār al-duwal* [Histories of nations], ed. Aḥmad Haṭṭīṭ and Fahmī Sa'd, 3 vols. (Beirut: 'Ālam al-kutub, 1992), 3:421, 422.

56. *Riḥlat al-shitā' wa-l-ṣayf* [The winter and summer journey], ed. Samīr al-Shinnāwī (Beirut: Dār al-Suwaydī, 2004), 159, 216.

57. *Akhbār al-'uwal* [Histories of the beginnings] (Cairo: n.p., 1883), 190.

58. "Hadhā kitāb dhikr kalām al-nās fī manba' al-Nīl," MS Landberg 365, reel 12, fol. 8r, Center for Bilād al-Shām, Jordan University.

59. Muṣṭafa As'ad al-Luqaymī, *Uns al-Jalīl fī Tarīkh al-Quds wa-l-Khalīl* [The glorious companion to the history of Jerusalem and Hebron], ed. Khalid Abdul Kareem Hamshari *[sic]* ('Akka: Mu'assassat al-aswār, 2001), 52.

60. As Professor Casale explained to me, "This is simply a *calque* of the Turkish name for the Mediterranean 'Ak Deniz,' meaning 'white sea.' It comes from the old Central Asian system of associating colors with directions: black is north, white is south. The Black Sea is called the Black Sea (also in English) because it is north of Anatolia, while the 'White Sea' is south."

61. Sonja Brentjes, "Mapmaking in Ottoman Istanbul between 1650 and 1750: A Domain of Painters, Calligraphers, or Cartographers," in *Frontiers of Ottoman Studies: State, Province, and the West,* 2 vols., ed. Colin Imber, Keiko Kiyotaki, and Rhoads Murphey (London: I. B. Tauris, 2005), 2:132.

62. *Al-Ḥulal al-sundusiyya fī al-akhbār al-Tūnisiyya* [The silk robes of the Tunisian accounts], ed. Muḥammad al-Ḥabīb al-Hīla, vol. 2, part 1 (Tunis: Dār al-kutub al-sharqiyya, 1973), 123.

63. "The Journey of Muḥammad Effendī," MS Arabe 2296, Bibliothèque nationale de France. See also the edition by Zayd Eid al-Rawāyḍ, *Safar ilā Faransā* (Travel to France) (Riyad: Markaz al-Malik

Faysal li-l-buḥūth al-ʿilmiyya, 2014); and Anonymous, "A Popular Account of Modern Russia," ISL 2449, India Office, British Library.

64. MS Arabe 312, fol. 40, Bibliothèque nationale de France.

65. *Al-Dhahab wa-l-ʿāṣifa* [The gold and the storm], ed. Nūrī al-Jarrāḥ (Beirut: Dār al-Suwaydī, 2001), 40, 41.

66. Abū ʿAbdallah Muḥammad al-ʿAbdarī, in his pilgrimage from Morocco in 1289, used the same terms, *Baḥr al-Sharq* and *Baḥr al-Gharb,* as the Syrian chronicler al-Qaramānī, who used *Baḥr al-Gharb* for the sea near Granada (*Akhbār al-duwal,* 3:264). But al-Qaramānī also referred to a conglomerate of two seas, *Mujammaʿ al-Baḥrayn,* which included the sea of Ceuta, near al-Andalus (*Akhbār al-duwal,* 2:309, 386).

67. Mīkhāʾīl Brayk, *Wathāʾiq tārīkhiyya li-l-kursī al-malakī al-Anṭakī-* [Historical documents of the Antiochean Melkite Church], ed. Qusṭanṭīn al-Bāsha (Ḥarīṣa, Lebanon: Maṭbaʿat al-qiddīs, 1930), 34, 39, 57.

68. al-Miknāsī, *al-Iksīr fī fikāk al-asīr* [The elixir in ransoming the captive], ed. Muḥammad al-Fāsī (Rabat: al-Muʾassassa al-jāmiʿiyya li-l-baḥth al-ʿilmī, 1965), 20.

69. *Riḥlat al-Miknāsī* [Miknasi's journey], ed. Muḥammad Bukabbūt (Abu Dhabi: Dār al-Suwaydī, 2003), 77, 78.

70. *Al-Tarjumāna al-kubrā fī akhbār al-maʿmūr barran wa baḥran* [The great history of the world, by land and sea], ed. ʿAbd al-Karīm al-Filālī (Rabat: Dār nashr al-maʿrifa, 1991), 294. See also his use of "Green Sea" (301). For a discussion of "Baḥr al-Maghrib," see the article by C. F. Seybold in *Encyclopedia Islamica.*

71. Al-Zayānī, *Al-Tarjumāna al-kubrā,* 129.

72. Al-Zayānī, *Al-Tarjumāna al-kubrā,* 130.

73. Al-Idrīsī, *Nuzhat al-mushtāq,* 2:526, and al-Zayānī, *Al-Tarjumāna al-kubrā,* 71.

74. Stephen Greenblatt, *Marvelous Possessions: The Wonder of the New World* (Chicago: Chicago University Press, 1991).

75. *Trinity House of Deptford Transactions, 1609–1635,* ed. G. G. Harris (London, 1983), 43, 45.

76. As Tiresias tells Odysseus, "Carry your well-planed oar until you come / to a race of people who know nothing of the sea." Homer, *Odyssey,* trans. Robert Fagles (New York: Penguin, 1996), bk. 11, ll. 139–42.

77. See chapter 1 in Moulay Belhemīsī, *al-Baḥr wa-l-ʿArab fī-l-tārīkh wa-l-adab* [The Arabs and the sea in history and literature] (Algiers: Manshūrāt ANEP, 2005).

78. *Riḥlat Ibn Ḥamadūsh al-Jazāʾirī,* ed. Abū al-Qāsim Saʿdallah (Algiers: al-Muʾassassa al-waṭaniyya, 1983), 255. For another meaning of *qūnās,* see note 66 in Svat Soucek, "Islamic Charting in the Mediterranean," in *The History of Cartography,*" ed. J. B. Harley and David Woodward, vol. 2, bk. 1 (Chicago: University of Chicago Press, 1992).

79. *Corrupting Sea,* 172.

80. Brummett, "Visions of the Mediterranean," *Journal of Medieval and Early Modern Studies* 37 (2007): 4.

81. The phrase comes from the call for papers to a conference entitled "The Information Fabric of the Pre-modern Mediterranean, 1400–1800," organized by Daniel Hershenzon and Wolfgang Kaiser, March 20–23, 2013, Mersin, Turkey. See also the earlier view by Sharon Kinoshita, who in commenting on Horden and Purcell's *The Corrupting Sea,* argued that there were "local, small-scale interactions and connectivities" in the basin. "Medieval Mediterranean Literature," *PMLA* 124 (2009): 604.

82. "The Mediterranean as a Borderland," *Review of Middle East Studies* 46 (2012): 54–63. See the earlier discussion of the Mediterranean as frontier in Kahlaoui, "Depiction of the Mediterranean," 44–46; and in section 2 of Ralph W. Brauer, *Boundaries and Frontiers in Medieval Muslim Geography* (Philadelphia: American Philosophical Society, 1995).

83. M.-N. Bourguet, *L'Invention scientifique de la Méditérrannée: Egypte, Morée, Algérie* (Paris: Ecole des hautes études en sciences sociales, 1998). See also Christopher Drew Armstrong, "Travel and Experience in the Mediterranean of Louis XV," in *Rethinking the Mediterranean,* ed. W.V. Harris (Oxford: Oxford University Press, 2005), 235–67. Armstrong credits the creation of a conceptual and commercial Mediterranean chiefly to French policies in place from Louis XV on.

84. MS Arabe 2249, 87v, Bibliothèque nationale de France.

85. *An Imam in Paris,* trans. Daniel L. Newman (London: Saqi, 2011), 114.

86. MS Orientale 48, St. Joseph University, Beirut, Lebanon, fol. 5v, from microfilm reel 754,Bilād al-Shām collection, University of Jordan.

87. *Riḥlat al-Saffār ilā Faransā* [The journey of al-Saffār to France], ed. Susan Miller and Khalid bin al-Ṣghir (Beirut: Dār al-Suwaydī, 2007), 118–19.

88. *Thalāth raḥalāt Jazā'iriyya ilā Bārīs* [Three Algerian journeys to Paris], ed. Khālid Ziyādeh (Beirut: al-Mu'assassa al-'Arabiyya li-l-dirāsāt wa-l-nashr, 1979), 50.

89. *Al-Riḥla-l-Ibrīziyya ilā al-diyār al-Inqlīziyya* [The golden journey to English lands], ed. Muḥammadal-Fāsi (Rabat: Jami'at Muḥammad V, 1967), 34.

90. *Al-Jinān* (August 1, 1873): 562.

91. *Ṣafwat al-i'tibār,* vol. 1 (Beirut: n.p., 1974), 41.

92. *Khizānat al-anām fī tarājim al-'idhām* [A depository of biographies of the great] (New York, 1899).

93. 'Īsā Iskandar al-Ma'lūf, *Dawānī al-qutūf fī tarīkh banī al-Ma'lūf* [A harvest from the history of the Ma'lūf family] (Ba'abda, Lebanon, 1907–8), 136.

94. Al-doctoor Najīb 'Abdū al-Lubnānī, *Dr. Abdou's Travels in America: al-Safar al-mufīd fī al-'ālam al-jadīd* (Washington, DC, 1907), 414.

95. *Al-Muqtabas* (1910), 221.

96. *Yawmiyyāt Khalīl al-Sakākīnī: Yawmiyyāt, rasa'il, ta'ammulāt* [The diary of Khalil Sakakini], ed. Akram Musallam, vol. 1 (Ramallah: Markaz Khalīl Sakākinī al-thaqāfī, 2003.

97. *Tarīikh al-Wilāyat al-Muttaḥida* [History of the United States] (New York: Maṭba'at Jarīdat al-Dalīl, 1913), 731.

98. *Ḥaḍārat al-'Arab fī-l-Andalus* [The civilization of the Arabs in al-Andalus] (Cairo: n.p., 1923), 149.

99. *Murshid al-ṭullāb ilā jughrāfiyyāt al-kitāb* [A student's guide to geography] (n.p., 1905), 1; *Tārīkh al-Nāṣirah* (History of Nazareth) (Cairo: Maṭba'at al-Hilāl, 1924), 191.

100. Esposito, *Narrative Mediterranean,* xviii.

101. I am grateful to professors Muhammad Asfour, Giancarlo Casale, Molly Greene, and Wadad Kadi for their comments and suggestions.

2

The Mediterranean of the Barbary Coast

Gone Missing

Julia Clancy-Smith

Ignacio Palombo and Dominique Delicata were in the business of ransoming North African slaves held in Malta; or, more precisely, they operated one link in a chain of brokers moving enslaved persons and ransom money around the central Mediterranean corridor during the eighteenth century. In 1710, the two men sailed from Valletta for Sousse, accompanied by five Tunisian Muslim captives. Before departing, Delicata placed his own (unnamed) wife under the peculiar guardianship of Joseph Gresafoulli, a fellow Maltese and kingpin of operations. In effect, the wife was labeled a *caution,* a deposit of good faith to guarantee that the men would not abscond with the funds that Tunisian families would hopefully hand over to free loved ones. Her status as *caution* served to spin the wheels (or sails) of the traffic in humans.[1]

Several decades later, during the spring equinox (March) of 1762, a season notorious for treacherous weather, the daughter of Shaykh Bil-Qasim al-Samadhi, a rich widow from Baja (or Beja), made ready to perform the pilgrimage to Mecca with her two sons. Free to manage her own financial affairs, she converted worldly possessions into merchandise, reserved places on a ship soon to depart La Goulette for Alexandria, and journeyed to the capital. Despite the widow's well-laid plans, she fortuitously missed the boat and narrowly escaped death, because violent winds hurled the ship into reefs off Mahdiyya with great loss of life. That same year, during the spring equinox, a ghost ship appeared off the coast between Tabarka and Bizerte. Its wreck funneled unimaginable wealth to hordes of scavengers on the shoreline. We take up tales of the traffic in humans, of vessels adrift, and of the pious female pilgrim momentarily.

These story fragments raise questions that have not been fully answered or even posed: how did women and men travel the Mediterranean? What mechanisms or

FIGURE 2. Fishermen on the wharf in Istanbul, ca. 1930. Courtesy of Branson DeCou.

arrangements channeled things, as well as people, to intended destinations—or to accidental ports of call? Was the "wife as *caution*" a common practice in trans-sea exchanges? Who were the on-the-ground brokers between North Africa and the wider maritime world, and what capillary strands of association and trust (or mistrust) did they draw on or violate? How did the Mediterranean as both geocultural frame and nautical actor—with its seasons, winds, and currents and its countless islands big and small, inhabited and uninhabited—dictate who went where, when, and how? What procedures and local conventions—the microlevel rules of engagement—governed the disposal of shipwrecks? And how does a view from the shoreline, where swimmers and Bedouins scrambled, either to save themselves from raging seas or partake of bounty floating in the waters, contribute to "reimagining the Mediterranean"? Owing to the paucity of evidence and scholarship for some places and periods, this essay seeks not to respond satisfactorily to these queries but rather to put them out on the table for historians to pursue.

But first, what does the early modern and modern maritime historiography for North Africa look like? And how might small hitherto unexplored spaces and unknown people located somewhere on the "southern rim" reconfigure understandings of the ways in which the Mediterranean was navigated and experienced elsewhere?

HISTORIOGRAPHIES

From Carthage to colonialism, narratives of the Mediterranean in certain eras suffer from a missing persons and places syndrome. Burbank and Cooper's 2010 *Empires in World History* is emblematic of the problem. This work completely erases Carthage from the story of imperial Rome ascendant.[2] Before the current second-wave surge of scholarly production on Ottoman maritime history, the sea's northern rim had long been privileged. Even with the present rush to the water by Ottoman historians, the eastern end of the Basin still attracts more notice than points west of Alexandria.[3] Until recently, the Maghrib was peopled mainly by shady Moors, Turks, renegades, captives, and pirates, as well as, after 1830, by "the colonized," although the historiography is shifting rapidly and moving in felicitous directions.[4]

The present tsunami of research on medieval and early modern Iberia, North Africa, and the Western Mediterranean has not only profoundly altered the narrative but also created new regional units of analysis for investigating unsuspected connectivities through comparative and world history methodologies.[5] Historians now argue that no community in Islamic Spain was hermetically sealed off from another because religious, legal, and political borders were porous and elastic. Reimagining the Mediterranean Basin as made up of contact zones of varying scales and tempos, rather than as a single unified sea, means that its Muslim shores are no longer quarantined from broader historical processes or patterns. This perspective resutures, for example, the previously severed histories of Islamic- and Norman-ruled Sicily (10th–11th centuries) and southern Italy with al-Andalous and the Maghrib.[6]

If the focus turns to key individuals or small-scale communities of men and women, slaves and free persons, converts and *conversos* (and not simply "Muslims, Jews, and Christians") in multireligious military borderlands, in crowded cities, in households, or on the high seas, North Africa appears not only as unexceptional but also as central to trans-Mediterranean political and cultural destinies in the periods characterized as "medieval," circa eighth century CE on. However, an unexamined assumption in most of the literature begs for reflection: the notion that "to be connected" was deemed desirable, something positive, by contemporaries. One might presume that the later construction of modern lighthouses along the Algerian and Tunisian coastlines in the nineteenth century was greeted with delight by many, dismay by some. The much older system of nocturnal flares, ostensibly to enlighten vessels regarding navigational positioning and maritime hazards, such as reefs, were manipulated to deceive unwary captains, yielding bounty to habitual coastal foragers as ships shattered on shoals or rocks. The prime example of unwelcome connections new to the nineteenth century that might have put some seamen out of business is the steamship, which could berth only in specific ports.[7] At the same time, the "age of steam" launched countless more sail- and oar-powered boats on the water. The point is that for communities in earlier or later epochs, novel linkages—whether nurtured by new transport technologies, instruments for credit or association, or "improved" means of warfare—were experienced differentially, a boon for some, a disadvantage or disaster for others. Some older, more comfortable connections succumbed to unfamiliar ones, but others were reinvented or reoriented.

A major flaw in current literature is that historians approach Mediterranean North Africa with a cadastral *mentalité.* A handful of port cities cum capitals—Algiers and Tunis—occupy center stage, while smaller ports, such as Tetouan, Tabarka, Bizerte, or Sousse, languish in obscurity. And we never get to the wharves, the beach, and the onboard ships or fragile boats. More significantly, sailing specialists—navigators, captains, coral divers, and seamen—are hardly, if at all, mentioned. Their written and orally transmitted knowledge—logs, manuals, and records composed in polyglot vernaculars—are rarely mined for data on how things at sea touched land. The identities of brokers are vague, and the view from the water's edge remains uncharted. Maritime "provinces" are severed from the indeterminate, vaguely threatening "interior," consigned to landlubber farmers and pastoralists. Mediation is cast solely as a human activity, often monopolized by religious or ethnic minorities. Yet I argue here that "natural" or geographical entities, such as islets, whether inhabited or not, might be conceived of as mediators. Seasonal climatic conditions and variations dictated who could go where, when they could go, and how they could get there. In brief, cultural or political explanations do not suffice to explain phenomena that necessitate geophysical, ecological, or environmental evidence and arguments.

What if conventional perspectives were skewed—if the mappable center, or centers, came to rest somewhere on the North African coast in the time before colonialism? Things slide momentarily out of focus, while others unexpectedly surface, which was the methodological point of my 2013 study, *Mediterraneans.* This vista flushes out second-tier ports, such as Sousse, whose location and small population have rendered it nearly invisible in colonial and nationalist narratives but which functioned as a node for ransoming Muslim slaves during the eighteenth century.

The first part of this chapter briefly retraces some of the journeys, departures, and detours that ultimately produced *Mediterraneans,* taking up the questions that arose along the way and those that are still pending. Directly related, the second section investigates the people, things, and places that remain archived as more or less "gone missing." In a sense, my query riffs on the challenge James Clifford posed some time ago: "Who is localized when the ethnographer's tent is pitched in center of a village?"[8] I ask, however, who and what is localized when the historian decamps from the Mediterranean's well-studied shores to peer into different centers, as well as margins.

THE QUESTION OF FRANCE: *LE MAUVAIS ITALIEN DE BARBARIE*

Let us first address the issue of France and North Africa during the early modern and modern eras. Imperial France looms large, perhaps too large, in historiography, in large measure because of Algeria and 1830. In the longue durée, what would later become "Italy" had always enjoyed the closest ties with "Greater Tunisia," roughly the territory of *Africa Proconsularis,* stretching from Bône (Annaba) to Tripoli. Treaties between Italian republics and the Hafsid Dynasty (1229–1574) dated to the thirteenth century, if not earlier. Compared with similar agreements of the time, the thirty-year commercial accord signed around 1229 by the king of Tunis, Abu Zakariya Yahya, with the Republic of Pisa was not unusual.[9] Among the so-called Barbary states, Tunisia boasted the most favorable reputation. In 1866, Louis de Mas Latrie, who analyzed centuries' worth of treaties that were concluded in Arabic and European languages, summed up the prevailing view: "Tunis has always been the principal center of relations between Europe and Barbary. . . . The government of the Hafsids preserved the country's ancient tradition of beneficence and trust with regard to Christian nations in general. The *funduqs* [residences and warehouses] of the Europeans in Tunis enjoyed complete security."[10]

Transport technologies, as well as shared maritime science, during the millennia-long "age of sail and oar" explain the close-knit relations between Greater Tunisia and Italian states and ports. But geography mattered. After all, the Strait from Tunis to Sicily measures a mere ninety miles at its narrowest point, although deadly currents, unfavorable winds, and semiconcealed shoals rendered the crossing perilous at certain moments. And as recent maritime archaeological evidence demonstrates, large ships had sailed directly on the open sea from North Africa to Italy since Punic times, but *cabotage,* or shorter, coastal hops and jumps to places hugging the shores of Sardinia, Sicily, and Malta, as well as numerous microislands, made possible innumerable commodity exchanges and human migrations.[11] In effect, this maritime nexus predated Roman advances into the sea and persisted into the modern and contemporary eras. However, the sixteenth-century Ottoman conquests of North Africa strengthened the west-east axes of exchange and produced, somewhat by accident, a new dynasty. Founded by the son of a Muslim from Venetian-ruled and subsequently Ottoman-controlled Crete, the Husaynid Dynasty (1705–1956) mirrored the larger play of trans-Mediterranean politics for two and a half centuries.[12]

At first the Husaynid beys (princes) strategically married women from the Tuniso-Algerian borders to cement ties with powerful tribal confederations, because the gravest dangers to the nascent state lay there, to the west. However, the rulers increasingly preferred "Italian" women as slaves, servants, concubines, or wives. Ali Bey (r. 1759–82) married a Genoese slave woman, as reported by a chronicler: "It came to pass that a ship belonging to the bey captured on the high seas a Genoese vessel with a beautiful young woman of twenty years on board. The *ra'is* (captain) took special pains that she be hidden from the sailors' gaze. As soon as the captain landed in Tunis, he informed the bey of the captive's presence"; she converted to Islam and married the ruler, bearing several sons who ascended the Husaynid throne.[13] Italian physicians and courtiers, many of them Jews from Livorno, were paramount at court. Built environment offers compelling clues regarding trans-sea cultural affinities. Many Tunis elites resided in palaces fashioned by skilled "Italian" (or Italianate) craftsmen and adorned them with immense Venetian glass chandeliers and other imported luxury furnishings—as well as Punic-Roman spolia. Indeed, I argue that the very existence of the "many Italies" until 1871 and after nurtured all manner of exchanges with Greater Tunisia and directly shaped the "French" protectorate.[14]

Until late in the nineteenth century, *le mauvais Italien de Barbarie* (the bad Italian of Barbary) constituted the regency's diplomatic language and lingua franca for expatriates and native residents dealing with the world outside, which by the eighteenth century included not only Europe but also the Americas. Although its lexicography remains obscure, one source characterized this means of communication as a "horrible mélange of languages." An eighteenth-century observer of the Husaynid court stated that, "the reigning bey speaks Italian or *petit moresque* a corrupted Italian mixed with French and Spanish."[15] This language, classified as a dialect, was in fact written. It was employed by a French notary in Tunis to narrate and legally verify the slave ransoming deal concocted by Palombo and Delicata in 1710. However bad it was (in the eyes of purists), "bad Italian" shaped European views of the "dominions of Tunis." Christian Windler advances an important argument regarding *petit moresque;* it made Tunisia appear less foreign, strangely near, to Europeans, in contrast to Cairo or Istanbul.[16] After 1881, Tunisian Italian was gradually, although never completely, replaced by Tunisian French, but surely this "new" (or old) language was overlaid onto its "impure" ancestor. Before and during the protectorate, Sicilians and Maltese in Tunis or provincial ports like Porto Farina (Ghar al-Milh) often used "dialectical" Arabic (*darja*) to compose letters, records, and petitions, as did Tunisian Jews of diverse backgrounds. One of the characteristics of vernacular Arabic was its inflection with Italian languages.[17] As imperial France learned with great reluctance, the Tunisian Italian attachment, while not always one of endearment, was enduring.

Related, although somewhat contradictory, questions driving my book were simply stated: Why leave home—home being mainly the Catholic islands and southern Europe—for North Africa if, until the 1820s, Barbary represented a land of danger, captivity, and apostasy, whose inhabitants were pitiless enemies of the Christians? How was North Africa transformed in the European or "Western" collective imagination into one of most active migratory frontiers in the Mediterranean—in less than two decades, from circa 1816 to 1830? And what historical forces—small, local, and large—converged to convince large numbers of Italian, Spanish, Maltese, or Sicilian peasants that this place of idolatrous oppression offered opportunities for good fortune, for making it? It took a long time to formulate these questions. Along the way, I had to consider changing modalities of empire and visual imperialism; networks of knowledge and displacement; technologies of movement (including something called passports); highly variable, unstable notions of protection; and where North Africa and Europe began and ended. Perhaps the nomenclature "North Africa," and "Europe" were in and of themselves part of the problem.

The challenge, then, became how to narrate the history of the modern Mediterranean World from simultaneous vantage points: people claiming to be "of the Maghrib" and those "in the Maghrib," whose status remained tantalizing, and even artfully, muddled: accidental sojourners, familiar strangers, the not quite indigenous, the not quite European, and creoles fashioned by cultural naturalization over time.[18] From the eighteenth century on, a relatively large number of Corsicans were born in Tunisia, and "ten women without husbands or whose husbands are absent" were registered with consular authorities. This was despite the fact that the Chambre de Commerce de Marseilles periodically forbade French women lacking male kin to police them from residing in the *Echelles de Levant et Barbarie.* Other categories of French subjects regarded Tunisia as "home," notably Protestant Huguenot trading communities, but were deemed "unauthorized" by the consulate in Tunis; they were expatriate "expatriates."[19] Therefore, close scrutiny of Europe's exiled, expulsés, and "shoveled out"—as well as the notorious "high rollers" of expanding imperialism—integrates the Mediterranean's northern rims into a Maghrib-centered narrative. But what has emerged from this exercise in inversion?

Even without France's 1830 invasion of Algeria, the counterintuitive (for today) north-to-south migrations would have transpired, owing to "population overshoot" on the big and small islands framing the Maghrib. Labor and other kinds of movements to the African littoral intensified from the early nineteenth century on—and to Tunisia as early as the 1820s—priming the pump for larger, wider migratory pulses across the Mediterranean and Atlantic. The life trajectories of settlers in Algiers or Tunis who returned to Sicily, only to strike out for the Americas or

Australia, represent a fund of data in need of recuperation. Migrants, who thought that they had settled permanently in North Africa, subsequently departed, leaving their mark there. Conversely, they took the Maghrib with them, whatever their ultimate destination. Of course, there was nothing innocent about any of this.

People abandoned homelands for many reason, frequently without meaning to do so. Leaving constituted an ever-present "adjacent possible," and migrants were always more than simply that: they were family members, soldiers on the lam, peasants, pilgrims, opportunists, spies, saints, and sinners. Directly related to this, the notion that a fatal divergence distinguished the ways in which Muslim and Western societies came to modernity is no longer credible. Viewing from below, wherever "below" was located, one perceives that the major eddies and flows structuring the long nineteenth century did not necessarily advantage only European "national" groups. Some reaped benefits from novel if menacing trends, while others managed to cut losses. Religious affiliation, an essential source of personal and communal legal and other identities, was not at all times the most decisive element in outcome. In other words, this is a cautionary note regarding the sly teleologies embedded in grand imperial narratives from above.

The century's major markers and ruptures—imperialism, invasion, territorial dismemberment, and subprime diplomatic agreements, such as the 1838 Anglo-Ottoman commercial treaty—mattered less in some places and times. Heterogeneous parties to microlocal deals that frequently incubated transnational disputes were oblivious to treaty obligations, or commanded an arsenal of dodges for evading interference. For the Algerian merchant Jacob Lasry, 1830 brought not disaster but a spectacular windfall. He reaped a fortune and amassed mounds of debt by supplying the French army with horses and foodstuffs, drawing on his expertise in older trans-Mediterranean circuits, notably the Gibraltar-Tetouan-Oran "smuggling" traffic.[20]

Ships, ports, and transient hinterlands functioned as interfaces between North African producers and trans-sea distribution networks, presenting the state with the first or last chance to tax, limit, or proscribe seaborne commerce and human displacements. The modern world is incomprehensible without a social history that factors in the workings of "oppositional cultures" among sailors or dock laborers, whose toil underwrote the global maritime economy. Yet, as mentioned above, sailors, captains, and fishermen remain almost completely absent from North African narratives, which is curious in light of the region's long, intense involvement in the sea. Why?[21] For these seafarers, the Mediterranean embodied a space of residence as well as transit, a place of resource extraction, livelihood, and identity. This often rendered them politically and morally suspect. Sea nomadism came with a price. Island folks also aroused deep suspicion on the part of land-based states claiming jurisdiction over floating bits of territory. Ships constituted a socioreligious, commercial, and legal universe. As seaborne republics, they shipped cargoes, human and otherwise, that mirrored the circumstances of warfare or peace, bad or good sailing weather, and boom or bust economic conditions.

For centuries, North African seamen ran pilgrimage tours from eastern Algeria, Tunisia, and Tripolitania to Alexandria; travelers, the pious and profane, and merchandise were embarked and unloaded here and there along the way. They generally followed similar routes determined by the existence of islets, food, and water but were greatly influenced by seasons and politics.[22] For these sea specialists, the Mediterranean represented less a space of unity, or of interconnections, than trodden microspaces and predictable behaviors. Some vessels were little more than floating prisons. During the nineteenth century, their numbers increased as laws and practices of protection or legal belonging congealed; some unfortunate devils were permanently exiled on the high seas.[23] Before and after the age of steam, a vessel's contents reflected both older social realities and shifts in local, regional, and global scales. Typical passenger manifests from circa 1850 to the 1870s for vessels docking in La Goulette registered a wide array of wares and products, as well as these individuals: North African, Ottoman, and European traders; military and diplomatic officers; engineers (including a Mexican national); bakers; servants; and "a hat-maker; a dentist; a watchmaker; a wine merchant; several carriage makers; and a manufacturer of fizzy lemonade drink, the cola of the day."[24] Of course, manifests camouflaged as much as they divulged.

In short, the book was about different types of navigation, how webs became lines—or vice versa—and ultimately about how microhistory, *alltagsgeschichte,* "history from below," and macrohistory might be reconfigured as traveling companions. What about other people, processes, and places still catalogued in the "gone missing" dossier? This brings us to the second part of my essay that offers avenues for future research.

GONE MISSING: DISSIMULATORS, PROTECTION, AND WOMEN

Displacements, whether voluntary or not, across sea or land—and often both—demanded creative dissimulation or risk aversion, which renders the historians' task daunting. Voyagers were neither who nor what they purported to be—nor were the ships that carried them. Uncertainty and borrowed identities were leveraged for profit or mere self-preservation. Traversing the Mediterranean without annoyance during the sixteenth and seventeenth centuries induced English Protestants to frequently dress, eat, and behave like Catholics as they entered Spanish, French, or Italian ports; some even attended Mass at Maltese churches.[25] In his early seventeenth-century travels from England to Constantinople, the English Levant Company chaplain William Biddulph described Malta, one of the most enthusiastic inquisition centers, in unflattering terms: "They [the Maltese] are such barbarous people," who would gladly consign to the fire "Protestants and good Christians," and "there are so many viperous people there . . . renegades and bandits of sundry nations."[26] In the same century, the Spanish Jew Girolamo, who had earlier purportedly converted to Catholicism, countered the Maltese inquisitor's charges of apostasy by pleading that he had only assumed the name Jacob Gomes of Tetouan and the guise of a Jew, into order to travel to "Algiers to baptize all those Turks who had not yet reached the age of reason."[27] The man alleging to be Gomes put forth a telling rationalization for his travels, demonstrating familiarity with such doctrinal positions regarding the conduct of legitimate conversions as "not yet reached the age of reason." Many who landed by design or serendipity in North Africa, or on nearby islands, could furnish an array of identities, culled from a rich menu of guises, depending on the urgency of circumstance and the contingency of whom they encountered. In 1870, Nicola Malinghoussy, allegedly a soldier in the pope's army, got into a barroom brawl in La Goulette and, threatened with prison, declared himself a protégé of France. He ultimately claimed five different national jurisdictions before being thrown aboard a French military vessel bound for Bone, for want of a cleaner solution.[28]

"Protection," *protégé,* and *himaya* had varying connotations across the Mediterranean World, depending not only on period and place but also on social class, profession, religion, and happenstance. The notion of protégé calls forth the state of the unequal, the vulnerable, but not the unequivocal. At times, the seekers of "protection" and those conferring it held dissimilar mental maps and sociolegal expectations. Thus, one strategy for historicizing the Mediterranean from below is to exhume local sociocultural and political customs governing protection, and the principles of engagement undergirding it, and triangulate them with the praxis of dissimulation, identity-marking, and movement. For the vast majority of women, gender conventions limited, and even proscribed, a range of physical displacements. Nonetheless, the unfortunate state of being female offered protection for women traveling unaccompanied. Two English Quaker ladies, Katherine Evans and Sarah Cheeves, failed (or chose not to) to disguise their true identities when they disembarked in Malta in the seventeenth century. Their presence caused a stir, so they were brought before the inquisitor on suspicion that they intended to proselytize among Catholics or captive Moors. Only the gendered opinion that their religious beliefs and brazen public preaching signaled an especially potent type of womanly madness spared them imprisonment. Mobility, and the perils that entailed, demanded subterfuge. Some women wore male garb to board or disembark from ships in Mediterranean ports.[29]

How did gender shape different kinds of physical and other displacements? For the early modern period, we are beginning to dimly understand women's participation in trans-Mediterranean exchanges, including collective confessional fears and rumors about female ransom captives or slaves.[30] Other kinds of involvement with and in the sea, however, remain largely unexplored. The Andalusian Moroccan woman Sayyida al-Hurra ibn Banu Rashid (ca. 1485–ca. 1542), whose life has generated much legend and lore, affords some clues. Known mainly in European sources as the "pirate-princess," her family fled Granada in 1492 for Chaouen in northern Morocco after the last Muslim kingdom fell to the Reconquista. Married to a notable, al-Mandari, the sultan of the restored port of Tetouan, al-Hurra assumed her husband's functions sometime after his death in 1515 (the exact dates are subject to dispute) and retained power until 1542. The female governor (*al-hakima*) concluded treaties with surrounding European states "as their partner in the diplomatic game" and negotiated the fates of captive Christians and Muslims. It seems that she accompanied ships into battle and on corsair raids. In one instance, al-Hurra's forces attacked Gibraltar with five boats, netting booty and many hostages, and around 1520 they captured a Portuguese governor's wife.[31]

The princess took an interest in politics to the east and apparently allied with Khayr al-Din Barbarossa (ca. 1478–1546). This "Turkish" ruler of the Ottoman military sanjak of Algiers (from 1517 on), had earlier employed La Goulette's strategic location and Hafsid patronage to become an admired naval strategist and feared privateer. Al-Hurra's second husband, Ahmad al-Wattasi, none other than the king of Morocco, agreed to a departure from dynastic nuptial protocols to marry al-Hurra in Tetouan, not in Fez. After governing for several decades, the hakima was overthrown by male members of her own family in 1542. Because of the paucity of historical research into women at sea, it is difficult to establish whether this female corsair, governor, and diplomat represented an anomaly.[32] Clearly, catastrophes, such as the fall of Granada, the Spanish seizure of Melilla in 1497, and Tetouan's near destruction by the Portuguese in 1490, created openings, however transient, for toppling socioreligious gender norms.

Yet environmental structures may have been a factor. Al-Hakima governed a semiautonomous maritime republic, where topography, ecology, and trans-Mediterranean politics had long fostered community-based sea raiding. Tetouan confirms a global pattern for niches where mountains and sea collide, fostering maritime raiding as a livelihood. Denied access to interior grain-producing plains by inhospitable terrain, residents of coastal microecologies resorted to coercion (sea raiding) or subterfuge (smuggling)—from the state's point of view. They were ideally suited to traffic in wider seaborne circuits, one of whose principal goods was human captives.[33]

At times, women's relationship to the sea can only be dimly perceived through anecdotal or stray documentation that forces open broader questions. One tidbit on the early modern Mediterranean is captivating but at first glance inconsequential. During his early seventeenth-century travels from Gibraltar to Tunis by way of Pantelleria, William Biddulph related that

> We saw also an isle called now Pantalarea, but of old it was called Paconia. . . . They say, that not only the men of the island but the women also are naturally good swimmers, but whether they be all so or not, I know not: but sure I am, we saw one woman come swimming from thence to our ship [being becalmed] with a basket of fruit to sell.[34]

Ethnographic depictions of exotic "foreign" women were by no means the exclusive purview of European men in motion across the sea. In his nineteenth-century account of the "customs of the Maltese," Faris al-Shidyaq barely mentions the garb worn by Catholic men but details the headdress and clothing of the islands' women, observing with surprise that "they frequent the suqs in order to deal in fruit, greens, fish, milk, and water."[35] We will return to the question of swimming and women taking to the sea as pilgrims and travelers momentarily, but first let us fix our gaze on ships in distress or run aground.

THINGS IN THE SEA: SHIPWRECKS, SWIMMERS, AND DIVERS

> *Perceived in the distance was a ship with masts but no flag flying which at times approached the shore, at others drew away. It was the month of April [1762] and the weather was unusually cold. . . . The next morning, we saw the vessel veer toward shore while a violent tempest raged.*
>
> —MUHAMMAD AL-SAGHIR IBN YUSUF, *TĀRĪKH AL-MASHRAʿ AL-MILKĪ FĪ SALṬANAT AWLĀD ʿALĪ TURKĪ*

Historians need to tease out unimagined ports-of-entry and social portals for probing land and sea relationships. Research has long demonstrated that people, enslaved and/or captive, constituted prime "merchandise" in the Mediterranean political economy.[36] A related approach would investigate how "objects"—naval stores, weapons, machinery, textiles, and novel comestibles—traveled, were recycled, or resold. In the mid-eighteenth century, the heir to the Husaynid throne, Muhammad Pasha, "sought with particular zeal objects of art and curious things found in Christian countries that did not exist in *Ifriqiyah* (Tunisia). He learned about these goods from people who had traveled in the interior of those countries."[37] Agents were dispatched to Europe to procure the coveted commodities. Ships along with their contents were seized, bartered, resold, repurposed, and ransomed in the same way that people were; their hulls, masts, and riggings were highly prized in wood-hungry North Africa. Many of these cherished objects circulated widely in gray or black markets as "contraband," violating state regulations and treaty obligations, whose precise remit was unknown or inconsequential to those taking possession. Wrecks offered an abundance of rare and precious goods as well as things never before seen.[38]

The scholarly archaeological literature on shipwrecks during antiquity is enormous, and much ink has been spilled on seafaring for the British Isles, navy, and Empire.[39] In literary/artistic studies, the shipwreck, as both metaphor and genre, has generated an enormous corpus of fiction, visual material, musical composition, and so on. In his magisterial work, Braudel emphasized winter's dangerous waters for both the Mediterranean and Black Seas: "In October 1575, a single storm sank a hundred of these little ships laden with grain. . . . Anyone sailing in winter knew he was at the mercy of the elements, had to be on the alert, and could expect to see hoisted on bad nights the storm lamps, the *fanales de borrasca*."[40] During the most fearsome months, an anticipated voyage from Marseille to Spain might land a traveler many days later in Tabarka thanks to the might of the January mistral. Yet there is virtually nothing on ships lost at sea for the Muslim shores of the Mediterranean, even for the modern era. Shipwrecks bring to light another category of specialist—invisible until now. Gone missing is the issue of who knew how to swim—a somewhat astonishing oversight—which was a critical factor not only for disposal of vessels, passengers, and cargoes but also for exploration and conquest.[41]

To reconnoiter this underwater universe, we turn to an improbable source—an eighteenth-century dynastic history by Muḥammad al-Ṣaghīr ibn Yūsuf (ca. 1693/94—ca. 1770/71), *Tārīkh al-mashraʿ al-milkī fī salṭanat awlād ʿAlī Turkī*. This chronicle, extant in several versions in mosque collections in al-Qayrawan and Tunis, was first translated into French by Mohammed Lasram and Victor Serres in serial installments in the *Revue Tunisienne* beginning in 1896. Its first book edition appeared in 1900 in Tunis under the title *Chronique Tunisienne du règne des fils d'Ali Turki (1705–1771)*.[42]

The author and his history are remarkable for a number of reasons. First, he was a *kulughli*, the son of a "Turkish" father attached to the *jund* (military) and a Tunisian woman, who hailed from Beja, a provincial town in the heart of prosperous grain-growing regions. Locally educated, he was not schooled in the capital city in the manner of the snobby *baldi* ʿulama. Social origins excluded him from standard biographical dictionaries of the period. Dialectical Arabic and grammatical infelicities explain, perhaps, why the manuscript was only very recently published in Arabic. (In addition, the author relates some unsavory details about his coreligionists' behavior during the pilgrimage fiasco, which may have discouraged publication.) Yet literary vice represents a windfall for the historian, because this vivid anecdotal account contains documentation unavailable elsewhere. Second, as a moderately prosperous merchant and cultivator, he was attentive to the deleterious effects of politics and adverse climatic fluctuations on fields and flocks. In theory enrolled in a military unit, Muḥammad al-Ṣaghīr evinced scant enthusiasm for combat, preferring to carefully tend his farms. Most of his chronicle is straight-up political history, but he also reported bad weather and sailing conditions, so critical for delivering harvests to markets.[43]

Muḥammad al-Ṣaghīr experienced some fairly dreadful reversals: Algerian invasions and internecine princely quarrels that rent the country, the loss of his monthly *jund* stipend after 1741 and part of his fortune, blighted crops, and flights with family to the safety of Tunis—in short, hardships and travails marked his life and account. Our author began composing the history around 1763, laboring away until 1771, presumably the year of his death. Yet he opens one of the few lengthy sections devoted to the sea with the following: "The most curious episode that transpired during the reign of Amir ʿAli Bey" was a shipwreck. In fact, he narrated two tragedies during the spring equinox of 1175 (August 1761–July 1762)—thus in March or April of 1762 when the Mediterranean was particularly hazardous.[44]

It is remarkable that ships foundering or running aground constituted the most "curious event" of a turbulent era. And this section concludes, for the most part, the chronicle, although these strange occurrences transpired earlier. While the circumstance is intriguing, it is impossible to know the reasons for the sequential placement of the material on wrecked vessels. Had the author himself imagined textual location as a sort of bookend (perhaps for dramatic effect)? Or did a later scribe decide that this arresting description of "land and sea" contributed little to dynastic history—thus making it a postscript? Of course, the question of audience or readership should be posed. It appears that the chronicle, written in a conversational style, was for the author's personal delight, rendering it even more valuable.

Historians have mined Muḥammad al-Ṣaghīr's work for documentation on the early Husaynid state—its finances, taxation, political factions, and military organization—but shunned the vessels battered by spring storms. More than a century after Muḥammad al-Ṣaghīr's disappearance, French officials and their beylical subalterns appreciated his account. The resident general René Millet, who was well disposed to Islam, patronized its translation and publication. It was prized as a detailed political, but not a nautical, record; the new colonial masters of Tunisia sought information on the interior, tribes, and borders.

Nevertheless, treaties and other arrangements had long regulated shipwrecks. The voluminous correspondence between Husaynid rulers and European powers is replete with contentious, but meticulous, negotiations over crews, cargoes, and ships lost at sea, in port, or smashed against the shoreline.[45] Let us begin with the sightings of the first doomed vessel that the chronicler deemed so bizarre:

> During the equinox, the sea threw a great ship onto the shore facing the territory of the Mogods. The people of this tribe ran to the bluffs to watch; finally, the sea hurled it upon rocks where it shattered and all the commodities of India and the Christian countries washed ashore with the currents. It is impossible to describe the vessel's treasures. . . . All riches of the East and the West scattered on the beach.[46]

For the locals, the tragedy proved a wondrous blessing. After the huge swells subsided, people came from everywhere: "A crowd of men and women hurried to comb the beaches for grey amber, musk, and precious stones, and European textiles. . . . The price for textiles dropped . . . because markets and homes were filled with these commodities . . . even the tents of the pastoralists."[47] Predictably people began talking about this strange incident. News traveled rapidly to the court where courtiers broached the matter with the bey who appeared oddly disinterested. Thus, Act I of this epic comprises a violent tempest, a wreck, the dash to grab things on the shore, and the repurposing of goods that triggered the rumor mill and international diplomatic wrangling.[48] A disquieting element was that the ship bore no flag identifying its national status.

In the following act II, the ruler reluctantly ordered that the cargo's remains be amassed and handed over to the *khaznadar* at the Bardo. Here the saga gets even better. The palace dispatched *hamba*s (gendarmes) to villages and tribal camps. "The most honest bribed the *hamba*s, handing over only one-tenth of what they had seized; the others denied having partaken of the goods at all." As a reward, the latter were imprisoned until they relinquished some beach booty. By now, the bey realized the treasure ship's worth. And so we witness act III. Hearsay had it that the ship's hull remained above water; surely the submerged part contained merchandise that had not yet been disgorged by waves and been snatched by beachcombers. The ruler decreed that "divers from Bizerte" go to the site and search the hold, which yielded little else but lead ingots and stones. What the folks in Tunis did not know was that other swimmers had gotten there first. This brings us back to the Mogod tribe that customarily grazed its flocks along the seaside in early spring and had initially espied the errant vessel tossed about by "a tumultuous sea."

At this point, Muḥammad al-Ṣaghīr acknowledged that other unnamed eyewitnesses had furnished details on the tragedy. In fact, our author must have collated oral testimonies from a range of informants. Even before the ship crashed, the son of the tribe's shaykh stationed guards day and night along the coast to survey its movements. With daylight, as the ship approached, "the shaykh asked men of good faith who knew well how to swim to go out to the vessel to see if anyone was alive. Three men disrobed and began swimming among waves as big as mountains. They reached the vessel but only found a dog barking; some said there were several pigs onboard." Unearthed in the cabins were "a hat decorated with precious stones set in gold and silver that appeared to belong to a noble Christian dignitary . . . a sword whose sheath was encrusted with gold, silver, and gems and two small pistols decorated with silver"—but no passengers.[49] Each swimmer helped himself to the goods and plunged into the water, but the surf proved so violent that they barely made it ashore. Their precious finds probably came to rest in the water's depths or later stocked the collective sand souk, thanks to winds and currents.

These reports folded into al-Ṣaghīr's narrative offer a panoramic view from small slivers of the water's edge. First, comes the matter of swimmers. Bizerte was reputed for its skilled divers, perhaps because it had long served as a hub for the ancient, lucrative coral industry. Yet that "pastoralists" took to the waves seems intriguing. The Mogods clearly boasted a well-oiled system for profiting from maritime adversity. Guards were immediately posted and, as soon as the ill-fated vessel broke open, trains of pack animals quickly carried away the spoils. Did the Mogods know that the spring equinox was an especially fortuitous season to reap "all of the riches of India and the West"? The mention of pigs on board may, or may not, represent actual "fact," but it marks the ship as Christian. Finally, the greatest mystery of all—what happened to the crew and passengers? Had they perished en route of disease or disembarked on one of the many small islets on their way from wherever to the Tunisian coast? We might speculate endlessly about this.

But we are getting ahead of our tale. The local people appeared unaware of the true value of the Indian white cotton, satin, and velour thrown up on the shore. But the folks in the capital knew. Putting aside traditional disdain for provincial bumpkins, the bourgeoisie of Tunis (or *baldis*) invaded the territory of the Mogod tribe, as did eager shoppers from Bizerte, Beja, Kef, and Ifriqiyah. "The merchants of Tunis soon had as much merchandise as they could handle . . . the poor became rich."[50] "Bedouins" harvested the masts to make fires until little remained of the skeletal hulk. For several years, stuff washed ashore. This spit of coastline must have attracted water gleaners from all over, and for a long time.

The convergence of intricate strands rendered possible the circulation of things from near and far—as they were lost, found, sold, and purchased. Some goods floating through global marketplaces were new, at least for certain social classes in the eighteenth century. Washed ashore and littering the beach was coffee preserved in small boxes, which was already widely consumed in North Africa. Other containers of white iron sheltered "unknown products . . . small round leaves, similar to the leaves of capers."[51] Traders in Bizerte identified the mystery plant as tea that when made into an infusion could be drunk in the manner of coffee. So we may have discovered from this snippet that tea was consumed in Tunisian ports, perhaps mainly by elites, but was largely unknown in rural households.[52] Significantly, the national identity of the ship and its owners were never ascertained.

Act IV of the first shipwreck concludes with the European consuls besieging the bey to open an inquiry into the identity of the vessel's owner, a story recounted elsewhere.[53] However, the issue of intermediaries, addressed more fully below, arose when the ruler ceded to consular pressure to determine proprietorship:

> The bey sent an educated Christian into each village of the mountain. Another one went to Beja where he used a ruse pretending that he had come to purchase wheat; the people showed him the textiles of velour, of satin, and cloth of all kinds; the envoy examined these materials but found no indication of provenance and the evidence was entered into a register. And thus it went in all the other cities.[54]

But another maritime catastrophe, involving the widow from Beja briefly introduced above, was unfolding during the inclement equinox.

Here is the preface to the second calamity: "In 1762, a certain number of bourgeois from Baja, Bedouins, Tunis notables, great merchants, and rich people pooled resources to perform the pilgrimage to Mecca. They rented a ship from the Christians of Doublet-Benadi that was taking to the sea for the first time."[55] Loading merchandise and passengers numbering between three and four hundred, the ship departed La Goulette. After two or three days, the vessel encountered a ferocious tempest that smashed ships at anchor. For several days and nights, the gale blew with such force that the ship nearly capsized; the captain lost all sense of direction. With daylight, the passengers spotted the village of Bekalta, fourteen kilometers northeast of Mahdiyya.[56]

Futilely, the *ra'is* scrambled to run up a new sail, but winds tore it to shreds. The pilgrims awaited death. Then with a mighty roar "like thunder," the boat smashed onto an outcropping; goods and people spilled into the water. On board, however, were "numerous Bedouins from Beja who swam, saving themselves, with the exception of two; a woman was also saved." Taken to Bekalta, "they were heated by a fire and given olive oil and food." Only fifty or sixty souls survived, including some Christians, but the captain perished. As with the ghost ship, the tragedy yielded "to the inhabitants of Bekalta a trove of incalculable worth; they filled their houses with goods and enriched themselves with the money belts of the pilgrims. Each cadaver that washed up on the shore was robbed and buried in the sand."[57]

Predictably, the disaster provoked a firestorm. The Husaynid ruler vainly sought to keep it a secret but the rumor mill churned out news until the consuls in Tunis made public that the vessel was lost. The families of the unfortunate pilgrims and traders with cargoes onboard levied charges against the qa'id of Bekalta. Brought before justice in the capital, he claimed to have taken nothing. After tumultuous proceedings, "large sums of money" were doled out to the wronged parties.[58] But what of the hapless (or happy) daughter of Shaykh Bil-Qasim al-Samadhi? Among other things, her travails allow a glimpse of how people *traveled to and from* ports of embarkation, at least according to the chronicler and his host of unnamed informants.

We already know that she had wisely prepared for the pilgrimage. "After bidding farewell to all in her native city, she left Baja for Tunis where she had her merchandise and provisions loaded onto the ship and then waited its departure. . . . She kept her silver [money] upon her person." In contrast to Alexandria or Algiers, Tunis proper had been shielded for centuries from the open sea by the *buhaira,* a marshy salt lake. Until the nineteenth century, transportation from city to port was by foot, by pack animal, or, for the well-heeled, by palanquin; small lighters transported them on board waiting ships. In the 1840s, horse-drawn carriages became available, and several decades later, a light-rail line connected Tunis to La Goulette. But in 1762, options were few.

When the moment came to head to La Goulette, the widow's son wheeled her in a cart, as she was a rather large woman. Making its way across the rutted tracks adjoining the *buhaira*, the cart hit a hole, pitching her into the mud. Only with great effort was she extricated; her clothes and bags were soiled and she nearly died. Her faithful son hurried ahead to implore the captain to delay departure, but the ship had already sailed, along with her possessions and dreams of visiting the holy cities. Informed of the misfortune, the widow "wept and comforted herself by cursing the ship and those aboard, then she forlornly climbed back into the cart."[59] To avoid embarrassment in the capital, she journeyed directly back home, stopping along the way at the zawiya of Sidi 'Abd Allah al-Sharif. There she learned of the wreck. In gratitude, she made generous offerings to the saint and "returned to Beja where she still lives in her home to this day."[60] This "just-so" story is deeply problematic in many ways; thorny questions arise about the sources and audiences for the tale of two wrecks, as well as about the related matter of narrative genres of the period.

What questions does the second shipwreck raise? First, this particular vessel took to the sea "for the first time." Does this mean that navigators and crewmen, whose identities are unknown, were unschooled in the maritime science to guide it through the Sicilian channel? Local knowledge was paramount: "Because depending on the season, a certain wind has supremacy. And these small commanders of vessels, almost walnut shells, have been passing on their experience for generations."[61] Second, we vaguely see how women as pilgrims moved about—or failed to do so—and how journeys to the Haramayn were arranged and financed. What comes into sight are the ways that objects circulated in the wake of disaster and that even the persons of the faithful en route to lands deemed holy were, in death by drowning, subject to plunder. These woeful incidents pose the issue of Islamic law and legal arenas for redress. Did Tunisian rulers and their courtiers, who seemed to have adjudicated many maritime contests, apply Maliki or Hanafi prescriptions for such critical matters as losses at sea, jettison, collision, salvage, and assignation of ownership? And how did long-established biateral commercial treaties with European powers come into play?[62]

The chronicler characterized the eventual fate of the pilgrim vessel bound for Mecca—minus the woman from Beja—as an anomaly. In an intriguing "throw-away" aside, Muḥammad al-Ṣaghīr observed that "never in collective memory had a ship en route to Mecca been lost; wrecks only occurred during the return voyage."[63] Here is an admittedly narrow window into a larger panorama of land, sea, and religious travel. People appeared to have believed that vessels headed for the holy cities were destined to arrive safely, yet those venturing home might be afflicted by the terrible vagaries of sea and seasons. Why they thought that divine protection shielded vessels headed for the holy cities deserves reflection and more research. Fast-forwarding several centuries, it appears that the chronicle narrating the eighteenth-century widow's plight landed in a special collections library in Saudi Arabia; the daughter of Shaykh Bil-Qasim al-Samadhi had made it to the Holy Land—as a story.[64]

Next let's take up our opening anecdote devoted to ransoming enslaved persons, which, similar to the shipwreck drama, raises issues of unsuspected mediation, mediators, and protection within the larger envelope of land and water connectivities and disconnections.

SLAVING AND A WOMAN AS SECURITY: MEDIATORS ON THE TUNISIAN-SICILIAN CHANNEL

The ransoming of Christians captive in North Africa followed well-established procedures that generated copious records. Conventional wisdom asserts that enslaved North Africans did not benefit from a similarly organized "system," and Muslims released from European bagnios or households hailed mainly from the ranks of the elite.[65] Crumbs of evidence from the early eighteenth century indicate how Muslims of modest social status sought liberty. Entered in French chancellery documents in Tunis is the saga of ʿAli ibn Ghassam captured with his family by Maltese corsairs. After laboring as a galley rower, ʿAli secured his own conditional freedom to return home. Around 1710, he landed in Tunis, where resident Europeans acting as intermediaries with the Husaynid palace, procured for him a travel permit or beylical *teskra.* ʿAli roamed the country, seeking alms at saints' shrines and importuning fellow believers for sufficient capital to return to Malta and free his wife and son. On his rounds, he stayed in the Tunis bagnio, where a Maltese tavern owner offered him shelter; he bought, sold, and bartered horses, grains, and other goods. Sadly, death surprised ʿAli in al-Qayrawan before his mission was accomplished.[66] The fate of his captive family in Malta remains unknown. It is significant that the amassing of ransom monies also entailed the microcirculation of commodities.

During the eighteenth century, a qadi resided in Malta but was apparently unable to bargain for the release of Muslims because obstacles blocked the transmission of funds. In contrast, transfers of rescue money from Europe to the Maghrib ran fairly smoothly, thanks largely to Catholic "Redemptionist" orders, such as the Trinitarian Brothers. On July 5, 1710, Jean-Baptiste Vitalis, chancellor of the French consulate in Tunis, drew up an affidavit composed in Sicilo-Maltese-Provençal that offers an admittedly cloudy lens. In it, Ignace Palombo declared that he had recently arrived from Malta accompanied by Dominique Delicata. Both claimed "power of attorney" (*mandat*) from a third individual, Joseph Gresafoulli, residing in Malta. In effect, Delicata and Palombo acted as paid "proxy guides" for Gresafoulli, who seems to have been a professional slaver, who purchased unfree persons from their masters on the island for resale or barter in North Africa. He hired vessels specifically for that

FIGURE 3. Photograph of Sousse, Tunisia, ca. 1899. Courtesy of Library of Congress.

purpose; a favored route was Valletta to Sousse because of the favorable sailing conditions and the fact that this port was not subject to strict beylical surveillance and offered direct access to the Tunisian interior. Clearly, Gresafoulli's designated agents were to receive a percentage of the fees charged for liberty.[67]

The boat with Delicata, Palomba, and five male slaves landed in Sousse. Two of the men wooed their Maltese guardians with promises of future monies. They were allowed to travel unaccompanied to al-Qayrawan and promptly disappeared. In Tunis, Palombo and Delicata extracted money from the remaining slaves' families, but then matters got murky. Delicata was indebted to some Tunisians from Djerba, the fruit of an earlier shady transaction gone amiss; the Djerbans pursued him in the capital city, thus stalling the slave enterprise. The Maltese had probably been wheeling and dealing among Tunisia, Djerba, and Valletta for a while. Then Delicata announced plans to go alone to al-Qayrawan "because he had left his wife as a *caution* to Gresafoulli and . . . he alone enjoyed the right to pursue the slaves."[68] Palombo smelled a rat. Foolishly he paid Tunisian agents up-front to track down the "escaped" slaves before Delicata. But his hired hands went missing. Out of luck and probably out of money, Palombo regained Sousse, where the boat had been moored while awaiting Gresafoulli's emissaries and the money; his coproxy remained behind to sort things out. If, when, and how that transpired, we will never know.

These ransom tales hint at how barter, bail agents, reputation networks, and guarantors maneuvered in tandem—or against one another. They suggest that North Africans were freed from Maltese bagnios to pursue other slaves, who had been previously liberated on a pledge of remitting funds; freedom was conditional and multistaged on a continuum. Moreover, the beylical *teskra* granting safe passage, and obtained through the offices of "foreign" consuls, comes up in other archival documents in Tunis and elsewhere. As a kind of internal passport, it facilitated people and things in motion across Husaynids realms and even the sea. The "wife as bail bond" demands further investigation, but this was surely not the first time that she had fulfilled such a purpose. And the ill-fated Palombo appears as a broker *manqué* who lacked know-how about a particularly fraught social universe. Perhaps these apparently routine methods for liberating Muslims constituted a "system"? Recall the role of go-betweens after the ghost ship cracked open. The bey dispatched "lettered Christians" (meaning educated) to the peoples of the mountains and to the tribes (i.e., the pastoral-nomadic folks or Bedouins). We now command a fuller palette of the agents of mediation: swimmers, pastoralists, captains, slaves, island folk, and so forth—not the usual suspects. By scratching the surface of labels, and looking at land and sea simultaneously, subterranean "others," whose actions undergirded local and global exchange circuits, surface.

Intermediaries forged specific trust niches that were highly tuned to changing spatial realities and politics. As Janet Ewald's work on the Indian Ocean trade demonstrated, trusted—or at least valued—brokers could rapidly fall from grace for paradoxically being too well connected, or conversely forfeit access to informational and reputational networks when they were physically displaced. At stake in all of these incidents was "risk aversion" in the face of flux and uncertainty. In a sense, reputation preceded transactions for ransoming North Africans and often endured long after the parties to a specific bargain ceased to exist.[69] Thus went the rules of engagement.

GEOGRAPHIES OF EXCHANGE: ISLANDS AS INTERMEDIARIES OF EXCHANGE OR IMMOBILITY

Another piece of the puzzle calls for additional field research. Several maritime subzones intersected to create the central Mediterranean corridor. Historically, northern ports, such as Annaba (Bone) and Tabarka, maintained intense relations with Sardinia and the Provence, while those on the Cap Bon's underbelly were more firmly tied to Sicily and Malta.[70] Located between mountains and sea, the interior city of al-Qayrawan guards the approaches to Ifriqiya's fertile lands, the western Maghrib, and Egypt. Its ports, Sousse and Mahdiyya, were close but not too much so, and lightly policed compared to La Goulette, rendering them attractive for all manner of trafficking.[71] Geographical features may elucidate al-Qayrawan's part in the ransoming racket—in addition to the fact that this Islamic pilgrimage hub counted pious benefactors, who would take pity on beggars like ʻAli. Yet nonhuman historical agents and motors were at work—prevailing winds and currents made for relatively easy sailing from Valletta or Marsala to these small ports.

Above it was suggested that more modest ports of call merit "land and sea" exploration. Excised from historical narratives as well are thousands of islets and uninhabited islands. The Galite Islands, eighty kilometers north-northeast of Tabarka, and 150 kilometers below Cape Spartivento in southern Sardinia, have played an unacknowledged role as places for finding refuge, water, fuel, and fish since prehistory.[72] Inhabited microislands like Lampedusa, Pantelleria, Favignana, and Lipari have long welcomed people and things in motion but paradoxically functioned as places of immobility—penal colonies for Italian anarchists in the nineteenth century. None of this is new. Since the rise of Carthage—and marching onward through Rome, the Vandals, Byzantines, and so on—Sardinia served as an incarceral island as well as a haven for those defeated by armies or condemned by religious authorities. The islet of Ponza off Naples was used as a place of exile for unruly galley slaves and "persons guilty of political offences."[73] Across from Tabarka, French colonial authorities repurposed an ancient goal on a small islet crowned by a Genoese castle to imprison Habib Bourguiba in 1952.

For millennia, Tabarka, whose cultural-linguistic fabric betrays Phoenician, Carthaginian, Roman, Arab, Italian, Spanish, and Ottoman influences, had been a bustling hub for trade, coral extraction, and privateering.[74] In 1540, the Genoese Lomellini trading family purchased coral rights from the Ottoman regime in Tunis; but subsequently the Husaynids controlled the lucrative coral business involving French, Sicilian, Maltese, and other interests. For reasons unknown, most of Tabarka's heterogeneous residents were forcibly relocated in the 1740s to the Sardinian microisland of San Pietro, where a Tunisian-Genoese dialect was spoken until recently. The Tabarkans remaining in North Africa were so acculturated that they were often referred to as (indigenous) "Tunisian Catholics."[75]

Like people and things, microislands, inhabited or otherwise, have functioned as arbitrators. Nonetheless, research on the Mediterranean has treated them as stowaways, despite the fact that they shaped maritime and therefore political destinies. Needless to say, uninhabited islands pose documentary problems. In addition, the big island of Sardinia, sparsely peopled compared to Sicily, hardly appears in historical studies. These scholarly omissions call for a cartographic reimaging of the spaces that make up the central Mediterranean corridor. Remapping centers, peripheries, and all of the land and sea spaces in between reveals a critical subregion running from the Provence, Sardinia, and western Sicily (Marsala) to Annaba, Tabarka, Bizerte, and Porto Farina, as well as their deeply indented hinterlands, whose purchase on the coastline shifted.

Finally, ports whose fortunes waned precipitously demand enquiry. Can maritime eclipse be tied to adverse environmental transformations, however tentatively? In his magisterial work, Faruk Tabak paid little heed to pirates and corsairs. But he calibrated the state's relative strength or weakness in relation to maritime raiding expeditions that created semideserted coastal villages, as people sought security upland. Human oscillations from seaside to mountains, he argued, were due in part to complicated large-scale environmental changes exerting local impacts.[76] Today Porto Farina is a sleepy town frequented by sun worshippers, although its beaches lie several kilometers from the open sea. But it wasn't always that way. Until the late eighteenth century, the port was a strategic corsair center in the Sicilian Channel, second only to Tunis. Porto Farina's fortunes plummeted as the Majarda River basin and watershed changed course, silting up the port and congealing into salt marshes; Porto Farino was severed from the sea. Only boatmen adept at operating light flat-bottomed boats (known as *sandali*) could navigate the newly created interface—marshes—between land and sea. Were these topographical transformations somehow connected to the end of the Little Ice Age? Can we interweave narratives of the rise and fall of specific ports and hinterlands—and their economic and political destinies—to seismic or incremental evolutions in ecological realities? And how could we even begin to investigate such a query?

Documentation has not yet been systematically collated; nevertheless the chronicles record strange weather events. Muḥammad al-Ṣaghīr ibn Yūsuf detailed anomalous seasonal fluctuations. At the beginning of 1726, "the rain fell continually for five months. . . . All the grain stored in silos and houses was spoiled by weevils . . . even the wheat conserved in high storage containers. . . . The people were obliged to throw it away in garbage dumps, bringing enormous loss." Again in 1762, from the fall harvests until spring, "the rain fell without cease, never stopping; the fields were submerged and the grain harvest rotted; few peasants were spared."[77] For the nineteenth century, Ahmad ibn Abi al-Diyaf described unfamiliar climatic patterns in his multivolume work. For example, in 1825: "a snowfall occurred in the kingdom that was unprecedented . . . and the harvest was plentiful . . . and the people (subsequently) referred to this time as the 'year of the snowfall.'"[78] More environmentally grounded, systematic studies, like the evocative work by John McNeill and Faruk Tabak, are needed. However, histories of the Maghrib that aspire to be simultaneously in, of, and on the Mediterranean might acknowledge that the sea's multiple hinterlands encompassed remote regions—such as the Chaambi Mountains, or the territory of the Mogods, where fluctuating tribal and ecological borderlands defined the fungible limits of states whose centers lay in Algiers or Tunis.

Like the holds of fragile vessels broken on rocks, Muḥammad al-Ṣaghīr ibn Yūsuf's account, and the stories of slave deals gone sour, are replete with precious little objects, shards of documentation awaiting verification and amplification by historians. As was true globally, wrecks were so common that they "created an entire underclass of scavengers who haunted the coast, waiting for the tide to deposit treasures."[79] Though well studied for the English and North American coasts, disasters at sea, or within sight of land, have not been considered for Mediterranean North Africa.

The dramas unleashed by a spring equinox illustrate how mediation was conducted. In addition, the centrality of water specialists with the know-how to swim or to navigate shoals and marshlands assumes significance. Other unsuspected actors, above all the unnamed bearers of local maritime knowledge, are churned up by this approach. Microislets, as well as winds, seasons, climates, and currents, become historical actors that shaped political and economic pulses. Pastoral-nomadic communities, "quarantined" until now in semiarid interiors, resurface as keen observers of ship movements that proved savvy actors in the arts of scavenging and redistributing water booty.[80] Directly related to ships in distress, "humanitarian" practices and codes for rescuing sailors, ships, and passengers call for illumination. Treaties stipulated how crews and vessels should be treated during foul weather and other natural disasters, but whether and how these agreements were implemented remain problematic.[81] Reputation, protection, and varying degrees of enslavement or conditional liberty greased trans-Mediterranean circuits that have remained below the historian's radar. Moreover, how different women traveled the sea and the ways in which gender norms shaped displacements beg for greater scholarly attention. And how did North Africans in the past see, experience, or imagine the Mediterranean? This remains a big question in search of its historian. While maps and map-making introduced state, military, and intellectual elites to the notion of the panoptic sea, one wonders about ordinary people. Was the sea imagined as webs of spaces that were both strange and familiar, auspicious and foreboding?[82]

One avenue for future research is to unearth ships' logs, charts, and manuals which may have gone unnoticed because they were composed in vernacular Arabic or other languages deemed too dialectical. Sometime in the World War II era, the Tunisian historian Bechir Mokadem came across a detailed "sea and route journal" written in infelicitous Arabic. Captain Mourad, whose title in the beylical army was "officier de l'ordonnance," served under General Rashid, whom the Husaynid ruler dispatched to Paris in 1853 on a diplomatic mission. Significantly, the delegation made a lengthy stop in Sardinia en route to Marseille. In his account, Captain Mourad digresses at length on the state of military preparedness in Sardinia, weather and navigational conditions, and shipping. As a navigational and travel report composed by a North African seaman on the cusp of the Crimean War, this account, even though it is fragmentary and in translation, is extraordinarily rich.[83]

The existence of a "hyperlinked" sea over a very long time has been well established. Even before the first Punic Wars (263 BCE), true connectivities across the Mediterranean and beyond meant that one commercial or population node could potentially be conjoined with others. Braudel's *Les mémoires de la Méditerrannée* reminds us that three transversal routes connected the basin's eastern limits with its western edges; all crossers of this land-sea bridge had to make passage through the Sicilo-Tunisian Strait: "Sicily and Tunisia cut the Mediterranean in two."[84] Until the sixteenth century, this strait operated as an Afro-Eurasian conduit, and subsequently as a global artery. These ancient lines of communication were reactivated during the mass North African exoduses to Lampedusa and Pantelleria that were triggered by the Tunisian uprisings of 2011.

Given the density, ubiquity, and longevity of cartographies of movement—the flows of people, objects, ideas, and species—it is challenging to ascertain what is or was genuinely new or novel. But dead-ends and cul-de-sacs also call for attention. One methodology pursued here is to engage in travel and coresidence simultaneously. *Anthropologie partagée* combined with *histoire croissée* represent an ethnohistorical approach to "land and sea" that seeks to set conventional narratives adrift, if only momentarily. In turn this demands critical re-evaluation of the historical carrying capacity of narratives that claim to be "Mediterranean" but fail to reach the water's edge.

NOTES

1. Pierre Grandchamp, ed., "Esclaves Musulmans rachetés en Chretienté," *Revue Tunisienne,* nos. 53–54 (1943): 239–45. Lucette Valensi was among the first scholars to raise the issue of slavery, in "Esclaves chrétiens et esclaves noirs à Tunis au XVIIIe siècle," *Annales* 22, no. 6 (1967): 1267–88. The immense destruction of World War II in Tunisia seems to have cracked open stashes of early modern and precolonial documents in numerous languages archived at the French residence in Tunis, as issues of the *Revue Tunisienne* and the *Revue Africaine* from the 1940s on indicate. At the same time, massive aerial bombardments of the port La Goulette destroyed precious documentation not only on North African but also on Mediterranean history.

2. Jane Burbank and Frederick Cooper, *Empires in World History: Power and the Politics of Difference* (Princeton, NJ: Princeton University Press, 2010) won an American Historical Association book prize in 2011. Carthage is characterized simply as "Rome's enemy" (29). Therefore, one major "missing" historical actor is the Carthaginian Empire, which had unified much of the Mediterranean and tutored the Roman state in maritime technology, border management, and agricultural arid-lands know-how. Nevertheless, in Burbank and Cooper's narrative, and in most scholarly literature, "we are all Romans." However, Robin Waterfield's *Taken at the Flood: The Roman Conquest of Greece* (Oxford: Oxford University Press, 2014) argues that Roman clashes with Carthage during the Second Punic conflict significantly impacted warfare with Greece, shaping the destiny of the eastern Mediterranean; see also Cyprian Broodbank, *The Making of the Middle Sea: A History of the Mediterranean from the Beginning to the Emergence of the Classical World* (Oxford: Oxford University Press, 2013).

3. Edmund Burke III was among the first historians to put environmental history and the Middle East together; see Edmund Burke and Kenneth Pomeranz, eds., *The Environment and World History* (Berkeley: University of California Press, 2009); for the late medieval and early modern Mediterranean,

Sharon Kinoshita and Brian A. Catlos have been leading the way, notably with their edited volume, *Can We Talk Mediterranean? Conversations on an Emerging Field* (London: Palgrave Macmillan, 2017). See also Stephen Ortega, *Negotiating Transcultural Relations in the Early Modern Mediterranean: Ottoman-Venetian Encounters,* Transculturalisms, 1400–1700 (Farnham: Ashgate, 2014); and Edwige Tamalet Talbayev and Yasser Elhariry, eds., *Critically Mediterranean: Temporalities, Aesthetics, and Deployments of a Sea in Crisis* (London: Palgrave, 2018).

4. For an overview, see Julia Clancy-Smith, "The Middle East and North," in *The New World History: A Teacher's Companion,* ed. Ross E. Dunn, 2nd ed. (Berkeley: University of California Press, 2016).

5. Older histories of Iberia under Muslim rule (ca. 711–1492) asserted that those centuries constituted a mere "occupation," thereby erasing reciprocal political, religious, and cultural transactions. However, "Mediterraneanism" has reawakened scholarly passion for the Inner Sea, which is both cause and consequence of related growth fields, such as migration and "neoimperial" studies, as well as women and gender studies and world history. Obviously present-day political agendas and crises drive Mediterraneanism. Peregrine Horden and Nicholas Purcell's *The Corrupting Sea: A Study of Mediterranean History* (Oxford: Blackwell, 2000) triggered the ongoing Mediterranean stampede. For a sophisticated treatment of how ideologies moved around, see Maurizio Isabella and Konstantina Zanou, eds., *Mediterranean Diasporas: Politics and Ideas in the Long 19th Century* (London: Bloomsbury, 2016).

6. Following are a few examples: Brian Catlos, *The Victors and the Vanquished: Christians and Muslims of Catalonia and Aragon, 1050–1300* (Cambridge: Cambridge University Press, 2004); Sharon Kinoshita, *Medieval Boundaries: Rethinking Difference in Old French Literature* (Philadelphia: University of Pennsylvania Press, 2006); Alex Metcalfe, *The Muslims of Medieval Italy* (Edinburgh: Edinburgh University Press, 2009); Ramzi Rouighi, T*he Making of a Mediterranean Emirate: Ifriqiya and Its Andalusis, 1200–1400* (Philadelphia: University of Pennsylvania Press, 2011); and Janina M. Safran, *Defining Boundaries in Al-Andalus: Muslims, Christians, and Jews in Islamic Iberia* (Ithaca, NY: Cornell University Press, 2013).

7. In "'The Great Event of the Fortnight': Steamship Rhythms and Colonial Communication," *Mobilities* 9, no. 3 (2014): 369–83, Anyaa Anim-Addo argues rightly that the spread of steam transport did not immediately or irrevocably transform older ways of conducting maritime exchanges.

8. James Clifford, "Traveling Cultures," in *Cultural Studies,* ed. Laurence Grossberg, Cary Nelson, and Paula Treichler (New York: Routledge, 1992), 98.

9. Louis de Mas Latrie, *Traités de paix et de commerce et documents divers concernant les relations des Chrétiens avec les Arabes de L'Afrique septentrionale au moyen âge recueillis et publiés par ordre de L'Empereur avec une introduction historique de M. L. de Mas Latrie* (Paris: Henri Plon, 1866), 31. See also Allen Fromherz, "A Vertical Sea: North Africa and the Medieval Mediterranean," *Review of Middle East Studies* 46, no. 1 (Summer 2012): 64–71.

10. De Mas Latrie, *Traités de paix,* 339–40; see also "Treaties and Other International Acts of the United States of America," in *The Barbary Treaties, 1786–1816,* ed. Hunter Miller, 2 vols. (Washington, DC, 1931).

11. The channel has long represented an arena for military engagement, political defiance, and demographic mixing that posed enormous navigational dangers. The Skerki Banks, or narrows, a zone of relatively shallow open sea, lie between Sicily and Tunisia, close by the Cap Bon. During the Little Ice Age, many known reefs, such as the Esquirques, volcanic outcroppings surrounded by sandbanks, receded under higher water levels; their location apparently disappeared from charts or inherited orally transmitted nautical knowledge, provoking numerous wrecks. Since 1988, archaeological surveys have revealed a concentration of shipwrecks, ancient and more modern, in this zone. Christian Weitmeyer and Hardi Döhler, "Traces of Roman Offshore Navigation in Skerki Bank (Strait of Sicily)," *International Journal of Nautical Archaeology* 38, no. 2 (2009): 254–80. See also Giuseppe M. R. Manzella, "The

Seasonal Variability of the Water Masses and Transport through the Strait of Sicily," *Seasonal and Interannual Variability of the Western Mediterranean Sea* (Washington, DC: American Geophysical Union Publications, 1994), 33–45.

12. The classic work on the dynasty's founder remains Mohamed Hedi Cherif, *Pouvoir et société dans la Tunisie de Husayn Bin 'Ali (1705–1740)*, 2 vols. (Tunis: Publications de l'Université de Tunis, 1984). Crete, or the Kingdom of Candia, had been an overseas colony of the Republic of Venice (*Regno di Candia* or *Ducato di Candia*) from 1212 until its fall to the Ottoman Empire in 1669. Husayn ibn 'Ali (r. 1705–40) was born in Tunisia to 'Ali al-Turki, who was from Candia, and a "native" Arab woman; he spoke no Turkish whatsoever, Tunisian Arabic being his mother language.

13. Muhammad al-Saghir ibn Yusuf, *Tārīkh al-mashra' al-milkī fī salṭanat awlād 'Alī Turkī*. This was translated and published in 1900 as *Mechra El Melki* and is now available in a modern edition: *Mechra El Melki: Chronique Tunisienne du règne des fils d'Ali Turki (1705–1771)*, trans. Mohammed Lasram and Victor Serres, 2nd ed. (Tunis: Editions Bouslma, 1978), 22–23.

14. Julia Clancy-Smith, *Mediterraneans: North Africa and Europe in an Age of Migration, c. 1800–1900* (Berkeley: University of California Press, 2011), 22–63.

15. Jean-André Peyssonnel, *Voyage dans les régences de Tunis et d'Alger* (Paris: La découverte, 1987), 442.

16. Christian Windler, *La diplomatie comme expérience de l'autre: Consuls français au Maghrib (1700–1840)* (Geneva: Droz, 2002).

17. Carmel Camilleri, "Une Communauté maltaise en Tunisie entre les groups arabo-berbère et français," in *Actes du premier congrès d'études des cultures méditerranéennes d'influence arabo-berberè*, ed. Micheline Galley (Algiers: Société Nationale d'Édition, 1973), 406–23.

18. Francesca Trivellato, *The Familiarity of Strangers: The Sephardic Diaspora, Livorno, and Cross-Cultural Trade in the Early Modern Period* (New Haven, CT: Yale University Press, 2010).

19. For an inventory of the "maisons de commerce Françaises et des Français en général établis à Tunis, Bizerte, et Porte-Farine," in 1796, see Eugène Plantet, ed., *Correspondance des beys de Tunis et des consuls de France avec la cour*, 3 vols. (Paris: Felix Alcan, 1899), 3:305–7; and Anne-Marie Planel, "De la nation à la colonie: la communauté française de Tunisie au XIXe siècle d'après les archives civiles et notariés du consulat général de France à Tunis," 3 vols. (Doctorat d'état, École des Hautes Études en Sciences Sociales, Paris, 2000), i, 20–21, published as *Du comptoir à la colonie. Histoire de la communauté française de Tunisie, 1814–1883* (Paris: Riveneuve éditions, 2015).

The scholarship on Huguenots in diaspora fails to mention that some found refuge in Tunisia. See, for example, Owen Stanwood, "Between Eden and Empire: Huguenot Refugees and the Promise of New Worlds," *American Historical Review* 118, no. 5 (December 2013): 1319–44.

20. Joshua Schreier, "From Mediterranean Merchant to French Civilizer: Jacob Lasry and the Economy of Conquest in Early Colonial Algeria," in "Maghribi Histories in the Modern Era," ed. Julia Clancy-Smith, special issue, *International Journal of Middle East Studies* 44, no. 4 (November 2012): 631–49. The Gibraltar-Tetouan-Oran triangle demands more research. In 1713, Great Britain seized "the Rock" from Spain and banished Jews from the place. However, in 1729, Britain and Morocco decided to permit Jews to reside and trade there, with some restrictions. By the end of the century, about one-third of Gibraltar's population was Jewish.

21. Among the first to flag the centrality of fishermen was Pierre Soumille, "Minorités et vie maritime: Pêcheurs Italiens et Français à La Galite (Tunisie) des Années 1870 aux Années 1940," *Colloque du Senanque* 10 (1978), no. 961.18 Sou Min., 181–96, Bibliothèque Diocesaine de Tunis. Naor Ben-Yehoyada's *The Mediterranean Incarnate: Region Formation between Sicily and Tunisia since World War II* (Chicago: University of Chicago Press, 2017) makes a significant contribution to the field. See also Sasha D. Pack, *The Deepest Border: The Strait of Gibraltar and the Making of the Modern Hispano-African Borderland* (Stanford, CA: Stanford University Press, 2018).

22. Clancy-Smith, *Mediterraneans*, 162–64.

23. Clancy-Smith, *Mediterraneans*, 225–29. Al-Saghir (*Tārīkh*, 74) notes that for the eighteenth century the Burj in La Goulette was employed as a temporary prison for undesirables awaiting expulsion on board a passing ship.

24. Clancy-Smith, *Mediterraneans*, 152.

25. Alison Games, *The Web of Empire: English Cosmopolitans in an Age of Expansion, 1560–1660* (Oxford: Oxford University Press, 2008), 52–55.

26. William Biddulph, *The Trauels of Certaine Englishmen into Africa, Asia, Troy, Bythinia, Thracia, and to the Blacke Sea: And into Syria, Cilicia, Pisidia, Mesopotamia, Damascus, Canaan, Galile, Samaria, Iudea, Palestina, Ierusalem, Iericho, and to the Red Sea: and to Sundry Other Places. Begunne in the Yeare of Iubile 1600. And by Some of Them Finished in This Yeere 1608. The Others Not Yet Returned. Very Profitable to the Help of Trauellers, and No Lesse Delightfull to All Persons Who Take Pleasure to Heare of the Manners, Gouernement, Religion, and Customes of Forraine and Heathen Countries*, ed. Theophilus Lavender (London: W. Aspley, 1609), 4.

27. See Frans Ciappara, "Society and the Inquisition in Malta, 1743–1798" (PhD diss., University of Durham, 1998), as well as numerous of his other works, including his chapter in Dionisius A. Agius, ed., *Georgio Scala and the Moorish Slaves: The Inquisition-Malta 1598* (Sta Venera, Malta: Midsea Books, 2013).

28. Clancy-Smith, *Mediterraneans*, 199–200.

29. A French national, Beaussier, who earlier in the 1790s served as *consul général et chargé d'affaires*, disembarked his mistress in La Goulette in violation of customary norms governing the introduction of "foreign" (i.e., nonsubjects of the bey) women into the kingdom. Disguising her as a man, Beaussier accompanied her to the Tunis souks, which caused a huge scandal; see Clancy-Smith, *Mediterraneans*, 30–31.

30. Gillian Weiss, *Captives and Corsairs: France and Slavery in the Early Modern Mediterranean* (Stanford, CA: Stanford University Press, 2011); Mary Elizabeth Perry, "Finding Fatima, a Slave Woman of Early Modern Spain," in *Contesting Archives: Finding Women in the Sources*, ed. Nupur Chaudhuri, Mary Elizabeth Perry, and Sherry Katz (Urbana: University of Illinois Press, 2010), 3–19; Joshua White, "Piracy of the Ottoman Mediterranean: Slave Laundering and Subjecthood," in this volume; Ellen G. Friedman, "Christian Captives at 'Hard Labor' in Algiers, 16th—18th Centuries," *International Journal of African Historical Studies* 13, no. 4 (1980): 616–32.

31. Osire Glacier, "Hakimat Tetouan (Tetouan's Governor)," *Dictionary of African Biography*, 5 vols. (Oxford: Oxford University Press, 2011); Fatima Mernissi, *The Forgotten Queens of Islam*, trans. Mary Jo Lakeland (Cambridge: Polity Press, 1993), 18–19; Chantal de la Véronne, *Sida el-Horra, la noble dame* (Paris: Hespéris-Tamuda, 1956), 222–25.

32. Glacier, "Hakimat Tetouan (Tetouan's Governor)"; Nada Mourtada-Sabbah and Adrian Gully, "'I am, by God, Fit for High Positions': On the Political Role of Women in al-Andalus," *British Journal of Middle Eastern Studies* 30, no. 2 (November 2003): 183–209.

33. Sebastian R. Prange, "A Trade of No Dishonor: Piracy, Commerce, and Community in the Western Indian Ocean, Twelfth to Sixteenth Century," *American Historical Review* 116, no. 5 (December 2011): 1269–93.

34. Biddulph, *Trauels of Certaine Englishmen*, 3.

35. Ahmad Faris al-Shidyaq, *Kitab al-rihla al-mawsuma bil-Wasita ila ma'rifat ahwal malita wa kashf al-mukhabba 'an funun Awrabba*, 2nd ed. (Constantinople: al-Jawai'ib Press, 1899), 30–34.

36. Molly Greene, *Catholic Pirates and Greek Merchants: A Maritime History of the Early Modern Mediterranean* (Princeton, NJ: Princeton University Press, 2013); Molly Greene, *A Shared World: Christians and Muslims in the Early Modern Mediterranean* (Princeton, NJ: Princeton University Press, 2002).

37. Al-Saghir, Tārīkh, 324–25; special breeds of horses from France and the Netherlands were of supreme importance to the prince. The history of things, a subfield of the history of consumption, is

currently a growth field. See Paula Findlen, ed., *Early Modern Things: Objects and Their Histories, 1500–1800* (New York: Routledge, 2013); and Alan Mikhail, "Anatolian Timber and Egyptian Grain: Things That Made the Ottoman Empire," in Findlen, ed., *Early Modern Things*, 274–93.

38. Julia Clancy-Smith, "A View from the Water's Edge: Greater Tunisia, France, and the Mediterranean before Colonialism, c. 1700–1840s," in "France and the Mediterranean in the Early Modern World," ed. Gillian Weiss and Megan Armstrong, special issue, *French History* 1, no. 29 (2015): 24–30.

39. For an overview, see Robert Lee, "The Seafarers' Urban World: A Critical Review," *International Journal of Maritime History* 25, no. 1 (June 2013): 23–64.

40. Fernand Braudel, *The Mediterranean and the Mediterranean World in the Age of Philip II*, 2 vols. (New York: Harper, 1972) 1:111, 249, 250. Horden and Purcell's *The Corrupting Sea*, 368–72, deals with wrecks from antiquity to the Middle Ages but privileges cargoes to address debates regarding "high commerce" versus cabotage. Weiss, *Captives and Corsairs*, deals extensively with shipwrecks and people seized on the North African shores, for example, the capture of an English girl by Algerian Kabyles in the eighteenth century (95). See also Cheryl Ward, "The Sadana Island Shipwreck: An Eighteenth-Century AD Merchantman off the Red Sea Coast of Egypt," *World Archaeology* 32, no. 3 (February 2001): 368–82; and Catherine Richarté-Manfredi, "Navires et marchandises islamiques en Méditerranée occidentale durant le haut Moyen Âge: Des épaves comme témoignages des échanges commerciaux entre domaines chrétiens et musulmans (IXe–Xe siècle)," *Mélanges de l'École française de Rome—Moyen Âge* 129, no. 2 (2017), published online April 3, 2018, https://journals.openedition.org/mefrm/3892.

41. Valentin Jeutner, "Of Islands and Sunny Beaches: Law and the Acquisition of Territory from the Fifteenth to the Nineteenth Centuries," special issue, *World History Bulletin* 24, no. 1 (Spring 2013): 7–12, mentions en passant that the ability to swim played a role in the sixteenth-century Spanish claims of sovereignty over an island off the Mexican coast.

42. The chronicle was comprised of a series of folios and in several renditions. After it was translated into French during the late 1890s, the original Arabic manuscript, which eventually made its way to the special collections of the Zaytuna University Library, was all but forgotten. I have relied on the second French printing by Editions Bouslma, Tunis (1978), which faithfully, as far as I can tell, duplicates the first edition. Only in 1998 did Ahmad Tawili put out an Arabic edition.

43. Ahmed Abdesselem examines the chronicler in depth in *Historiens Tunisiens des XVII, XVIII et XIX siècles: Essai d'histoire culturelle* (Paris: Klincksieck, 1973), 243–59. In their introduction to the translation, Mohammed Lasram, Directeur de l'Administration des Forêts d'oliviers, and Victor Serres, Contrôleur civil attaché à la Résidence Générale à Tunis, provide additional biographical details (1–5). One of the manuscripts (or a copy?) was discovered in al-Qayrawan in the early 1890s by an Italian, Arabic-speaking interpreter named Canova, who served the military and contrôleur civil in that city. Upon learning of the chronicle's existence, Canova set about translating it into French. Misfortune brought about his transfer to Tozeur, where he died of cholera during the 1893 epidemic. Apparently Canova flagged the chronicle's importance to Lasram and Serries.

44. Al-Saghir, *Tārīkh*, 438.

45. See de Mas Latrie, *Traités de paix* and the massive correspondence among the diverse foreign consuls and consulates in Tunis in the precolonial series National Archives of Tunisia, "Correspondence of the Beys."

46. Al-Saghir, *Tārīkh*, 438.

47. Al-Saghir, *Tārīkh*, 438–41.

48. Al-Saghir, *Tārīkh*, 438.

49. Al-Saghir, *Tārīkh*, 440.

50. Al-Saghir, *Tārīkh*, 441–42.

51. Al-Saghir, *Tārīkh*, 441.

52. Helen Saberi, *Tea: A Global History* (London: Reaktion Books, 2010), 79–80. The first mention of tea consumption in the Ottoman Empire comes from the pen of Evliya Çelebi. He noted that around

1631, customs houses in Istanbul frequented by merchants in the eastern trade, particularly with Russia, offered tea to guests. After the Crimean War, British commercial interests sought new markets in the western Mediterranean, where they introduced tea to Morocco.

53. Clancy-Smith, "View."

54. Al-Saghir, *Tārīkh,* 441–42.

55. Al-Saghir, *Tārīkh,* 441–42.

56. Al-Saghir, *Tārīkh,* 442–43.

57. Al-Saghir, *Tārīkh,* 443.

58. Al-Saghir, *Tārīkh,* 443–44.

59. Al-Saghir, *Tārīkh,* 444–45.

60. Al-Saghir, *Tārīkh,* 444–45.

61. Enrico Pea, *Vita in Egitto* (Milano: Mondadori, 1949), 43. Quoted in Lucia Carminati, "The Bourgeoisie Is More International Than We Are: Transnationalism in the Mediterranean, a Snapshot from 1898" (unpublished paper). Cited by permission of the author.

62. Hassan S. Khalilieh, *Islamic Maritime Law: An Introduction* (Leiden: Brill, 1998), deals with classical law and the fundamental question of legal dictates versus actual practice.

63. Al-Saghir, *Tārīkh,* 444.

64. Thanks to Ms. Kamilia Rahmouni, PhD candidate, School of Middle Eastern and North African Studies, University of Arizona, for this information.

65. Weiss, *Captives and Corsairs.*

66. Grandchamp, "Esclaves Musulmans," 239–45.

67. Grandchamp, "Esclaves Musulmans," 239.

68. Grandchamp, "Esclaves Musulmans," 240.

69. Janet Ewald, "Crossers of the Sea: Slaves, Freedmen, and Other Migrants in the North-Western Indian Ocean, c. 1750–1914," *American Historical Review* 105, no. 1 (2000): 68–91. One major reason for captivity was the imperative for access to information from local and regional maritime specialists; Katip Çelebi's *History of the Maritime Wars of the Turks,* expanded, edited, and annotated by Svatopluk Soucek (Princeton, NJ: Markus Wiener, 2012), 171, states that "during this victorious [Ottoman] raid [in 1560 against Malta] individuals were seized for intelligence interrogation." In *Staying Roman: Conquest and Identity in Africa and the Mediterranean, 439–700* (Cambridge: Cambridge University Press, 2012), Jonathan Conant notes that under the Vandals "ship captains—whose role in the dissemination of information rendered them a politically suspect group—were also deprived of their ships" (168).

70. E. de Fages and C. Ponzevera, *Les pêches maritimes de la Tunisie,* 2nd ed. (Tunis: Editions Bouslama, 1903).

71. Among the tales in Giovanni Boccaccio's *Decameron* is the story (day 5, tale 2) of the star-crossed lovers Gostanza and Martuccio from Lipari, who later end up in Sousse owing to winds, currents, and piracy.

72. As with the history of things, the history of animals represents a "growth" subfield; for examples, see Martha Few and Zeb Tortorici, eds., *Centering Animals in Latin American History: Writing Animals into Latin American History* (Durham, NC: Duke University Press, 2013); and Alan Mikhail, *The Animal in Ottoman Egypt* (New York: Oxford University Press, 2013). But what about maritime animals? According to Lilia Zaouali, *Medieval Cuisine of the Islamic World* (Berkeley: University of California Press, 2007), "fish occupied a place of honor in medieval Islamic cuisine" (96). A source of protein, creatures of the sea provided sustenance to crews, passengers, islanders, and many others. Rich coral banks and fisheries increasingly drew European imperial powers to the North African coasts from the early modern period on. Did local or regional maritime knowledge concerning the location and seasonality of fish resources—what we now call "aquaculture"—determine sailing patterns?

73. Grenville T. Temple, *Excursions in the Mediterranean: Algiers and Tunis,* 2 vols. (London: Saunders and Otley, 1835), 1:4; Soumille, "Minorités et vie maritime," 181–96.

74. Fiorenzo Toso, "Tabarchini e tabarchino in Tunisia dopo la diaspora," *Bollettino di Studi Sardi* 3 (December 2010): 43–73.

75. Grandchamp, "Les corailleurs," 83–96.

76. Faruk Tabac, *The Waning of the Mediterranean, 1550–1870: A Geo-historical Approach* (Baltimore: Johns Hopkins University Press, 2008).

77. Al-Saghir, *Tārīkh,* 34, 445.

78. Ahmad ibn Abi al-Diyaf, *Ithaf ahl al-zaman bi-akhbar muluk tunis wa ʿahd al-aman,* 6 vols. (Tunis: al-Dar al-Tunisiya lil-Nashr, 1989), 3/4:200. Solomon Hsiang, "Essays on the Social Impacts of Climate" (PhD diss., Columbia University), UMI Dissertations Publishing, 2011, argues that while climatic variations must be studied at the regional and transregional levels, social communities were often affected by very local patterns and forces; directly linking social violence, for example, with unfavorable natural conditions raises the issues of evidence and causation.

79. Nataniel Rich, "To the Lighthouse," review of *Brilliant Deacons, New York Review of Books* 63, no. 9 (May 26, 2016): 26; Eric Jay Dolin, *Brilliant Beacons: A History of the American Lighthouse* (New York: W. W. Norton, 2016).

80. A long report dated 1846, and entered into a deposition from the National Archives of Tunisia, carton 206, dossier 87, armoire 21, "Correspondence of the Beys with the Consuls of France," details in numerous pages of nautical data the complex itinerary of a vessel (*gondole*) from Ajjacio during the spring equinox (late March). While the ship was headed for Bone and Philippeville, huge seas drove it from island and islet across the central Mediterranean until violent storms forced it to beach on the Cap Negro in Tunisia. What becomes clear from the unusually detailed ship's log is that the captain was islet hopping as a strategy for coping with intemperate weather.

81. Out of numerous examples, the treaty of 1781 granting France's Compagnie Royale d'Afrique a six-year exclusive right to exploit Tunisian coral fisheries is typical. Article 6 stipulates that "the Tunisian government will provide full protection to ships and to sailors . . . in the case that these ships are afflicted by bad weather." *Catalogue of Documents,* Tunis, 1994, 53, National Archives of Tunisia.

82. See the numerous publications by Palmira Brummett, including *Mapping the Ottomans: Sovereignty, Territory, and Identity in the Early Modern Mediterranean* (Cambridge: Cambridge University Press, 2015); and "The Ottomans as a World Power: What We Don't Know about Ottoman Sea Power," *Oriente Moderno* 20 (81), no. 1 (2001): 1–21; Miriam Cooke, Erdağ Göknar, and Grant Parker, eds., *Frogs around a Pond: The Mediterranean World from Delos to Derrida* (Durham, NC: Duke University Press, 2007); and Julia Clancy-Smith, *Women Travel the Mediterranean from Queen Dido to the Twenty-First Century,* in preparation. There is virtually no scholarship on how North African women traveled the sea, although elite European women wrote numerous accounts; the Atlantic crossing is well documented in, for example, Stephen R. Berry, *A Path in the Mighty Waters: Shipboard Life and Atlantic Crossings to the New World* (New Haven, CT: Yale University Press, 2015).

83. Bechir Mokadem, "Une mission Tunisienne à Paris (February–May 1853)," *Revue Africaine* 90 (1946): 58–98. The journal may have been exhumed during the early 1940s from the old French consulate's basement in Tunis, which Mokadem and Pierre Grandchamp excavated because it warehoused disparate unarchived documents. Unfortunately, Mokadem did not translate the entire manuscript but only selected sections of it; whether the original Arabic manuscript is still extant in any form remains a mystery.

84. Fernand Braudel, *Memory and the Mediterranean,* trans. Siân Reynolds (New York: Vintage Books, 2001), 181–90; Braudel, *Mediterranean,* 1:114.

3

The Mediterranean of Modernity

The Longue Durée Perspective

Edmund Burke III

MEDITERRANEAN MODERNITIES: FINDING THE WAY FORWARD

The Mediterranean is a research space long established in classical studies, and to a lesser extent in anthropology. Yet despite Fernand Braudel's magisterial two-volume work *The Mediterranean and the Mediterranean World in the Age of Philip II,* there has been surprisingly little scholarly work that takes it seriously as a zone of historical interaction, or as a laboratory in which to view how that ubiquitous thing "the modern" emerged within the Mediterranean.[1] While the Mediterranean is the place where European, Muslim, and African civilizations converge, most authors have tended to emphasize the boundaries between civilizations, not their histories of interaction. Clearly the fact that the region is one of more than a dozen important languages, each with its own literature, has inhibited the emergence of broader perspectives. So too has nationalism, which has fostered the development of multiple tunnel-vision histories, while undermining attempts to see across cultural and political boundaries. While important, these factors only begin to explain why Braudel's project of a comparative history of the Mediterranean died stillborn. Most crucial was the shadow cast by colonialism, which divides the Mediterranean into two allegedly monolithic blocs: the Christian and the Muslim Mediterraneans. The cultural struggle within today's Europe over the presence of large Muslim populations is for Braudel but the tip of a vast iceberg of mutual incomprehension. Related to this is the way in which northern Europeans have tended to view even the societies of southern Spain, France, Italy, and the Balkans through orientalist spectacles. The result has been to distort not only the histories of the colonized peoples of the Muslim parts of the Mediterranean but also those of Mediterranean Europe.

This chapter represents an effort to bridge the gap between mutual incomprehensions and to reimagine the Mediterranean as a zone of comparative historical inquiry. The Mediterranean is one place where an interdisciplinary approach can help us make headway against both the dominant state-centered nationalist narratives by which the different societies of the region have told their stories and the orientalist representations that still durably intervene to cloud our understanding. As this essay is a reprint of a 2013 article published in the *Journal of World History*, some readers may wish that I had taken the time to update the references for its publication in this volume.[2] As a place to begin the revisions, some have proposed (not unreasonably given the rapid emergence of this much-needed new field) the environmental history of the Mediterranean region.[3] Given that elements of this essay come from versions that were published more than a decade ago (including in Italian and French), there is potentially no end to the updating.[4] When I set out to write what became an explicitly nonculturalist history of the Mediterranean, it was with the sense that such a project was too great for any one scholar. My hope was that it might spark a congenial collective project among the emerging generation of scholars.

Historians, literary scholars, art historians, and social scientists all have perspectives that can mutually enrich one another. Where a particular disciplinary or regional literature leaves off, others can intervene to provide new questions, new sources of intellectual stimulation. Recently historians have shown some signs of interest in reviving the Braudelian project. But for Peregrine Horden and Nicholas Purcell, British medievalists whose *Corrupting Sea* is the most ambitious of recent attempts, this takes the form of a systematic avoidance of master narratives, for fear of tumbling into the vice of orientalism.[5] My approach here is in some respects the opposite: to "world" the transformations of the Mediterranean, instead of breaking it into microecological segments. Efforts to examine the modern period remain few and have been mostly limited to the eastern Mediterranean.[6]

The Mediterranean is central to the process of Europe's reinvention. As the first recipient of the nineteenth-century liberal reform project in its political and economic forms, it was therefore also the site from which to begin the process of rethinking European modernities (in the plural). For some, it may also be a place to observe the ways in which Europe is being transformed today. For all these reasons we find the Mediterranean an important site for research and reflection in our present conjuncture. That this task is an urgent one is clear from a consideration of the ravages of divisive nationalisms in the recent past and the rise of various forms of Islamism in the present. As the proportion of Muslims steadily increases in the new Europe, the need for a "Europe" that generously incorporates the southern and eastern ends of the Mediterranean (perhaps even the interior of Africa) has increasingly made itself felt. However, because of the persistence of European racism and the legacy of colonialism, the political project of integrating the Mediterranean into the new Europe remains stalled. Arab suspicions of European motives in calling for a new Mediterranean (and the persistence of European racism, as well as European hegemonic aspirations) remain all too obvious. If the Mediterranean is to be only a European "security zone," then sincere Arab and Muslim partners will be difficult to find.

A central problem in writing about the Mediterranean is that its history has been primarily written by northern Europeans. For example, as Marie-Noelle Bourguet and her collaborators have noted, the invention of the Mediterranean as an object of study dates from eighteenth-century Enlightenment thinkers.[7] It was the Napoleonic expedition to Egypt in 1798 that for the first time enabled Europeans to imagine the Mediterranean as a scientific laboratory (a conception closely bound to French imperialist aspirations of the time). The Saint-Simonian technocratic vision of a Mediterranean made modern by French capital and know-how continues to inspire contemporary Euro-Mediterranean discourse.[8] In view of this prior history, thinking about "Mediterranean modernities" from the vantage point of the Muslim Mediterranean must inevitably appear either as a naive exercise in denying history (the history of colonialism) or a cynical effort to annex the histories of the modern Muslim Mediterranean to the progress-oriented narrative of the new European globalization. The project of Mediterranean modernities carries a lot of historical baggage.

Northern Europeans typically came to the cultures and peoples of the region with a set of agendas and expectations that shaped the histories and anthropologies they wrote. We need to be alert to the existence of these agendas and to the ways they continue to deform our own vision even as we seek to place the Mediterranean in its world historical contexts. The problem of orientalism is thus more encompassing than previously imagined. For the populations of the Muslim Mediterranean were not the only ones to be inspected by the lens of power, and this inspection has not occurred just under conditions of colonial rule. As Jane Schneider argues in *Italy's "Southern Question,"* the lens of power has significantly deformed knowledge about southern Italy as well.[9] Much the same can be said about southern Spain, Portugal, and Greece. Moreover, once internalized, orientalist discourse became a self-lacerating search for "what went wrong." Throughout the region, local intellectuals became obsessed by the ways in which their society failed to measure up to northern European models of modernity. Orientalist histories operate as if the West were fated to achieve modernity thanks to its superior cultural attainments (the Greeks, science, democracy, and such) while other societies as a result of their inferior culture remain trapped in the realm of the traditional, leaving the South (pick a South, any South) as the realm of tradition and stasis.

The present intervention is an attempt to rethink the place of regional histories in world history using the Mediterranean as an example. As a historian of

Mediterranean Islam as well as of modern Europe, I believe that a comparative history of Mediterranean modernities can provide a number of benefits.[10] By relocating the experience of colonialism in the Mediterranean within the larger story of the hegemony of northwestern Europe over the region, it brings some important commonalities into view, and well-known differences between the "Christian" and "Muslim" Mediterraneans take on a different character. When viewed in a broad comparative context, such a study may make it possible to discern the existence of Mediterranean models of economic modernity appropriate to Mediterranean conditions. Finally, a comparative study of the Mediterranean may allow us to perceive the blocked narrative of Muslim modernity in a different light. Sufficiently capacious to deprovincialize core narratives, but sufficiently limited in range and extent to enable plausible comparisons: the Mediterranean is such an area. Thus, for example, it has the potential to weaken the power of the northern European narratives and of ubiquitous culturalist explanations for the backwardness of the region, such as amoral familism (Banfield), patronage networks, or religion.[11] Bad culture (amoral familism, Islam, take your pick), there's the problem! But if so, then how can we explain the common historical experience of all Mediterranean countries from 1500 to 1800? While culture no doubt is usefully invoked as one element in a historical explanation, it is by no means the full story.

Where is the Mediterranean? The question, apparently innocent, leads us away from the familiar Inner Sea of the classical era and toward the realization that it depends upon when and why we ask the question. We imagine, rather than a fixed space, a Mediterranean with differing modalities (*à géometrie variable*). In a striking metaphor Braudel called for us to imagine a Mediterranean opened to the Sahara and the West African interior. In a similar spirit, given the well-attested connections (cultural, economic, and political) between the eastern Mediterranean civilizations and those of the Indus Valley, world historian Ross E. Dunn has suggested that it may be useful to imagine the rise of the classical civilizations of antiquity as occurring in the supraregional space he calls *Indo-Mediterranea.*[12] With the Iberian voyages at the end of the fifteenth century, the Mediterranean increasingly opened into (and was subsequently subsumed by) the emergent Atlantic World even as Mediterranean cultural, economic, and political institutions crucially shaped the New World (including shaping the slave trade in important ways). We are all familiar with the way Mediterranean institutions helped shape the emergent culture of modernity in northwestern Europe. Finally, with the opening of the Suez Canal (1869), the onset of steamship navigation, and the laying of the telegraph cables that linked Europe with the world, we arrive at the Mediterranean of modern times. At this point we might ask, in what sense is the concept of the Mediterranean still useful? I would reply that it depends upon what you are interested in explaining. By expanding the frame we are able to imagine how the migrations of Mediterranean workers (especially Italians) gave rise in the early twentieth century to an

FIGURE 4. Satellite view of the western Mediterranean. Courtesy of NASA.

"anarchist Atlantic" (Jose Moya), and how closely the emergence of the middle class in many parts of the region (Spain, Sicily, and Lebanon come to mind) was linked to the migrations of the late nineteenth century.[13] So one important intellectual move in imagining the way in which the Mediterranean came to modernity is to leave behind older, more static notions of a Mediterranean frozen in time and space in favor of a more open and extensible idea of the region.

MEDITERRANEAN MODERNITIES: A DEEP-HISTORICAL APPROACH

To understand why the Mediterranean as a world region (and not just the Muslim parts) was economically marginalized during the long sixteenth century, we need to view it in its global context. To do so we need to insert the Mediterranean into the deep history of Eurasia. From this perspective, one can notice a family resemblance among the states and empires that emerged in Eurasia from China to the Mediterranean from circa 1500 BCE. The origins of agriculture, cities, and civilizations mark the transition of humanity to a new phase, the Agrarian Age, which Braudel called the Biological Old Regime.[14] Periods of prosperity in which populations burgeoned, agricultural production soared, and trade flourished were followed by periodic subsistence crises in which famines and disease provoked downturns. In effect, the Biological Old Regime governed human affairs from the first millennium BCE until circa 1750 CE. But already starting around 1450 CE some changes can be observed. Human populations across Eurasia expanded at a faster rate, states developed new military and organizational capabilities, and communications capabilities (printing as well as transportation) developed in unprecedented ways. As the changes pyramided, states that were able to adapt to the new conditions of warfare, commerce, and communications achieved unprecedented power. Although these changes were hemisphere-wide, they were particularly important in China, where the Ming dynasty (1367–1644) had just replaced the Mongol Yuan (1280–1367); in India under the Mughals (1526–1707); and in western Europe (just emerging from the Black Death). To fully comprehend what occurred, it is useful to compare the ecohistorical predicament and specific strategies of Mediterranean states with those of China, India, and Europe on the eve of modernity. Here is where a global and environmental perspective has much to offer.

Let's begin by examining the ecohistorical context in which the Mediterranean region came to modernity. By 1450 CE, the ecological constraints on growth were emerging in states all across Eurasia. Kenneth L. Pomeranz has argued that China (we might add India) and western Europe pursued contrasting approaches to the growing ecological limitations.[15] Western Europe's solution to the contradictions of population increase and ecological overshoot was to exploit its maritime advantage through overseas expansion, as a result of which it achieved levels of wealth and power well beyond Agrarian Age norms. Overseas colonies gave Europe a strategic advantage in the new global struggle for empire and resources, with the availability of colonial raw materials (above all the silver of the Americas) allowing it to participate in the new global market from a position of strength. First Europe muscled in on the Asian spice trade; then, as the sugar revolution (1650–1800) transformed the Atlantic economy by linking Africa, the Americas, and Europe, it was able to channel profits from the slave trade and sugar production in the Caribbean into an unprecedented source of economic growth. The emergence of a truly global market in spices, sugar, and other commodities did not lead to a definitive break with the material limitations on growth that had characterized the agrarian age, but it did allow western Europe to transcend at least some of the limitations of its ecological situation.

In this regard the ecohistorical situation of the Mediterranean region makes an interesting contrast to China, India, and western Europe.[16] Situated at the junction point of Asia, Africa, and Europe, the Mediterranean region as a whole long enjoyed a central position in the topology of exchange within the Eastern Hemisphere. Well endowed with agricultural and (initially) forest resources, the region contained the earliest centers of agriculture and civilization. The vigor and dynamism of the complex social forms that flourished within the Mediterranean facilitated a sustained interchange between agricultural, mercantile, and pastoralist

World Populations by Regions: 500 BCE–1900 CE

	Region (Millions)				
Date	*China*	*S Asia*	*Mediterranean*	*NW Europe*	World
500 BCE	19	30	60	29	153
0	70	46	75	23	252
500 CE	32	33	67	15	207
1000 CE	56	40	57	15	253
1500 CE	89	95	50	49	461
1600	110	145	65	69	578
1700	150	175	65	90	680
1800	330	180	70	125	954
1900	415	290	103	137	1634

SOURCE: Colin McEvedy and Richard Jones, eds., *Atlas of World Population History* (Harmondsworth: Penguin Books, 1978); and Carlo Cipolla, ed., *The Fontana History of Europe*, vols. 2–3 (London: Fontana/Collins, 1973 and 1974).

societies. For millennia the prosperity of the region was assured by the social power inherent in large, well-organized populations exploiting a varied resource base and exploiting a central position in the currents of exchange within Afro-Eurasia. All this changed around 1450 CE, when, for complex reasons it is useful to briefly detail, the Mediterranean became increasingly undermined by secular as well as conjunctural vectors of change and began to lose momentum.

The cumulative secular decline in agricultural productivity within the Mediterranean region as a whole (especially severe in the Fertile Crescent) marks a first aspect of the predicament of Mediterranean societies. This was nothing new. Primarily a consequence of irreversible processes of siltation and salination consequent to the introduction of irrigation, the decline in agricultural productivity was already evident by Roman times.[17] As agricultural productivity gradually slowed and even reversed, the population of the Mediterranean, which in 500 BCE had been more than double that of China (60 vs. 19 million) was by 1000 CE already falling behind (56 million for China vs. 33 million for the Middle East alone) (see table 1).[18] By 1500, China and India had vastly larger and more dynamic populations (ca. 84 million and 95 million respectively, versus ca. 50 million in the Mediterranean region). What I am calling western Europe had a population in 1500 of ca. 49 million). By 1800, China had four times the population of the Mediterranean (ca. 330 vs. 70 million), while Europe's (ca. 125 million) was almost double that of the Mediterranean region. The causes of this growing demographic divide are complex. In addition to the long-term trends alluded to above, they include important changes in land use, consequent to the increased relative importance of pastoralist production in the post-Mongol (and post–Black Death) period. Fernand Braudel was the first to note that the rise of pastoralist economic interests after 1500 (notably the wool trade) was a region-wide Mediterranean phenomenon.[19] As pastoralist power increased, agricultural lands were taken out of cultivation and land tax revenues declined. While the rise of the social power of pastoralism is also observable in India and China in the same period, it was especially important in the Mediterranean region. This would have long-term consequences for the future.

From an ecohistorical perspective there was a second reason for the decline of the Mediterranean region relative to the rest of Eurasia: a shortage of forest resources, a basic raw material and an important source of energy for most of human history. Historians tell us that by Roman times (if not before) the forests of the Mediterranean were already significantly depleted.[20] The biomass resources of the region declined further during the Little Ice Age (1350 to 1850 CE) because of the prolonged drought conditions that were the region's lot.[21] The depletion of forest resources affected the Mediterranean two ways: a shortage of building materials and a slowly building energy crisis. Both of these became fully apparent after 1500. From this date onward we can observe all across Eurasia a new dynamism in the rise of early modern states and empires. Their resource needs for warfare, major construction projects (among them vast navies), and wood/charcoal drastically accelerated regional deforestation.[22] To summarize thus far, the Mediterranean region in the period 1500–1800 witnessed the regional dominance of the rival Hapsburg and Ottoman empires. In this rivalry the Ottomans were fatally disadvantaged. For unlike the Spanish Hapsburgs, who for a time could draw upon the natural resources (and silver!) of the Americas, the Ottoman Empire had neither an inner frontier area to exploit (like China, India, and Europe) nor any colonies. As a consequence, by 1800 the Mediterranean region as a whole (and not just the Ottoman zone) faced an incipient energy crisis due to its growing wood shortage.

A third important ecohistorical factor that eroded the competitiveness of the Mediterranean versus the other major regions of Eurasia was major long-term climatic shifts.[23] Attention has recently focused on the role that shifts like El Niño and the advance and retreat of glaciers have played in world history, and increasingly historians now recognize the impact of the climate changes attendant upon the Little Ice Age (1300–1850) in late medieval and early modern Europe.[24] Glaciers re-formed in the Alps (and other major European mountain chains), unprecedented periods of freezing temperature were noted, and the growing season became shorter. More recently attention has turned to the effects of the Little Ice Age onto the Mediterranean region. In *The Waning of the Mediterranean,* historian Faruk Tabak argues that the Little Ice Age had a cumulatively devastating impact upon Mediterranean agriculture, as torrential rains destroyed irrigation works and as swamped coastlands became the site of endemic malaria. When combined with contemporary political changes (the decline of empires and the rise of piracy in the seventeenth century), it led to the long-term depopulation of large swaths of the Mediterranean coast.[25]

More important still in the relative decline of the Mediterranean region after 1450 is the transformation in its place in the topology of the world economy. For millennia, the Mediterranean region had profited greatly from its position astride the trade routes linking inner Asia, South and Southeast Asia. and western Europe. However, even before the voyages of discovery at the end of the fifteenth century, the Indian Ocean was already emerging as a larger and more important Mediterranean.[26] The European navigation revolution of the sixteenth century led to the emergence of the Atlantic as the center of the emergent world economy and subordinated the Indian Ocean and Mediterranean systems to it. The rise of a capitalist world economy centered upon the Atlantic was a major world historical development. It transformed the place of the Mediterranean in the emergent global system of exchanges in three major ways. First, from playing a central role in the exchange of goods, ideas, and people within Afro-Eurasia, the Mediterranean became increasingly marginal to the new global communications network. The region's land transport advantages (via the Middle Eastern caravan trade) became redundant, while its fading dominance over the internal seas of Eurasia made it increasingly irrelevant in the new age of oceanic transport.[27] Second, as Europeans acquired direct access to American silver and West African gold, they marginalized the Muslim-dominated trans-Saharan routes that had previously been an important source of gold for Europe. Third, American silver and West African gold allowed Europeans to participate in the global market.[28] The discovery of the Americas benefited Spain during a period of sharpened competition between the Hapsburgs and the Ottomans. Although the Hapsburgs were initially able to profit from their American empire at the expense of the Ottomans and enjoyed untrammeled access to the resources of the Americas, including mining, timber, and vast agricultural lands, this was not fated to last. The cumulatively ruinous expense of the sixteenth-century wars of the Hapsburgs and the Ottomans ultimately worked to the advantage of the British, Dutch, and French, who were better able to navigate the increasing cost curve of the fiscal/military revolution.[29] In the longer-term perspective, as Pomeranz has argued, access to colonies provided crucial advantages to western Europe. The Mediterranean region, already suffering from a relative shortage of forest resources and agriculturally depleted from millennia of intense cultivation, was without a viable alternative strategy. With the emergence of a global world economy, the Mediterranean became increasingly sidelined.

Already put in an untenable position by its demographic decline and its reduced place in the topology of global exchanges, the Mediterranean region suffered a third major setback as a result of changing ecohistorical conditions. Around 1550 Britain (western Europe a century later) found itself facing a looming energy crisis caused by rapidly increasing deforestation. The crisis threatened to jeopardize the remarkable economic growth that had accompanied the establishment of the colonial empires in the Americas, maritime Asia, and Africa. Just at this point the fortuitous discovery of abundant deposits of coal located adjacent to northwestern Europe's water transport network sparked the transition from biomass energy to fossil fuels. As a result, the previous environmental constraints on economic growth were burst asunder and an unprecedented new relationship of humans to the environment was forged.

It was the dawn of the Age of Coal (and its essential correlate, steam power). The new global energy regime was to prove as significant for humanity as the mastery of fire and the discovery of farming.[30] No longer limited to the availability of biomass, human, and animal energy, humans acquired vast capabilities never before known. The new energy regime proved crucial for the subsequent course of human development, placing humans in an altogether different relationship with the environment.[31] Access to fossil fuels (in the first instance coal) became critical to the industrial revolution (without which indeed the latter is unimaginable). Northwestern Europe's privileged access to coal (and its location conveniently near its water transport network) was to shape global ecohistorical conditions in the long nineteenth century (1750–1918), and thereafter. Absent fossil fuels, the material limits upon growth of the solar energy regime would inevitably have asserted themselves to muffle and delay the installation of the industrial revolution.

How did the advent of the age of fossil fuels and steam power play out in the Mediterranean? Already poorly endowed in wood, the Mediterranean's transition to industrialization in the long nineteenth century was greatly handicapped by the absence of significant deposits of coal: little in the Ottoman domains, and not much more in Italy, Spain, and Greece. As a result the Mediterranean was a major loser in the transition of the early modern period. Although today the Middle East is a major player in the world energy game, it had to sit out phase 1 of the fossil fuel revolution (the Age of Coal). Only when the fossil fuel revolution moved on to phase 2 (petroleum and natural gas) did the situation of the region change (helping those with petroleum but not those without). But by this time European imperial powers dominated the region, so the oil of the Middle East was not "theirs" to dispose of as they saw fit and instead was controlled by multinational corporations.

Thus we do not need to seek cultural explanations for the decline of the Mediterranean region after 1500. All the will in the world and all the good capitalist intentions could not compensate for centuries of demographic decline, agricultural downturn, and deforestation. The undermining of agriculture by the Little Ice Age further weakened the position of the Mediterranean in world terms. Nor could Mediterraneans gain advantage from their location in the topology of global exchange. Nor, finally, could they atone for the fact that when Mother Nature was distributing her gifts, the Mediterranean came up short in the coal department. Because it lacked both the ecological resources and the strategic position to make the transition to the new ecohistorical context of the age of fossil fuels, the Mediterranean was one of the major regional losers within Eurasia after 1500. The recounting of this history necessarily leads to a reproblematization of the work of culture in Mediterranean "backwardness." After 1500 the entire region, and not just part of it, was "underdeveloped": increasingly semiperipheral with respect to the Atlantic-centered world capitalist system and characterized by weak state structures, delayed or weak class formation, agrarian backwardness, and the persistence of pastoralism.[32] The coming to modernity of the Mediterranean makes it an ideal vantage point from which to assess the costs and consequences of the transformation of northern Europe. As well, the internal unity within diversity foreshadows the historical experience of what used to be called the Third World.

TOWARD A DEEP-CULTURAL HISTORY OF THE MEDITERRANEAN

Despite the appearance of divergence in the paths pursued by individual states within the Mediterranean region, a deep-cultural filiation can be perceived to underlie the paths by which the Mediterranean came to modernity. Viewed from East Asia, the Mediterranean appears as one place, with one history, not several. It is a region shaped by the heritage of ancient empires, by Hellenism ("Greek thought"), and by monotheism (the Chinese word *hui hui* refers to Western monotheists, not just Muslims). Should the sword and the scepter (the state and religion) be united? Jews, Christians, and Muslims have struggled among themselves over this question for millennia. What should be the relation between a revealed scripture and rational thought? Again, in somewhat different forms, the question occurs in all three religious traditions. The heritage of Roman law embraced the entire region and left historical residues in the religious laws of Islam, Christianity, and Judaism.

Cultural explanations of Mediterranean backwardness are widespread. The national histories of most Mediterranean states tend to attribute their delayed modernization to cultural weaknesses internal to their respective national histories.[33] This predilection for internalist accounts connects the modern histories of Mediterranean states to those of the rest of the Third World. One reason for the repeated recourse to cultural explanation lies in the continuing power of the myth of the European miracle, according to which the "rise of the West" derived from the superiority of Western culture (science and rationalism).[34] Societies that failed to conform to this pattern were suspected of being culturally defective. In the post-9/11 world such civilizational thinking unfortunately has enjoyed a renewed life. Thus Samuel P. Huntington has argued that the divisions between rich and poor states in modern world are best explained as a clash of civilizations.[35] Similarly, Bernard Lewis's *What Went Wrong* finds the explanation of Middle Eastern backwardness in Islam (rather than the complex legacy of colonialism and petroleum politics).[36] At this point we have left the realm of history for that of ideology. Clearly we must look elsewhere for a more satisfactory explanation.

One place to begin this task is by noting the underlying unity in the responses of Mediterranean elites and peoples to the forces of the dual revolution (the industrial and democratic revolutions of modern times). The deep-cultural shifts of the period can be described as a kind of historical plate tectonics. Since I'm a Californian, seismic metaphors come naturally. I've already noted how monotheism, Hellenism, and the legacy of ancient empires (including especially Roman law) distinguish the region from the rest of Asia. By the late medieval period especially in Spain, France, and Italy we can observe the strengthening of an impulse toward enforced cultural homogeneity within the emerging states of the region—or at least the Christian ones. With the rise of the Iberian empires (Portugal, Castile, Aragon—earlier the Cathars and Albigensians), religious differences between groups became increasingly fraught. The search for religious homogeneity culminated in state projects of ethnic cleansing in Iberia of their Jewish and Muslim minorities. While the Ottoman record of religious tolerance in the period stands in sharp contrast to that of the Iberians, if we roll the cameras forward to the emergence of linguistic nationalisms in the Balkans and the Ottoman Empire during the long nineteenth century, we note the reappearance of projects of ethnic cleansing in the service of enforcing cultural homogeneity. The history of linguistic minorities within the states of the region had more complex but equally fraught dynamics. We might evoke in this connection the contrasting histories of the Basque and Catalan speakers of Spain, or of Greek, Armenian, Kurdish, and Arab speakers in Ottoman lands. I do not have the space to explore the urge for linguistic uniformity here. Suffice it to say, the persistence of submerged linguistic ethnicities remains an important element in the national politics of many Mediterranean countries. But exclusivist nationalisms are only one aspect of the underlying similarities that linked the eastern and western regions of the Mediterranean, the worlds of the Catholic Iberians and the Muslim Ottomans.

LINEAMENTS OF MEDITERRANEAN MODERNITY IN THE LONG NINETEENTH CENTURY

In this section, I want to focus on the striking family resemblance of Mediterranean societies in the "group photo" of their encounter with modernity over the course of the long nineteenth century (1750–1914). Let's look again at the deep history of Mediterranean, this time viewed as a zone of tectonic interaction.

By 1750 all around the rim of the Inner Sea we find weak states with strong hinterlands ("explosive countrysides").[37] An older historiography, perhaps impressed with the sheer scale of the Iberian Hapsburg and Ottoman empires, saw them as all powerful, world-bestriding colossi. Today's historians are more apt to describe them as pitiful, muscle-bound giants.[38] A closer diagnostic reveals states chronically incapable of exercising their control beyond the walls of the provincial capitals, reduced to governing through a plethora of placeholders and middlemen who exercised a rough-and-ready justice (generally for a price).

We next discover a dense thicket of hedge-priests and urban clerics intent upon making sure that liberal reform in all its myriad forms remained at bay, while they busily connived with landlords, military elites, and urban gentlemen to guarantee this outcome. In the countryside the world tended to be divided between macrofundia and microfundia in which (as the century wore on) absentee landlords and their local henchmen faced down an increasingly numerous and obstreperous peasantry. This was much less true in Muslim parts of the Mediterranean, where relative indivision of land tended to be the norm until modern times. Here we find ourselves on the terrain of Eric Hobsbawm's *Primitive Rebels*, the Mezzogiorno, Sicily, and Andalusia. But with a little imagination we can detect similar social forms all around the region, from Greece and Anatolia to Mount Lebanon and the Hawran, from Upper Egypt to the Maghrib.[39] (Nonetheless it is important not to draw this picture too sharply, as the Mediterranean countryside was, as Braudel has shown, infinitely various and complex.)

The rise and fall of empires (the Ottoman and the Hapsburg, and all those that came before) had a lasting effect on the history of the modern Mediterranean. This heritage left durable historical residues—legal and administrative structures, urban types, characteristic approaches to difference (linguistic and religious)—that distinguish the historical trajectory of Mediterranean lands from those of Northwest Europe, East Asia, and South Asia. On the question of difference, we might notice that the modern history of the region begins with the ethnic cleansing of Jews and Muslims from Iberia by Isabella la Catholica and concludes in the 1920s with the ethnic cleansing of Armenians and Greeks from Anatolia by Ataturk. Bracketed by these dual ethnic cleansings, the search for an ethnically coherent nation is a defining feature of the ways in which the region came to modernity. Here, we might say, the political plate and the cultural plate rammed up against one another.

The more historians have studied the Old Empires of the Mediterranean (the Hapsburg and the Ottoman), the more they appear to have been coalitions of interests, patchwork quilts of institutional structures, veritable museums of politics past whose strategy seems to have ensnared internal rivals in webs of privilege (or if that did not work, to expel them), while fostering subimperialisms (like that of the House of Aragon in Italy). By the eighteenth century the old structures were badly in need of an update, to which the Spanish Bourbon reforms and the various abortive reform projects of the Ottomans testify. But the path to reform was strewn with obstacles. Entrenched agrarian elites and their allies in church and state sought to oppose encroachments upon their traditional privileges. It was in this context that the liberal reform project (as I call the loosely connected bundle of political and economic reforms associated with the Enlightenment and the French Revolution) burst upon the scene.

Until now, despite the well-acknowledged deep-structural historical unity of the Mediterranean, two important facts (and their attendant deeply interconnected historical narratives) have intervened to derail any effort to imagine the history of the modern Mediterranean as a whole. One is Islam. The other is colonialism. However, while colonialism has ended at least formally (independent states now exist around the rim of the Mediterranean, although local elites remain in the thrall of European and American masters), Islam has not. The result is that the colonial past continues to shape the ways in which we understand the modern histories of the eastern and southern Mediterranean (of Turkey, the Balkans, and the Arab Mediterranean), placing them in parenthesis, apart from the history of the western and northern Mediterranean. This has made it difficult to perceive the underlying unities in the ways the Mediterranean came to modernity. Yet as we'll see in this section, these paths to modernity, as well as the characteristic conflicts to which the modernizing process gave rise, have important underlying structural similarities. The Mediterranean experience foreshadows the historical experience of the Third World in its unity and diversity.

All national histories are by definition unique. But their underlying structures can bear a family resemblance. In this section I'd like to explore the architecture of political modernity in the Mediterranean. The liberal reform project compelled Mediterranean elites to take positions on reform. For reform-minded elites, the state-led development project held out the possibility of defeating entrenched rivals, and a path to modernity. Their opponents viewed the reform package as a threat to age-old privileges and economic ways of life. Because the entire region and not just part of it experienced the age of liberal reform and economic modernization, there is an underlying similarity in the reforms and the opposition they engendered. At the risk of oversimplifying, the Mediterranean region was transformed over the course of the long nineteenth century by the intersection of three main kinds of change: (1) the rise of the modern state; (2) the deepening of the incorporation of the region into the world economy; and (3) the unprecedented revolution in communications and transport. The struggle over the liberal reform package divided Mediterranean elites against one another, sparking both strong advocacy and passionate resistance. As the vectors of change ricocheted among different social groups, alliances shifted now one way, now another. Let's consider the larger context of reform before moving on to a discussion of the ways in which social change produced social upheavals and contention around the region.

The primary engine of political change over the course of the long nineteenth century was the state. Inspired by the successes of the Enlightenment French state, Spain, Italy, and the Kingdom of the Two Sicilies sought to introduce liberal reforms in the eighteenth century. So too did the Ottoman Empire, though with minimal success until the advent of Mahmud II (1808–39), and Greece, to a lesser extent, would introduce reforms after 1830. To this end all drew on the French political tool kit in an attempt to fashion political modernity. Central to the reform package was the disestablishment of the church's control over land: church lands and *waqf* properties were legally taken over by the state. Reformers also sought to replace older military and governmental elites rooted in patron-clientage with newer ones for whom efficiency, discipline, and laisser-faire were the key watchwords. Under the aegis of the liberal state, bureaucracies sought to increase their control of the population, modern armies were established, and modern higher schools and methods of communications were encouraged.

It is important to recognize the relatively recent origin of the political boundaries of the region and the highly contested nature of the reform process. In 1800, the Hapsburg Empire (in both its Spanish and Austrian incarnations) as well as the Ottoman Empire remained heteroclite and poorly integrated assemblages, and the boundaries of their domains were porous and subject to change without notice. The Kingdom of the Two Sicilies and the Egypt of Mehmet Ali enjoyed a contingent independence. The rise of the modern nation-state with its homogeneous narrative still lay in the future. Neither Greece nor Italy existed as independent states. Nor indeed did the modern states of the Balkans (which emerged at the end of the century) or the Arab Middle East. To speak of the adoption of the reform project is therefore primarily to speak about the imperial auspices of reform, which from the point of view of the "captive nations" secreted within their frontiers would vastly disrupt their path toward independence.

As modern states emerged along the Mediterranean's north bank, they developed new, more efficient, and more intrusive fiscal systems. These brought them into collision with old agrarian elites and established religious elites. Within this history, the Ottoman case (along with the cases of Egypt and Tunisia) differs primarily in degree. Its would-be state builders were no less jealous of their power and no less eager to demolish entrenched interests, and by the latter third of the nineteenth century they had some solid achievements. The Ottoman reform process (known as the *tanzimat*) provoked a collision between reform-minded state bureaucrats and local elites eager to defend their traditional rights and liberties. It also stimulated conflict with peasants and artisans, for whom the encroachment of the state was experienced primarily in the form of military conscription and increased taxation. Egypt and Tunisia had their own quasi-autonomous state-building programs (though both were juridically part of the Ottoman Empire, they possessed their capabilities of change). The reform impulse was weaker in precolonial Morocco, despite the accomplishments of Hasan I (1876–94), and in Qajar Persia. Finally, we must recognize the colonial auspices under which reform was introduced especially in the Maghrib, starting with the French invasion of Algeria in 1830.

While little recognized, the cultural struggle set off within the region by the introduction of liberal reforms (whether in the Ottoman Empire, in France, Spain, and Italy, or in the Maghrib) pitted reformist officials against rural interests. Appointed from the metropolitan centers, reformists were politically unaccountable to local groups. Culturally distinct from the local populations, they spoke different languages and operated in terms of different cultural assumptions than those under their charge. Endowed with a sense of their own superiority to the locals by dint of their self-evident modernity, agents of reform suffered epic frustrations. Sharing orientalist stereotypes and racial prejudices about those whom they administered, they often resorted to force to carry out their objectives. In the process they provoked much resistance. Unable to speak the local language or comprehend the diffuse structures of local power, other officials found themselves isolated and stopped trying, or retreated into their own privatistic worlds. The profound cultural abyss that separated reformist officials and progressive landlords in their respective "Souths" from their local administrative charges can be observed in Carlo Levi's *Christ Stopped at Eboli* and the novels of Marcel Pagnol and Yashar Kemal. But one finds a similar suspicion and hostility in the experiences of colonial officials in North Africa, Egypt, and Palestine. Here the writings of Amin Maalouf, Abdel Rahman al-Sharqawi, and Mouloud Mammeri provide a useful guide.[40] Something deeply colonial links the experiences of Mediterranean populations at the hands of the modern state.

The incorporation of the Mediterranean into the world economy stimulated a second and in some ways more far-reaching type of change that cumulatively affected even relatively isolated regions with weak states. However, its impact was differentially greater upon urban areas, like the Marseille area, northern Italy, Barcelona, Salonica, Istanbul, and the littoral of the Arab East that stood astride major world communications links. Incorporation into the world economy encouraged the rise of new urban middle classes whose fortunes were linked to northern European elites. The incorporation also fostered the emergence of an urban-based class of landowners engaged in commercial agriculture for export and provoked the decline of artisans and peasants unable to adapt to the changing economic tides. To the fiscal and other pressures of the centralizing state were added, therefore, pressures based on incorporation in the capitalist world market. As with the enactment of state reforms, it is possible to detect the presence of semicolonial patterns in the economic histories of the various "Souths" of the European Mediterranean: Andalusia, parts of Languedoc, Corsica, the Mezzogiorno, Sicily. There is a semicolonial element as well in the dominance of the various Mediterranean "Souths" by financial groups and institutions headquartered in the North, and in the transformation of the systems of landholding by liberal elites linked to northern Europe. But while the economic modernization of the Mediterranean region can be seen to have been structured by colonial relationships, at least in part, this is not the full story.

Recently, historians Jordi Nadal, Gérard Chastagnaret, Olivier Raveux, and Luigi de Rosa have begun to challenge the standard history of how economic modernity came to the Mediterranean region. They have taken aim at the one-size-fits-all British model of textile-led industrial development, according to which the Mediterranean was seen as irrevocably backward since it did not conform. Instead, they have argued for the existence of a specifically Mediterranean path to economic development.[41] They note that already by the 1830s (and not the 1870s, as earlier historians have claimed), the metallurgy, food-processing and vegetable oils industries in Barcelona, Marseille, and Naples were centers of dynamism in the emerging modern economy of the Mediterranean.[42] Upon closer inspection it appears that even latifundist proprietors in Calabria in the eighteenth century, long portrayed as hopelessly out of step with the new economic music, were more economically dynamic than previously believed.[43] Can one find sprouting seeds of capitalism in the Ottoman Empire? A scan of the literature suggests that it too looks more modern and less sidelined than previously held.[44] The patterns of economic change were broadly similar in Ottoman domains, though with some important nuances. Lebanese silk entrepreneurs, sugar and cotton industrialists in Egypt, and Ottoman entrepreneurs (most of whom were Greek and Armenian) participated in the industrialization of their respective economies, in partnership with (and often under the tutelage of) foreign (especially French) interests.[45] By the last third of the nineteenth century, in Ottoman lands as well as in France, Spain, and Italy (and perhaps Greece as well), these enterprises were "colonized" by "northern" capital. More or less at the same time, thanks to the steam navigation revolution and the opening of the Suez Canal (1869), they also were drawn into colonial circuits of exchange (West African ground nuts, for example).

In general they appear to have participated in the industrialization of their respective economies, but generally in partnership (and often under the tutelage) of foreign (especially French) interests. Although the colonial pattern of development remains clear, we must recall as well that in other ways the worldview and aspirations of the liberal elites of precolonial Egypt, Tunisia, and the Ottoman Empire were broadly shared with the Euro-Mediterranean elite. Historian Albert Hourani's *Arabic Thought in the Liberal Age* (1964) is in many respects a group biography of this cosmopolitan ruling group. These individuals were often educated in Europe, spoke English and French among themselves, and often sat on the boards of directors of the same enterprises, such as the Sucreries d'Egypte.[46] Quintessential liberals, they had a nationalist vision that readily accommodated European difference. The emergence of more deeply rooted cultural populist and radical nationalisms starting with Ataturk in Turkey in the interwar period sounded the death knell for this class.

The nineteenth-century communications revolution, our third vector of change, profoundly transformed Mediterranean lives as well. It constituted a third major vector of change. In contrast to the sixteenth-century voyages of discovery, which rendered the Mediterranean increasingly peripheral to the new North

Atlantic-centered world economy, the introduction of the railroad, the steamship (regular steamship service between the Middle East and Europe dates from the 1840s), and the telegraph (London was linked to India as early as 1857) changed the place of the Mediterranean in the topology of global exchange once again. The formative vision for modernizing the Mediterranean's role in the global circuit of exchange was provided by French Saint-Simonian technocrats.[47] Most of the railroads around the region were constructed by French capital and with French engineering expertise.[48] Railroads helped bring Egyptian cotton to the world market, along with Lebanese silk, Palestinian soap and olive oil, and Sicilian and Andalusian grain. As a result of all these changes in communications, shipping times between Europe and markets in Asia were drastically reduced. Regular steamship transport linked the region to the Atlantic World and facilitated large-scale migrations of people to North America, South America, and Australasia. And along with the inauguration of the American Transcontinental Railroad six months earlier, the opening of the Suez Canal (1869) made it possible to circle the globe in record time. These innovations restored the place of the Mediterranean in the topology of global exchange. To summarize, the nineteenth-century communications revolution profoundly altered the spatial context of economic development of the region, securely linking it to the global market.

LINES OF SOCIAL CLEAVAGE

The onset of modernity in its diverse manifestations from 1750 on provoked a series of bitter struggles along the southern cultural fault lines of Europe. Everywhere in the nineteenth-century Mediterranean, the liberal reform project raised up certain groups in the society and pitted them against others. Those possessing privileged ties to the state or to European business interests were often in a position to profit disproportionately, while urban artisans and rural agriculturalists found themselves squeezed from all sides. Following the establishment of European political control, groups willing to serve as intermediaries gained substantially, while overt opponents suffered from various forms of political and economic discrimination. The complex sequence of changes thus set in motion intersected with one another, generating powerful crosscurrents and back eddies that eroded old established interests and remolded new. Social protest and resistance found fertile ground in the circumstances thus created. Over the course of the long nineteenth century, elites, the church, workers, and peasants found themselves divided along a number of lines of cleavage. Coalitions were continually reshaped even as they persisted. In the end, all people were affected, though not all to the same degree.

If we abstract from the dense thicket of local specificities that shaped these struggles and the cleavages they provoked and exposed, it is nonetheless possible to observe some basic patterns.[49] In particular, the struggles center on three major arenas: the place of religion in the state, gender (especially sexuality and the public role of women), and the land question. It is crucial is to understand that these struggles (and cleavages), beyond their complex local characteristics, derive from common sources.[50] Let us briefly examine each in turn.

The land question was incontestably the major source of conflict in the nineteenth-century Mediterranean. It pitted a relatively small group of wealthy landlords holding vast tracts of land (macrofundia) against throngs of smallholding peasants holding tiny uneconomic strips of land (microfundia) and an even larger array of day laborers and unemployed rural workers. The development of commercial agriculture (whether under the auspices of colonialism, as in the Maghrib, or under local landlords (as in the European Mediterranean, eastern Anatolia, Egypt, and greater Syria) provoked continual resistance. Throughout the nineteenth century the Mediterranean region as a whole was plagued by peasant violence. This took a variety of forms, as memorably evoked for Italy and Spain in Hobsbawm's *Primitive Rebels:* millenarianism, social banditry, and somewhat later (more worryingly for landlords) peasant leagues like the Sicilian *fascii,* Andalusian anarchists, and leftist labor organizers.[51] The dynamics depended upon local contexts, but peasant violence was an endemic feature of the history of Andalusia, Sicily, Greece, Lebanon, and Kabylia (among other regions).

As modernity came to the region in the nineteenth century, the place of religion (previously a central element of ethnic identity everywhere) became a second focal point of struggle. Starting with the sixteenth-century wars of religion and the introduction of secularizing measures, religious identity continued to underpin the emerging political order and religion as a marker of identity and was if anything strengthened by the dynamics of change.[52] But it was not only Latin Europe that was ravaged by the struggle between clerical and anticlerical interests in the nineteenth century. Here we may distinguish between three main historical experiences: a Latin Mediterranean (France, Italy, and the Iberian states), an Orthodox Mediterranean (mostly the Balkans and parts of Anatolia), and a Muslim Mediterranean (the Ottoman domains, including Anatolia and the Arab East and Arab West). Distinctive historical legacies, including religious institutions, legal systems, and conceptions of the state and the individual, differentiated these three groups. Although not usually recognized, the same cultural confrontation also forms a leitmotif in the deep structural history of modern Turkey.

Across the region the liberal project stigmatized religion as backward and marked it for elimination. At opposite ends of the Mediterranean, popular anticlerical passions spilled over in attacks against Spanish convents and Turkish Sufi lodges. The bureaucrats of the *tanzimat,* no less than the liberal bureaucrats of nineteenth-century Spain, France, and Italy, saw in priestcraft the enemy of all reform. And thus they gave it no quarter.[53] In response, religious elites, whether Muslim, Christian, or Orthodox, sought to block efforts to abolish old privileges or to undermine old classes (including old military elites, old landowning elites, and old religious classes). In some respects we can think of them as the cultural equivalent of tectonic plates, now colliding, now slipping alongside one another over a very long historical perspective. However, despite what may appear to be their enormous power, in fact the civilizational blocs were riven by the religious complexities and local syncretisms that were a central organizing feature of the Mediterranean social order. Against the expectations of the progressive narrative, linguistic nationalisms failed to supplant religious identity. The extremely secular Spanish anarchists find their homologue in the Ataturkian bullyboys of Turkey. Like the return of the repressed, Islamist groups now terrify the holders of power all around the rim of the Muslim Mediterranean in the name of populist virtue and justice. As I have suggested elsewhere, the torments of contemporary Algeria must be seen in the context of a Jacobin French colonial state that all too efficiently demolished the central institutions of Algerian Islam.[54]

A final arena of struggle in the region during the long nineteenth century focused upon loosening patriarchal control of female sexuality and permitting women to participate in the public square. It had two main foci. One was the struggle over the legal status of women in Mediterranean societies, where deeply rooted local customs and religious laws restricted progress. In Catholic Europe, where French code law gave women some limited rights, the struggle was long and messy but ultimately successful. In Orthodox Europe, it was delayed until after World War II, though those countries where there was some code law tended to be more advanced. In the Muslim Mediterranean, this meant efforts to modernize the *shari'a* through the enactment of a new family code regulating marriage, the family, divorce, and inheritance. A second arena of confrontation was over women's suffrage. Spain was the first Mediterranean state to afford women the right to vote in national elections in 1931. Turkey followed in 1934, then France and Yugoslavia in 1945, Italy in 1948, and Greece in 1952. With the end of colonialism, the rest of the Arab Mediterranean soon followed.

THE IMPACT OF MIGRATION ON THE MEDITERRANEAN REGION

The communications revolution had other effects within the Mediterranean region. It greatly facilitated the movement of people as well as goods—a process that shows no signs of abating any time soon. Four broad types of migration can be distinguished. In the first category are the migrations from the Euro-Mediterranean region primarily to the Americas and Australasia. Thus five million Spaniards emigrated to the Americas in the period from the 1820s to the 1930s, where they were joined by more than ten million Italians. Lesser numbers of Greeks, Armenians, Lebanese, and Syrians left the Ottoman Empire in the nineteenth century. All told, close to twelve million Mediterranean men and women emigrated over a period of a century and a quarter, with the majority of departures coming after 1870. A second type of migration involved the movements of Mediterranean people within the Euro-Mediterranean arena. While the numbers of people involved were substantially lower than the numbers of long-distance travelers, they were nonetheless significant. Already by the 1830s, hundreds of thousands of Italian migrant workers were seeking economic opportunities in French (and later in the nineteenth century, German) cities. Prior to World War I thousands of Spanish and Portuguese as well as Algerian Kabyles had already found their way to French industrial job sites. These migrants were to be the forerunners of the waves of Iberians, Maghribis, and others who would come after World War II. Because these movements are relatively well known they need no further comment here.

Less well known are the large-scale movements of the Turkish-speaking populations of the Black Sea region and the Caucasus who flooded into Anatolia and the Balkans from the end of the eighteenth century onward. Eventually Russian military incursions into this region would propel more than seven million Muslims to seek refuge in Ottoman Turkey between 1783 and 1913. Of these refugees 3.8 million were Russian subjects, most of them Turkish-speaking Muslims (including some two million people from the Caucasus). With the emergence of nation-states in the Balkans, more Muslim and Turkish populations were displaced. Large numbers of Greek and other Christian groups went in the opposite direction. Not until the exchange of populations in the 1920s between Greece and Turkey did these movements of peoples come to an end. The large-scale ethnic killings of Armenians, especially during World War I, when between 700,000 and 1.2 million perished at the hands of the Turks, permanently altered the demography of modern Turkey. As a result of these massacres and movements of peoples, the Balkans and Turkey became more homogeneous (the former more Christian, the latter more Muslim), and the cultural fault lines became more pronounced.

Still less well known are the precolonial movements of southern Italians, Sicilians, Corsicans, and Maltese to North Africa (especially Tunisia) that Julia Clancy-Smith has studied. She estimates that these migrations were made up of thousands of individuals, mostly misfits of one kind or another—draft dodgers, criminals, speculators, fortune hunters, lovers on the lam. When the French protectorate was established in 1881, the Beylik of Tunisia was home to some seventy thousand Sicilio-Italians and twelve thousand Maltese. It is well to recall that until the unification of Italy and the consolidation of European states, there was nothing odd about this. Here Clancy-Smith lifts the rug to enable us to see the hybrid cultures of the not yet quite modern Mediterranean.[55]

Khedival Egypt attracted similarly impressive numbers of Levantines (as they were called at the time), though in this case the polyglot and heterogeneous population of Europeans and not-quite-Europeans incorporated earlier sedimentary layers of Italians and Greeks who were attracted to Egypt by the spice trade, if not the Crusades. The nineteenth-century European migrants were attracted by the prospect of riches attendant upon the construction of the Suez Canal (1867) as well as a refuge from hardship. (Not for nothing was this period in modern Egyptian history known to Europeans as "Klondike on the Nile"; such were the visions that attracted a horde of speculators and con men.)[56] The descendants of these individuals populate the pages of Lawrence Durrell's *Alexandria Quartet.*

Finally, large numbers of European settlers migrated to North Africa and Palestine. On the eve of the independence movements of the 1950s and 1906s, North Africa counted a European population of 1.5 million settlers (chiefly French, Italian, and Spanish) who arrived over the course of the nineteenth century (Zionist settlers in Palestine in the first half of the twentieth century should also be included in this group). Nowhere was the settler colonial population greater than in Algeria, which on the eve of the revolution totaled some 1.2 million. It is a well-known secret that the "French" population of Algeria comprised a majority of people whose ancestors had arrived from Spain, Italy, and Malta—and not the hexagon itself. David Prochaska has evoked the Algero-French patois of the settler populations and their sense of themselves as a new "Mediterranean" race in his book *Making Algeria French.*[57] The European population of Morocco, Tunisia, and Libya (the other Maghribi societies) totaled around 350,000 individuals.

With decolonization, more than 1.5 million settlers of European origin (most of them middle class) relocated to southern France, Italy and Spain, and the Americas. This constitutes the third major wave of migration that has reshaped the Mediterranean. The reintegration of former settler populations into contemporary European societies has posed an enormous challenge. This is especially true of southern France, where ex-Algerian settlers form one of the major constituencies behind Le Pen. By an irony of history southern France is also heavily populated by large populations of recently arrived North African Muslims, as well as Spaniards, Portuguese, and Italians all attracted by the prospect of a better life. Studies of labor migration from the Mediterranean to northern Europe and the wider world reveal the complexity as well as the deep historical roots of this phenomenon.

The post–World War II period has seen the large-scale migration of Spaniards and Portuguese to France, of Turks to Germany, of southern Italians to northern Italy and Germany, and of Maghribis to western Europe. With the onset of globalization, a far more massive and heterogeneous wave of migration has brought larger numbers of people from the Arab East, Turkey, eastern Europe, and the interior of Africa to western Europe. The size of this cohort as well as its diversity has demographically transformed western European society. It has also posed a powerful challenge to European nationalisms predicated upon the myth of homogeneity.

How are we to understand the impact of the large-scale migration within and from the Mediterranean region? I have two thoughts. Both refer us, though in different ways, to the social context of migration. As we have seen, the nineteenth-century Mediterranean region as a whole was plagued by peasant violence in response to the development of commercial agriculture. In this historical context, migration served to defuse the agrarian time bomb when peasantries were struggling against grasping landlords (*latifundistas*, colonial settlers) and the inexorable pressures of rapid demographic increase. A second thought proceeds from the observation that Mediterranean migration patterns are also complexly interwoven into the social fabric of peasant society. Throughout the Mediterranean, worker remittances made possible the reinvention of the neotraditional family and the renegotiation of gender norms. As numerous scholars have argued, the traditional Mediterranean family is in fact the result of dynamic processes closely connected to family strategies of investment in land and the maintenance of control of women and minors by migrant men. Akram Khater's book *Inventing Home* explores how this happened for Lebanon. He examines the gendered impact on Maronite Lebanese peasant society of the silk boom (and bust) and links it to a careful study of the impact of Lebanese emigration on the household economy.[58] Khater argues that Lebanese rural women's responses to the tensions generated by the massive changes of the period lie at the core of new understandings of how modern Lebanon was made. Gender and the family, he argues, were the sites of contention over a changing Lebanese cultural identity. Both were intimately linked to histories of migration.

This chapter is part of an effort to reexamine against the background of world history how the Mediterranean came to modernity. It is intended to stimulate further thought, not foreclose debate. Modernity, I suggest, was the product of global processes of interaction of the societies of Eurasia, rather than the result of the genius of any particular society. Against the grain of interpretations of the European past that view it as the beneficiary of a foreordained destiny and impute moral superiority to the fact that the modern world was first fully instantiated in Europe, I suggest an alternate reading. It begins with the notion that something is seriously flawed about models of causality that view societies as changing in accord with built-in civilizational motors. While "the rise of the West" makes great ideology, it is poor history. Like Jared Diamond, I believe that we need to situate the fate of nations in a long-term ecohistorical context. Unlike Diamond, I believe that the ways (and the sequences) in which things happened often shaped what came next. The Mediterranean is a particularly useful case in this light. An ancient center of economic and cultural dynamism, its history provides part of the authorizing documentation that undergirds the European miracle literature, according to which once the bouncing ball of historical change jumped to northwestern Europe, the Mediterranean dropped out of the narrative. The secular decline and deindustrialization of the

Mediterranean prefigures the fate of the Third World. No longer a center of progress after the sixteenth century, the Mediterranean experienced a decline usually ascribed to its inherent cultural deficiencies. While the specific cultural infirmity varies with the historian (amoral familism, patron/clientelism, and religion are favorites) the civilizationalist presuppositions of this approach are clear. In this respect the search for "what went wrong" typifies national histories across the region.

In this chapter I have argued that we can observe numerous points of convergence within the Mediterranean region. For example, I have suggested strong resemblances in the transformation of the Mediterranean countryside (and responses to this process), as well as in the enormous growth of cities (and responses to it) and the characteristic divisions among the elite over the utility or not of adopting the liberal reform package. Broadly similar as well were the new lifestyles, a trend especially marked of course among the elites, some of whom indeed frequented the same spas, casinos, and opera seasons and (occasionally) sat on the same boards of directors and were members of the same Masonic lodges. However, once one discounts for the intense specificity of local customs, similar broad trends can be observed among workers and peasants as well. New political identities circulated throughout the Mediterranean, including nationalism (mostly avowedly secular) but also, overwhelmingly for the emerging middle classes and above, consumerism. New ideologies too were beginning to appear, including populism, anarchism, socialism, and the beginnings of what would become in the interwar period fascism. Is the Mediterranean fated to be a zone of cultural and civilizational conflict? If we consider the deeply rooted drive for cultural homogeneity that lurks within even French universalism, it is difficult to give a positive answer to this question. However, as I have suggested here, other histories exist, other ways of thinking about the region and its confrontation with modernity. It is important to encourage the development of these alternative histories if we do not wish to relive the dilemmas of civilizational history.

NOTES

A slightly different version of this chapter was published as "Toward a Comparative History of the Modern Mediterranean, 1750–1919," *Journal of World History* 23, no. 4 (2013): 907–39.

1. Fernand Braudel, *La Méditerranée et le monde méditerranéen à l'époque de Philippe II* (Paris: Presses universitaires de France, 1947), translated as *The Mediterranean and the Mediterranean World in the Age of Philip II,* 2 vols. (1978; repr., New York: Harper's, 1995).

2. Edmund Burke III, "Toward a Comparative History of the Modern Mediterranean, 1750–1919," *Journal of World History* 23, no. 4 (2013): 907–39.

3. See, among others, Sam White's *Climate of Rebellion in the Early Modern Ottoman Empire* (Cambridge: Cambridge University Press, 2013); Alan Mikhail's *Nature and Empire in Ottoman Egypt: An Environmental History* (Cambridge: Cambridge University Press, 2011) and *Water on Sand: Environmental Histories of the Middle East and North Africa* (Oxford: Oxford University Press, 2013); and recent work by Christopher Gratien, notably his "The Ottoman Quagmire: Malaria, Swamps, and

Settlement in the Late Ottoman Mediterranean," *International Journal of Middle East Studies* 49, no. 4 (November 2017): 583–604.

4. Edmund Burke III, "Elementi di modernità nel Mediterraneo nel lungo xix secolo," in *I Sud: Conoscere, capire, cambiare,* ed. Marta Petrusewicz, Jane Schneider, and Peter Schneider (Bologna: Il Molino, 2009), 71–88, and "Modernité," in *Dictionnaire de la Meditérrannée,* ed. Dionigi Albera, Maryline Crivello, and Mohamed Tozy (Marseille: Actes Sud, 2016), 950–66.

5. Peregrine Horden and Nicholas Purcell, *The Corrupting Sea: A Study of Mediterranean History* (Oxford: Blackwell, 2000). See also, by the same authors, "The Mediterranean and the New Thalassology," *American Historical Review* 113, no. 3 (2006): 722–40.

6. Here Ottoman historians have taken the lead. See, for example, Molly Greene, *Catholic Pirates and Greek Merchants* (Princeton, NJ: Princeton University Press, 2010).

7. Marie-Noelle Bourguet, Daniel Nordman, Vassilis Panayotopoulos, and Maroula Sinarellis, eds., *L'Invention scientifique de la Mediterrannée: Egypte, Morée, Algérie* (Paris: École des hautes études en sciences sociales, 1998). See also Marie-Noelle Bourguet, Daniel Nordman, Vassilis Panayotopoulos, and Maroula Sinarellis, eds., *Les expéditions françaises d'Egypte, de Morée et d'Algérie: Actes du colloque, Athènes-Nauplie, 8–10 Juin 1995*, Enquêtes en Méditerranée (Athens: Institut de recherches néohelleniques, 1999), and B. Panagiotopoulos, ed., *Les expéditions françaises en Méditerranée* (Athens: Centre de recherches néohelleniques, n.d.).

8. On Michel Chevalier's Saint-Simonian vision of the Mediterranean, see Michael P. Murphy, "Envisioning Romantic Political Economy: The Formative Years of Michel Chevalier (1806–1879)" (PhD diss., University of California, Santa Cruz, June 2011).

9. Jane Schneider, *Italy's "Southern Question": Orientalism in One Country* (Oxford: Berg, 1998).

10. Edmund Burke III and David Prochaska, eds., *After the Colonial Turn: Orientalism, History and Theory* (Lincoln: University of Nebraska Press, 2007).

11. Edward C. Banfield, *The Moral Basis of a Backward Society* (Glencoe, IL: Free Press, 1958); Bernard Lewis, *What Went Wrong? The Clash between Islam and Modernity in the Middle East* (New York: Perennial, 2003).

12. Ross E. Dunn, "Indo-Mediterranea: Thinking about the Geography of World History," lecture, Planetary Perspectives Series, Rutgers Center for Historical Analysis, Rutgers University, November 2005.

13. Jose Moya, personal communication, May 7, 2005.

14. Fernand Braudel, *Civilization and Capitalism, 15th–18th Century,* vol. 1, *The Structures of Everyday Life* (New York: Harper and Row, 1985).

15. See, more generally, Kenneth R. Pomeranz, *The Great Divergence: China, Europe, and the Making of the Modern World Economy* (Princeton, NJ: Princeton University Press, 2000), and Andre Gunder Frank, *Reorient: Global Economy in the Asian Age* (Berkeley: University of California Press, 1998).

16. The analysis that follows draws on Edmund Burke III, "The Transformation of the Middle Eastern Environment, 1500 B.C.E.–2000 C.E.," in *The Environment and World History,* ed. Edmund Burke III and Kenneth L. Pomeranz (Berkeley: University of California Press, 2009), 81–117.

17. Peter Christensen, *The Decline of Iranshahr: Irrigation and Environments in the History of the Middle East, 500 B.C. to A.D. 1500* (Copenhagen: Museum Tusculanum Press, 1993).

18. For the purposes of this table, I have added the population figures from McEvedy and Jones for the Middle East and North Africa with the figures from Cipolla for Spain, Portugal, and Italy. I have then subtracted the Spain, Portugal, and Italy figures from those given for "Europe" in McEvedy and Jones. A finer-tuned statistical definition of the Mediterranean awaits! In the meantime, this rough cut will have to do.

19. Braudel, *Mediterranean,* pt. I, chap. 4.

20. Oliver Rackham and A. T. Grove, *The Nature of the Mediterranean Europe: An Ecological History* (New Haven, CT: Yale University Press, 2001).

21. Brian Fagan, *The Little Ice Age: How Climate Made History, 1300–1850* (New York: Perseus, 2000).

22. Burke and Pomeranz, *Environment and World History.* See also John R. Richards, *The Endless Frontier: An Environmental History of the Early Modern World* (Berkeley: University of California Press, 2003). On Spain in this period, see David Ringrose, *Transportation and Economic Stagnation in Spain* (Durham, NC: Duke University Press, 1990).

23. Brian M. Fagan, *The Long Summer: How Climate Changed Civilization* (New York: Basic Books, 2004). See also Emmanuel Le Roy Ladurie, *Times of Feast, Times of Famine: A History of Climate since the Year 1000* (New York: Noonday Press, 1988).

24. Fagan, *Little Ice Age.* Jean M. Grove, *Little Ice Ages: Ancient and Modern* (New York: Routledge, 2004), provides an authoritative scientific summary.

25. Faruk Tabak, *The Waning of the Mediterranean, 1550–1870: A Geohistorical Approach* (Baltimore: Johns Hopkins University Press, 2008).

26. See, among other works, Janet Abu-Lughod, *Before European Hegemony: The World System A.D. 1250–1350* (New York: Oxford, 1991), and K.N. Chaudhuri, *Trade and Civilization in the Indian Ocean World: An Economic History from the Rise of Islam to 1750* (Oxford: Oxford University Press, 1971).

27. Niels Steensgaard, *The Asian Trade Revolution of the Seventeenth Century: The East India Companies and the Decline of the Caravan Trade* (Chicago: University of Chicago Press, 1974).

28. Dennis Flynn and Arturo Giraldez, "Born with a Silver Spoon," *Journal of World History* 6, no. 2 (1995): 201–21; also Andre Gunder Frank, *Reorient: Global Economy in the Asian Age* (Berkeley: University of California Press, 1998).

29. Geoffrey Parker, *The Army of Flanders and the Spanish Road, 1567–1659* (Cambridge: Cambridge University Press, 2004). See also the same author's *The Military Revolution: Military Innovation and the Rise of the West, 1500–1800* (Cambridge: Cambridge University Press, 1996).

30. The concept of energy regime is developed by Johan Goudsblom, *Fire and Civilization* (London: Allen Lane, 1992), and Fred Spier, *The Structure of Big History* (Amsterdam: Amsterdam University Press, 1996). See also David Christian, *Maps of Time: An Introduction to Big History* (Berkeley: University of California Press, 2003).

31. The rest of this paragraph draws upon Edmund Burke III, "The Big Story: Human History, Energy Regimes, and the Environment," in Burke and Pomeranz, *Environment and World History,* 33–53.

32. On the persistence of pastoralism, see Edmund Burke III, "Pastoralism and the Mediterranean Environment," *International Journal of Middle East Studies* 42, no. 4 (2010): 663–65.

33. For some examples, see Banfield, *Moral Basis;* Julian Pitt-Rivers, *Mediterranean Countrymen* (Paris: Mouton, 1963); and Raphael Patai, *The Arab Mind* (New York: Scribner, 1976).

34. Eric M. Jones, *The European Miracle: Environments, Economies and Geopolitics in the History of Europe and Asia,* 3rd ed. (Cambridge: Cambridge University Press, 2003).

35. Samuel P. Huntington, *The Clash of Civilizations and the Remaking of World Order* (New York: Touchstone Books, 1997).

36. Lewis, *What Went Wrong?*

37. See Edmund Burke III, "Changing Patterns of Peasant Protest in the Middle East, 1750–1950," in *Peasants and Politics in the Modern Middle East,* ed. Farhad Kazemi and John Waterbury (Gainesville: University of Florida Presses, 1991), 24–37.

38. The literature is vast. On the Spanish Empire, see Leslie Bethell, ed., *Colonial Spanish America* (Cambridge: Cambridge University Press, date); J.H. Elliott, *Imperial Spain, 1469–1716* (London: St. Martins, 1968); and John Lynch, *Spain, 1516–1598* (Oxford: Blackwell, 1992). On the Ottoman Empire, see Halil Inalcık and Donald Quataert, eds., *An Economic and Social History of the Ottoman Empire* (Cambridge: Cambridge University Press, 1994); and Suraiya Faroqhi, *The Later Ottoman Empire, 1603–1839,* vol. 3 of *The Cambridge History of Turkey* (New York: Cambridge University Press, 2006).

39. E.J. Hobsbawm, *Primitive Rebels* (New York: Harper and Row, 1958) and many subsequent editions.

40. Compare Carlo Levi, *Christ Stopped at Eboli* (New York: Farrar, Strauss and Giroux, 1947) and subsequent editions; Amin Maalouf, *Origines* (Paris: Grasset, 2004); Abdel Rahman al-Sharqawi, *Egyptian Earth* (London: Saqi Books, 2005); and Mouloud Mammeri, *The Sleep of the Just* (Boston: Beacon Press, 1958).

41. The British model, best summarized in Walt W. Rostow's *Stages of Economic Growth: A Non-Communist Manifesto* (London: Cambridge University Press, 1961), stressed the lead role of the industrialization of textile production. In the 1980s, Patrick O'Brien and Caglar Keyder argued for the existence of a French road to capitalist development (based on the northern French experience). See their *Economic Growth in Britain and France, 1780–1914: Two Paths to the Twentieth Century* (London: G. Allen and Unwin, 1978).

42. For an overview, see Gérard Chastagnaret and Olivier Raveux, "Espace et stratégies industrielles aux XVIIIe et XIXe siècles: Exploiter le laboratoire méditerranéen," *Revue d'Histoire Moderne et Contemporaine,* nos. 2–3 (2001): 11–24. More generally, Olivier Raveux, Gérard Chastagnaret, and Paul Aubert, *Construire des mondes: Elites et espaces en Méditerranée, XVIe–XXe siècle* (Aix-en-Provence: Publications de l'Université de Provence, 2005). See also Jordi Nadal, *Moler, tejer y fundir: Estudios de historia industrial* (Barcelona: Ariel, 1992); Gérard Chastagnaret, ed., *Crise espagnole et nouveau siècle en Méditerranée: Politiques publiques et mutations structurelles des économies dans l'Europe méditerranéenne, fin XIXe–début XXe siècles* (Madrid: Casa de Velázquez, 1998); and Luigi de Rosa, *La rivoluzione industriale in Italia* (Rome: Laterza, 1985).

43. Marta Petrusewicz, *Latifundium: Moral Economy and Material Life in a European Periphery* (Ann Arbor: University of Michigan Press, 1996).

44. See for example, E.R.J. Owen, *The Middle East in the World Economy, 1800–1914* (London: Methuen, 1981), and Charles Issawi, *An Economic History of the Middle East and North Africa* (New York: Columbia University Press, 1982).

45. Faroqhi, *Later Ottoman Empire;* Akram F. Khater, *Inventing Home: Emigration, Gender, and the Middle Class in Lebanon, 1870–1920* (Berkeley: University of California Press, 2001); Ellis Goldberg, *Tinker, Tailor, and Textile Worker: Class and Politics in Egypt, 1930–1952* (Berkeley: University of California Press, 1986); Robert Vitalis, *When Capitalists Collide: Business Conflict and the End of Empire in Egypt* (Berkeley: University of California Press, 1995).

46. Goldberg, *Tinker, Tailor.*

47. Phillippe Régnier, *Les Saint-Simoniens et Egypte, 1833–1851* (Cairo: Banque de l'Union Européenne, 1989); Magali Morsy, ed., *Les Saint-Simoniens et l'Orient* (Aix-en-Provence: Edisud, 1989); Antoine Picon, *Les Saint-Simoniens: Raison, imaginaire et utopie* (Paris: Belin, 2002).

48. Jacques Lajard de Puyjalon, ed., *L'influence des Saint-Simoniens sur la realisation de l'Isthme de Suez et des chemins de fer* (Paris: L. Chauny et L. Quinsac, 1926), and Clement Henry Moore, *Images of Development: Egyptian Engineers in Search of Industry* (Cambridge, MA: MIT Press, 1980). See also Pierre Robert Baduel, ed., "Modernités arabes et turque: Maîtres et ingénieurs," special issue, *Revue de l'Occident Musulman et de la Méditerranée,* no. 72 (1994), on engineers in the Mediterranean.

49. Burke, "Changing Patterns."

50. Burke.

51. Anton Blok, *The Mafia of a Sicilian Village, 1860–1960: A Study of Violent Peasant Entrepreneurs* (Oxford: Blackwell, 1974); Roderick Aya, *The Missed Revolution: The Fate of Rural Rebels in Sicily and Southern Spain, 1840–1950* (Amsterdam: Universiteit van Amsterdam, Antropologisch-Sociologisch Centrum, 1975); Temma Kaplan, *Anarchists of Andalusia, 1868–1903* (Princeton, NJ: Princeton University Press, 1977).

52. See C.A. Bayly, *The Birth of the Modern World, 1780–1914* (Oxford: Oxford University Press, 2004), chap. 9.

53. Niyazi Berkes, *The Rise of Secularism in Turkey* (Montreal: McGill University Press, 1964).

54. Edmund Burke III, "The Terror and Religion: Brittany and Algeria," in *Colonialism and the Modern World*, ed. Gregory Blue, Martin Bunton, and Ralph Croizier (White Plains, NY: M. E. Sharpe, 2002), 40–50.

55. See Julia Clancy-Smith, *Mediterraneans: North Africa and Europe in the Age of Migration, c. 1800–1900* (Berkeley: University of California Press, 2010).

56. David Landes, *Bankers and Pashas: International Finance and Economic Imperialism in Egypt* (Cambridge, MA: Harvard University Press, 1958).

57. David Prochaska, *Making Algeria French: Colonialism in Bône, 1870–1920* (Cambridge: Cambridge University Press, 1990), and "History as Literature, Literature as History: Cagayous of Algiers," *American Historical Review* 101 (1996): 670–711.

58. Akram Khater, *Inventing Home, Emigration, Gender, and the Middle Class in Lebanon, 1870–1920* (Berkeley: University of California Press, 2001).

4

Piracy of the Ottoman Mediterranean

Slave Laundering and Subjecthood

Joshua M. White

In 1617, troubling reports reached Istanbul from the Ottoman district (*sancak*) of Karlieli (present-day Aetolia-Akarnania in Greece) concerning the conduct of its former governor (*sancakbeyi*) Mahmud. The Imperial Council (*divan-ı humayün*) learned that Mahmud Bey, recently rotated out of office and replaced, had devised an innovative and illegal way to make his tenure more profitable. Posted to the edge of the empire and far from the watchful eyes of their superiors in Istanbul, Ottoman governors like Mahmud and other high-ranking military and administrative officials on the Adriatic and Ionian coasts enjoyed a great deal of discretionary power and minimal supervision. Thus those who were sufficiently enterprising could, if so inclined, dabble in extortion, racketeering, and simple theft to supplement their salaries. The Imperial Council frequently heard complaints about such practices. But Mahmud Bey had not been satisfied with the usual abuses of stealing from those he ruled or demanding money. Instead, he and his deputy had seized the most valuable commodity in their district: its Christian inhabitants.[1]

Slaves were always in demand in the early modern Ottoman Empire and often commanded high prices; because manumission was common and slave status was rarely inherited, a constant supply of captives was required to meet the needs of the market. The strict rules in place to regulate the Ottoman slaving industry restricted who could be captured and imposed taxes, notably the *pencik* (one-fifth) duty, on imported captives.[2] By the standards of both Islamic and sultanic law, the enslavement of tax-paying, non-Muslim Ottoman subjects (*harac veren reaya*) like those resident in Karlieli was patently illegal. They were *zimmis* (Arabic, *dhimmī*), people of the pact (*ahl al-dhimma*), and their submission to Muslim rule, signified by the payment of a tax (*cizye;* Arabic, *jizya*), guaranteed them protection.

Only "enemy infidels" (*harbi kafirler*), non-Muslims from outside Ottoman domains, could be legally enslaved. Until the eighteenth century, enemy infidel captives were obtained directly through prisoner-taking in wartime and, more consistently, through Tatar slaving expeditions north of the Black Sea and through the trade in slaves from the Caucasus and sub-Saharan Africa.[3] These regular, licit channels for the acquisition of slaves—all of which involved significant risk or financial investment—were supplemented with frequent amphibious and cross-border raids in the Mediterranean and central Europe. Yet the number of sources from which enemy infidel captives might legally be obtained in peacetime was, in fact, severely limited. The sultan's commercial and peace agreements with foreign powers, called *ahdnames*, contained clauses guaranteeing the recipients' subjects protection from Ottoman enslavement. By 1612, the subjects of Venice, Dubrovnik (Ragusa), France, England, the Netherlands, and Poland-Lithuania were formally off-limits, as were those of the Austrian Habsburgs, according to the terms of the peace agreement between them, though divided Hungary still sustained a vigorous cross-border, ransom-slavery industry.[4]

The contents of the sultan's treaties did not deter many a pirate or border raider—Ottoman-subject slavers frequently targeted Venetian subjects in the sixteenth and seventeenth centuries, for example—but the complaints of European powers' diplomatic representatives in Istanbul could lead to undesirable scrutiny for high-ranking Ottoman provincial officials accused of facilitating their capture and sale.[5] In contrast, news of the disappearance of a number of Ottoman Christian subjects settled on the Adriatic-Ionian frontier might never reach the imperial center. Mahmud Bey was not the first Ottoman official in the region to recognize the potential for free labor and easy profit residing in his district.[6]

When the rewards of war—measured in captives and pilfered booty—were not forthcoming, proximity and convenience made the capture of non-Muslim Ottoman subjects an attractive proposition for unscrupulous Ottoman officials like Mahmud and the military personnel charged with their protection. It was a practice already favored by small-scale bandits and pirates, who used locally obtained Ottoman captives to build and row their ships.[7] Despite its unambiguous illegality, capturing Ottoman subjects was a comparatively low-risk venture. It was their sale as legal slaves on the open market—turning the commodity into cash—that presented the real challenge. No potential buyer would knowingly purchase his erstwhile neighbor, in part because slaves, and their relatives and friends, could sue masters for their freedom. As Mahmud Bey knew well, any Ottoman court would order the slaves' release if their provenance were discovered and proven, even if they had already changed hands multiple times. Defrauded slave buyers would then sue their way up the chain of sellers to recover their investment, potentially exposing the culprits and endangering their profits.[8]

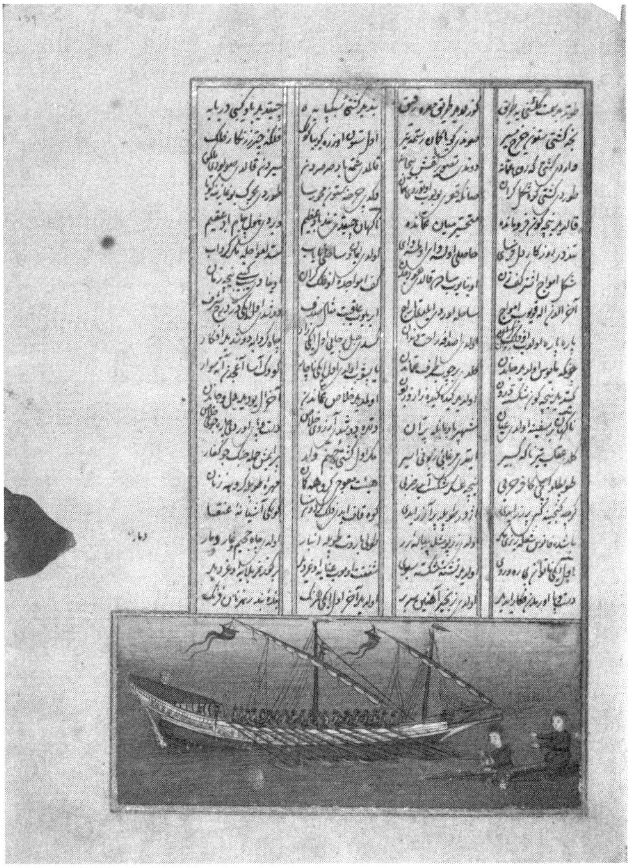

FIGURE 5. A Mediterranean galley as portrayed in a 1721 illuminated manuscript of the *Ḫamse* of Nevizade Atai (d. 1634). MS W.666, fol. 137a. Courtesy of the Walters Art Museum.

Thus, to get around this problem, Mahmud Bey innovated: Mahmud, his deputy, and their men abducted numerous Ottoman Christian subjects from every village in the district, marched them to the sea, embarked them on the governor's personal galley, and put them to the oar. Mahmud then forced his captives to row the ship across the Mediterranean to North Africa. Upon arrival, he exchanged them, his captive Ottoman subjects, for "enemy infidel captives," whom the North African corsairs had *legally* enslaved, since the corsairs enjoyed political and religious license to raid and enslave designated enemies of the faith and the state. Mahmud then transported these slaves of acceptable provenance back to Karlieli, where he could employ, distribute, or sell them on the open market without subterfuge.[9] It was the equivalent of money laundering—but with slaves.

In the late sixteenth and seventeenth centuries, along the Adriatic, Ionian, and Morean coastlines and further inland, Ottoman naval irregulars, amphibious strongmen, and the agents of district governors conducted raids on Ottoman Christian villages, capturing Ottoman subjects for use or sale as slaves.[10] To disguise the provenance of their captives and realize maximum profits with minimal interference, human traffickers engaged in what I call "slave laundering," shipping those illegally enslaved to distant locales, especially North Africa, where they could pass them off as legally enslaved enemy infidels, and where the Ottoman center would be hard-pressed to find or redeem them. Camouflaged by the much larger, licit trade in bodies, rapid turnover and frequent aftermarket resale soon made them functionally indistinguishable from those legally enslaved. Without identity cards or passports, only in-person Muslim testimony sufficed to prove these captives' free origin in Ottoman courts, a logistical challenge that could easily prove insuperable.

In the case of Mahmud Bey's slave-laundering expedition, however, transporting the Ottoman subjects to nominally "Ottoman" North Africa did not simply obfuscate their subjecthood; it rendered it moot. The Ottoman central administration might attempt to recover Ottoman subjects "laundered" within the empire's core, in spite of the challenges involved in proving their subjecthood in the courts, but for both Mahmud and his captives, the port cities of North Africa existed, for all practical purposes, outside the protective umbrella of Ottoman law and beyond the reach of its agents. Although Mahmud Bey's crime was eventually discovered, there would be no rescue or return for the lost villagers of the *sancak* of Karlieli.

The growing size and reach of North African corsairing operations in the late sixteenth and seventeenth centuries have been well documented, and the seventeenth- and eighteenth-century captivity of Britons, French, and Spaniards among others has received plenty of attention from scholars working with European-language sources like captivity narratives.[11] And certainly the capture and enslavement of the *ahdname*-protected subjects of Venice, England, and France by the forces of Algiers and Tunis give us some indication of the geographical limits of Ottoman law and the sultan's peace.[12] Nevertheless, the trans-Mediterranean trafficking of Ottoman-subject captives complicates the received narrative on the Mediterranean slaving industry, which has largely failed to integrate the contributions of Ottoman sources.

Framed by the story of Mahmud Bey's slave-laundering ring, this chapter examines the early modern, intra-Ottoman trade in illegally enslaved Ottoman subjects. Besides being an unrecognized facet of an understudied phenomenon—the illegal enslavement of Ottoman subjects[13]—slave laundering sheds light on the dynamic, often difficult relationship between the Ottoman center and its periphery, and the uneven reach of Ottoman legal precepts and administrative directives. The events of 1617 exposed the lack of central oversight and control in the Adriatic-Ionian region and the dramatic divide between North Africa and the Empire's core, with the littoral seemingly viewed by both slavers and the Ottoman central administration as a place beyond the reach of Ottoman law. They thus force us to reexamine what it meant, legally and across time and space, to be "Ottoman." Amid larger debates about the unity or incoherence of the Mediterranean, the tragic story of the villagers from Karlieli and its unhappy ending simultaneously reveal close linkages and a deep disconnect between supposedly unified shores of the Mediterranean. For slave laundering and the illegal slave trade to be possible, the sea had to both connect and divide.

SUBJECTHOOD AND SLAVERY

As Mahmud's trans-Mediterranean slave-laundering venture makes clear, the question of the targets' subjecthood was as much a concern as their religious identity for Ottoman slavers in the late sixteenth and seventeenth centuries, with Mahmud swapping one set of captive Christians in North Africa for another with acceptable origins. Scholars of Mediterranean piracy and trade have long highlighted the tug-of-war between the competing promises and demands of subjecthood and religious identity in a divided sea.[14] North African corsairs routinely disregarded the limits imposed on them by the sultan through his *ahdname*s, and by the early seventeenth century had arrogated to themselves the right to determine which non-Muslim powers were enemy infidels open to attack, though in so doing they still considered their targets' subjecthood.[15] At the same time, France obtained huge numbers of Muslim slaves—primarily under Maltese cover—to serve as oarsmen, circumventing the reciprocal antislaving clauses of the *ahdname,* which had been in effect since 1569 and which required the release of all Ottoman subjects among them.[16] Although both Catholic and Muslim corsairs claimed religious legitimation for their actions, those operating out of North Africa typically eschewed the blanket targeting of the religious other, irrespective of subjecthood, adopted by their Catholic rivals.[17]

For Jews and Ottoman Christians who straddled the uncomfortable space between the religiopolitical battle lines of the Mediterranean corsairing industry, the right combination of subjecthood and religious identity could be a boon; the merchants, brokers, and interpreters whom Natalie Rothman has called "trans-imperial subjects" could reside in both worlds and travel freely between them.[18] Even though the reciprocal rights to trade enshrined in the *ahdname*s made no distinction between the sultan's subjects, as a practical matter non-Muslims enjoyed far greater access to European markets than Ottoman Muslims and could profitably exploit the connections with their coreligionists abroad. Inscribed from above, these legal identities were often rather fuzzy on the ground and might be exchanged. In many instances, Greek merchants and others could make credible claims to be either Venetian or Ottoman subjects, depending on who was doing the asking. At the same time, the inherent ambiguities of early modern subjecthood made Ottoman non-Muslim subjects vulnerable to opportunistic attacks from both directions. Maltese corsairs routinely targeted Ottoman Greek Orthodox merchants, in spite of their charge to despoil only Muslims, and Ottoman corsairs sometimes attacked Ottoman subjects, including Muslims, in total violation of Islamic and sultanic law.[19]

For those taken captive, religious affiliation, status, and loyalty more so than subjecthood governed the world of ransom slavery practiced across the Mediterranean and in Central Europe.[20] Although the repatriation of captives became an increasingly important point of pride for European states toward the end of the seventeenth century, efforts to free captives were still couched in religious terms, and notably there was little interest in retrieving converts to Islam—a reminder that in Europe conversion to Islam, "turning Turk," automatically read as a switch in subjecthood.[21] How different then was the situation within the Ottoman Empire, where subjecthood did not necessarily overlap with religious identity and where conversion to Islam, though irrevocable, neither validated captivity nor ended it? Mahmud Bey's slave laundering underscores the fact that these were not simply interimperial issues but rather that the tension between subjecthood and religious identity permeated Ottoman domains as well.

How did Ottoman jurists define Ottoman subjecthood? How could it be obtained and lost and how did the challenge of Ottomans enslaving Ottomans sharpen the debate? What, if anything, could the Ottoman central administration do to combat this phenomenon? Given the stringent evidentiary requirements of the Islamic law that governed Ottoman courts and the political and military limits of Istanbul's ability to project power in an age of significant foreign and domestic challenges to its authority, fighting illegal slaving was no simple task. As the empire was buffeted by back-to-back wars, financial crises, peasant rebellions, widespread brigandage, endemic piracy, environmental catastrophes, and existential dynastic distress between the 1570s and 1630s, the center's control and oversight of its provincial governors weakened while its reliance on irregular, amphibious paramilitary forces for intelligence gathering and defense increased.[22] The results were disastrous. The Ottoman government could not do without these men stationed along the borders and at strategic points along the coasts, but neither could it fully control them. The Sublime Porte had long been forced to tolerate a certain amount of illegal violence from its servants in order to preserve its broader security arrangements, but the system teetered on the edge of collapse through the early seventeenth century.

More importantly, the Ottoman center's preoccupation with more pressing concerns allowed for the emergence of an increasingly independent North Africa after 1580. Well connected to the Ottoman mainland by trans-Mediterranean trade routes, bonds of patronage, and military and political connections, yet often unencumbered by Ottoman foreign policy and centrally appointed legal and administrative personnel, Ottoman North Africa's ports provided increasingly safe markets for cargo and captives of all stripes seized in contravention of Ottoman law.[23] Even as their corsairs augmented the Ottoman navy during the annual "sea season" and engaged in raids on the sultan's enemies in the central and western Mediterranean, the North African ports' connections with Ottoman officials and naval irregulars along the Adriatic, Ionian, and Morean coasts actually exacerbated the illegal enslavement problem, enabling both pirates and corrupt governors like Mahmud Bey to profitably expand their illegal slaving operations and circumvent the thorny issue of their captives' subjecthood.

The tension between subjecthood and religious identity, and the danger inherent within it, extended farther inland within the Ottoman sphere. After all, in frontier zones like the Adriatic—divided among the Venetians, Ottomans, and Habsburgs—it was often only subjecthood that separated populations, professing the same faiths and speaking the same languages, that straddled porous, ill-defined, and often violently contested borders. The heightened potential for abuse here, for armed men to willfully conflate those who at times might legally be taken as prisoners of war with those who had the sultan's protection, was often realized.[24] Natalie Rothman has noted that early modern Venetian (and other European) commentators were often unable to "imagine Christian Ottoman subjects as truly 'Ottoman.'"[25] The activities of some Ottoman Muslim frontier officials suggest that view may have held to some extent on the other side of the border. But here we must distinguish between any sort of sociocultural "Ottoman-ness," however that might be defined in different places and times, and the early modern Ottoman political-legal understanding of subjecthood generally, and Ottoman subjecthood specifically. In spite of its limits in practice, and the countervailing view that "unbelief is one nation," the concept of juridical subjecthood defined the Ottoman legal and administrative view of the world around it. There were tax-paying Ottoman subjects, the sultan's flock, or *reaya* (the same word was used for the subjects of other powers, friend or foe); the subjects of powers to which the sultan had granted his *ahdname;* and, only then, the undifferentiated mass of "enemy infidels."[26]

The secular concept of subjecthood, expressed in the *ahdname*s and imperial correspondence and shared with the sultan's Christian treaty partners, coexisted in the Ottoman sphere with the Islamic binary division of the world into mutually exclusive zones of peace and continuous war: the Abode of Islam (*darülislam*), the lands under Muslim rule, and the Abode of War (*darülharb*), the lands yet to be conquered. The attendant body of Hanafi legal theory, known as *siyar,* governed relations between the two.[27] For non-Muslims, Ottoman subjecthood and the protections it provided came at a cost—obedience to the sultan and payment of the *cizye* made them *zimmi*s and *reaya.* Revolt or flight to the enemy constituted repudiation of the pact (*nakz-ı ahd*) between the sultan and his flock and resulted in the loss of Ottoman subjecthood, turning the erstwhile *zimmi* into an enemy infidel, who might be legally enslaved. Indeed, Ottoman policy toward rebellious locales was usually to view them as having abandoned *darülislam*. The central government routinely ordered that disobedient towns or villages, having effectively reverted to *darülharb*, be destroyed—with the "troublemakers" slaughtered, the women and children enslaved, and the moveable property and livestock carried off—if they did not promptly resubmit (thereby reestablishing the *ahd*).[28]

This policy could be opportunistically abused. For example, in May 1579, it was reported that the *sancakbeyi* of the district of Albanian Iskenderiyye (the region surrounding present-day Shköder) had taken it upon himself to identify "rebellious" villages to punish, sacking the peaceful and paid-up village of Klemente, killing some women and enslaving others. After the survivors complained of their treatment to the imperial center, the government instructed the nearby *kadi*s (magistrates) to investigate the unwarranted attack and find and free the slaves.[29] Evidently, the *sancakbeyi,* impatient with his obedient *reaya* and the consequent lack of opportunities for licit plunder, had decided to invent a revolt to crush, so that he could treat the district's inhabitants as if they were enslaveable enemy infidels. In an effort to legitimize his plot, he had previously forwarded to Istanbul a list of villages he described as being on the brink of rebellion that, upon examination, proved to be fabricated.[30] Ultimately the Iskenderiyye governor's attempt to legally strip his captives of their Ottoman subjecthood was unsuccessful. We can see, then, why Mahmud Bey of Karlieli, similarly tempted by the promise of easy captives decades later, looked to the sea for a lasting solution to the problem of his slaves' subjecthood.

Without the jurisdictional anchorage of land and the relative physical and legal security it provided, the sea rapidly diluted the strength of Ottoman subjecthood's promise of protection. An Ottoman Christian from an Ottoman village in Ottoman-administered territory was a known entity, but at sea the same Ottoman Christian could be, with a minimum of willful ignorance, construed as an "enemy infidel" and thus a legitimate target. The same practical ambiguity of subjecthood that "trans-imperial subjects" often used to their commercial advantage could easily cut the other way. To sixteenth- and seventeenth-century Ottoman jurists, however, Ottoman subjecthood was made of more durable stuff. Although they recognized that the transition from land to sea made the *zimmi* vulnerable to the unscrupulous, they categorically rejected the view that an Ottoman *zimmi's* subjecthood was contingent on his remaining on land or even within the Ottoman Empire.

A fatwa (an Islamic legal opinion) issued by Ebu Suʿud Efendi (d. 1574), the renowned long-serving *şeyhülislam* (the title of the mufti of Istanbul, who headed the Ottoman religious-legal hierarchy and served as the empire's chief jurisconsult), illustrates that vulnerability. Written with the brevity and anonymized format characteristic of early modern Ottoman fatwas, it anticipates the principal practical problem associated with Ottoman subjecthood: proving it.

> *Question:* In order to come to Islam, Zeyd the *zimmi* boards the ship of Captain Amr. While they are coming to *darülislam,* the captain wants to sell the aforementioned *zimmi,* saying "he is my slave." If the *zimmi* proves his freedom to the captain's face, is he freed? *Answer:* It is not permissible to interfere with someone who is undertaking emigration by his [own] choice.[31]

As Ebu Su'ud's ruling makes clear, even if the person represented by the Zeyd alias had been an enemy infidel traveling to Ottoman domains for the express purpose of becoming a Muslim, his enslavement would not have been permissible.[32] The fatwa thus reveals that the captain was doubly guilty, first, for attempting to enslave an Ottoman subject, who had proven his free origin, and second, for obstructing his intended conversion to Islam. However, his expansive ruling sidesteps two trickier questions. First, how would Zeyd "prove" his freedom? Second, what if Zeyd had simply been a *zimmi* traveling between Ottoman ports for trade, who was similarly threatened with sale and enslavement once at sea; would it then be incumbent on him to "prove his freedom to the captain's face" to prevent his enslavement? To the latter question, the legal tradition gives a clear, unambiguous answer: no. Another fatwa from Ebu Su'ud holds that it is the would-be captor who must be able to prove his captive's unfree—that is, non-Ottoman—origin and that, in ambiguous circumstances, the potential captive who claims Ottoman subjecthood should be given the benefit of the doubt.[33] Ebu Su'ud was following centuries of Islamic legal precedent, which held that the presumptive status of all people is free, not slave.[34]

The jurists did not consider Ottoman subjecthood and its protections to be restricted to Ottoman domains. Rather, subjecthood inhered with the loyal, taxpaying *zimmi.* As a fatwa from the *şeyhülislam* Çatalcalı Ali Efendi (d. 1692) makes clear, neither abduction nor removal of the *zimmi* from Ottoman territory by force could abrogate it:

> *[Question:]* Enemies (*harbiler*) capture Zeyd the *zimmi.* After they import [him] into *darülharb,* some of the people of Islam [i.e. Ottoman Muslims] take Zeyd from the enemies by force. If they export [him] to *darülislam,* can they enslave Zeyd simply by saying "we exported [him] from *darülharb* to *darülislam?*" *Answer:* They cannot.[35]

Whereas only an enemy infidel (*harbi kafir*) captured in the Abode of War and removed to the Abode of Islam—in this case, the Ottoman Empire—could be made a slave, simply being an infidel within the Abode of War did not automatically make one an enemy infidel. Though he may have been captured alongside enslaveable enemy infidels, Zeyd's legal status as an Ottoman subject and *zimmi,* and the immunity from enslavement that came with it, were not affected by the violent trips back and forth across the invisible line separating *darülislam* from *darülharb*. Thus, the slave laundering practiced by Mahmud Bey of Karlieli could never, in religious-legal terms, transform his Ottoman captives into enemy infidels. It could only obscure the difference.

Ottoman subjecthood did have limits. Just as Ottoman villagers deemed rebellious by Istanbul effectively became enemy infidels in their own homes, the *zimmi* who abandoned Ottoman domains to fight for the enemy "repudiated the pact" and thereby renounced his subjecthood. In so doing, he lost the ability to appeal to the protections of his former status, as a fatwa from a mid-eighteenth-century compilation demonstrates:

> *Question:* Zeyd the *zimmi* repudiates the pact (*nakz-ı ahd edüb*) and goes over to *darülharb* and enters a Christian pirate ship. While cruising in *corso* with the followers of the enemy, they do battle with a ship of the people of Islam [i.e., the Ottomans] and the people of Islam overcome the frigate with the help of God. Since they seized [it] by force, if they also seize Zeyd, can Zeyd simply say, "since I was previously a *zimmi,* I am of free origin," and thus free himself from slavery? *Answer:* No.[36]

This fatwa, in which the *zimmi* joins up with Christian pirates to raid and pillage Ottoman ships and shores, illustrates the contingent nature of Ottoman subjecthood. His free origin, to which the wrongfully captured Ottoman *zimmi*s in the previous examples could appeal, offers no legal protection here. It must be emphasized that this was true for all Ottomans who abandoned *darülislam* by choice in order to join with the enemy. For Ottoman Muslims, renunciation of Ottoman subjecthood was inevitably bound up with apostasy; the apostate from Islam who joined up with Christian pirates, if subsequently captured by Ottoman forces, could be legally enslaved just as the former *zimmi* could be—the only distinction being that he must first re-embrace Islam to avoid the death penalty for apostasy.[37] Seventeenth-century court records from Ottoman Crete demonstrate that, with large numbers of Ottoman-subject Cretan Christians and converts to Islam joining the Venetian privateers based on small fortress islands only a stone's throw from the Cretan coast during the 1684–99 war, these were not simply theoretical concerns.[38] Yet it is crucial to note that in these cases it was the voluntary actions of the Ottoman subject that resulted in the loss of Ottoman subjecthood. Enemy conquest of Ottoman territory would also result in a change of subject status for the residents who remained behind, but otherwise Ottoman subjecthood was, at least in theory, rather durable and water resistant.

The reality, however, was very different. Ebu Suʿud's fatwas might suggest that in ambiguous circumstances the *zimmi* was to be given the benefit of the doubt, but it is clear that even when the jurists favored a certain outcome, the man with the sword usually had his way. Furthermore, although *zimmis* threatened with enslavement were not legally obligated to prove their free origin to avoid this fate—not that it would necessarily have made a difference if they could have or did—the situation changed dramatically as soon as the captives were sold off. Unless the government intervened promptly to secure their release, responsibility for adjudicating ownership disputes over slaves fell to the Islamic courts. Enslaved *zimmis* had to sue their owners to regain their freedom, and in a system designed to protect the financial interests of slave owners from specious claims of wrongful enslavement, they had to meet the evidentiary standards of the courts to prove that they were "of free origin" (*hurrü'l-asl*).

Early modern Ottoman court records preserve hundreds of such freedom suits. Indeed, freedom suits (*dava-yı hürriyet*) of this sort were so common that contemporary Ottoman judicial praxis manuals typically contained examples, often several, to guide judges and their scribes in how to hear, decide, and record them.[39] The frequency of resale and the practice of registering major purchases with the courts probably provided many illegally enslaved persons with their opportunity to sue, though all slaves theoretically had access to the courts. But only those plaintiffs who were able to round up trustworthy, male Muslim witnesses to attest to their free origins won their cases and their freedom. Perhaps surprisingly, many successfully did so. Others failed to meet the burden of proof and returned to servitude. Untold numbers, perhaps the majority, never managed to bring their cases to court. It is not difficult to imagine that many illegally enslaved women and children (the categories most desired by slave buyers), sequestered in their masters' households, were too restricted in their movements or too young to find their way to the courts.

Family, neighbors, friends, and local officials often trekked long distances to testify in court on behalf of those who sued for their freedom. For example, in November 1633, Fatima Hatun bint Viko, originally from a village near Rusçuk in present-day Bulgaria, sued her owner in the court of the military judge (*kazasker*) of Rumeli in Istanbul. This was the empire's highest court, second only to the Imperial Council. Several Muslim witnesses from her village traveled to Istanbul to testify on her behalf. The suit was recorded six months after her previous owner, Ayşe bint Mehmed, sold Fatima to the defendant, Mehmed Ağa bin Abdullah, for eighteen thousand *akçe;* the time it took for Fatima's witnesses to receive the summons and make the journey may account for the six-month lag between the sale, which probably gave her the chance to file suit, and the hearing at which her freedom was declared.[40] How or by whom Fatima had been captured was not noted in the court's record, but it is safe to assume that Ayşe bint Mehmed was not her original captor—a reminder that slaves, especially women, frequently changed hands.

However, for many of those carried far from their homes or who hailed from areas with limited Muslim settlement or Ottoman administrative presence, such as the smaller Aegean Islands, proving Ottoman subjecthood and thus "free origin" through normal legal channels could be virtually impossible. The case of a certain Cafer, who claimed that his mother was a Christian Ottoman subject resident in

France and that his father was a *zimmi*, is instructive. In the winter of 1617–18, Cafer accused Süleyman Çelebi of illegally enslaving him and sued for his freedom in the court of the Rumeli *kazasker* in Istanbul. For his part, Süleyman stated that he had bought Cafer for 320 pieces of gold two years earlier in Tunis, from a man named Receb, and summoned two witnesses to testify to that effect. Cafer, who strenuously denied that he was a legal slave when Süleyman purchased him, could do nothing when the court asked him to provide evidence of his free origin.[41] Whether he had been captured by pirates, betrayed by a ship captain, or laundered by an Ottoman provincial official, Cafer could not deny that he had been sold as a slave in Tunis, and he could not prove that his sale had been illegal. However he got there, passage through Tunis had effectively washed away his subjecthood and condemned him to continued servitude. Likewise, if any of Mahmud's victims were brought to Istanbul from North Africa by their new owners, it is unlikely that they would have prevailed in court absent substantial financial and logistical support to secure witnesses.[42]

Thus, frontier slave raiders could exploit the gap between Ottoman subjecthood's theoretical durability and its intangible, difficult-to-prove nature. Isolated incidents could easily slip through the cracks, but larger raids were harder to conceal and the Ottoman government, once notified, often tried to rectify such incidents. Nevertheless, the logistical hurdles involved and the stiff local resistance these efforts often faced exposed the limits of the center's ability to project its authority, as well as its uneven, and sometimes tenuous, grip on a maritime perimeter that was sustained economically in large part through the interimperial and trans-Mediterranean traffic in captive bodies and pilfered goods.

OTTOMANS ENSLAVING OTTOMANS

The illegal enslavement of Ottoman subjects was a perennial problem throughout the Ottoman Empire, and it was not unheard of during the supposedly golden years of Sultan Süleyman's reign (1520–66). Incidents became more frequent, however, after the 1570–73 war with Venice and were most concentrated in coastal or frontier areas with substantial Christian populations and significant numbers of naval irregular and other paramilitary forces, known as *levends*.[43] In the western Aegean and especially along the southern Adriatic, Ionian, and Morean coasts (making up present-day coastal Montenegro, Albania, and Greece), the task of providing coastal defense and gathering intelligence was left largely to *levend*s, who after 1573 were denied permission to raid their erstwhile Venetian enemies. With the return of an inconvenient and unprofitable peace, which stretched until 1645, many of these underemployed, poorly supervised *levend*s turned (or returned) to piracy and to raiding nearby Ottoman villages, often in addition or as a precursor to staging attacks on Venetian and Ragusan shipping; many worked profitably with local governors and judges, who turned a blind eye to their crimes and shared in their profits.[44]

Mahmud Bey's district of Karlieli had long been one of the biggest problem areas, for it included Lefkada, the sole Ionian island in Ottoman hands, and the adjoining fortress of Aya Mavra (Santa Maura), a notorious corsair base. In 1599, the Ottoman bureaucrat and social commentator Mustafa Ali specifically called out the island for its role in Ottoman-on-Ottoman piracy and identified successful operations there as a common entry on the resumes of *levend*s seeking to move up in the world of Mediterranean piracy to a more profitable and honorable captainship in Algiers. Karlieli's governor's seat was located just across the water at the mainland coastal fortress of Angilikastri (Angelokastro), but since the reign of Süleyman, many *sancakbeyi*s had taken up residence at Aya Mavra itself.[45] The close proximity of the district's administration had the potential to intensify rather than curtail the *levends*' illegal activities; Mahmud Bey was no doubt aided in his venture by the naval irregulars stationed on Aya Mavra, and he was likely able to capitalize on their connections with their corsair colleagues in North Africa to effect his plan.

By then, the paramilitary forces operating out of Lefkada had been a scourge of Venetian, Ragusan, and Ottoman shipping and shores for decades. Already in the spring of 1573, with the ink barely dry on the treaty ending the war with Venice, *levend*s based at Aya Mavra fortress were reported to be building frigates to raid Ottoman subjects settled in the area, just as they had done before the war.[46] Shortly thereafter the *sancakbeyi* of the Morea informed the government that pirates sailing from Aya Mavra fortress and Inebahtı (Nafpaktos) had been plundering his district and taking Ottoman captives. In response, Istanbul ordered the governor of Inebahtı to apprehend the pirates and put them to the oar.[47] Clearly, not all Ottoman governors were abetting piracy, but complaints to the center seem to have accomplished little. The recipients of these orders certainly knew about the *levend* raiding beforehand, but they were either collaborating with the pirates or were unable to stop them. Since the *levend*s still fulfilled a vital security function and did so virtually for free in an era of constant war and fiscal crisis, the center was unprepared to force the issue and intervened only in the most extreme instances.

Mahmud Bey was not the first governor of Karlieli to develop a warm working relationship with his district's perennially piratical corsairs. For instance, in 1591, Mustafa, the by-then former *sancakbeyi* of the district, was found to have been "disobeying the noble *şeriat* [i.e., Islamic law]" by "always committing corruption" and working in concert with the "rebel *levends*" based at Aya Mavra. He had been bankrolling them, equipping their frigates for raids, and enslaving Ottoman subjects from his district and from nearby islands and coasts. He put his Ottoman-subject slaves to work building larger galliots with which to harass passing merchant vessels, for the traffic in and out of the Adriatic offered higher-calorie prizes

FIGURE 6. The fortress of Aya Mavra (Santa Maura) on the Ionian island of Lefkada, held by the Ottomans from 1479 to 1684. From Alain Manesson Mallet, *Les Travaux de Mars ou l'Art de la Guerre* (La Haye: Moetjens, 1696), 319.

and more opportunities for ransoming than interdicting small-fry coastal shipping. In so doing, he was adopting the standard career trajectory of the ambitious, upwardly mobile coastal pirate. Unlike the local amphibious strongmen he emulated, however, he was a sitting governor.[48]

The Ottoman central government learned about his criminal activities only after he had been routinely rotated out of his position and his newly arrived successor, Murad, informed the government of what had been happening. The Sublime Porte instructed Murad Bey and the commandant (*dizdar*) of the fortress of Aya Mavra to see to it that any Ottoman-subject captives held there be immediately freed, to put a stop to the Aya Mavra *levend*s' attacks on Ottoman islands and merchants, and to write if the problem persisted. But, of course, the activities of the *levend*s stationed at Aya Mavra fortress were not news to its commandant, and since no attempt was made to replace him and no force was sent to restrain the men who sheltered their ships under his cannon, the decree may have had only a limited impact—if any.

Murad, the new *sancakbeyi* of Karlieli in 1591, may have been more honorable than his predecessor, whose misdeeds he exposed, but he ultimately failed, if he ever tried, to squelch piracy and illegal slaving in the area. History was simply repeating itself in 1617, when the Imperial Council received a letter from Hasan, the recently appointed *sancakbeyi* of Karlieli, concerning the depredations of his predecessor, Mahmud, and his deputy.[49] Once again, the central government was caught completely unaware. Unlike Mustafa Bey in 1591, however, Mahmud had not abducted the Ottoman villagers to work in his arsenal but rather for the money that could be obtained from their sale. Had Mustafa attempted to sell large numbers of Ottoman slaves close to home, he might have been discovered sooner, much as the *sancakbeyi* of Iskenderiyye had been with his invented rebellion in 1579, or he might have struggled to find willing buyers.

Mahmud Bey engaged in trans-Mediterranean slave laundering to dispose of the evidence, selling his captives in the larger, more robust slave markets of North Africa, where a quick turnaround was assured and potential buyers were unlikely to ask inconvenient questions. Presumably neither Mahmud Bey nor his contacts in North Africa were especially concerned about intervention from Istanbul; there is no evidence that any attempt was made to retrieve the villagers from Mahmud's district. Ports like Tunis were sufficiently outside the purview of the Ottoman center by this point that such efforts would be fruitless and would require the expenditure of scarce diplomatic capital, which otherwise had to be reserved for coaxing the release of wrongfully captured European notables in accordance with the *ahdname*.[50] As for the slaves imported from North Africa by Mahmud, there was nothing objectionable about their capture, enslavement, or sale that would have required government action. Thus, in response to Hasan Bey's disturbing revelations, the center simply ordered him to investigate further and not abuse his office as his predecessor had.[51]

It is noteworthy that the copy of the 1617 sultanic decree to Hasan Bey, which provides us with our only extant record of this incident, never mentions where in North Africa the captives were taken. We are given neither an indication of the total number of slaves transported there, though it was likely at least in the low hundreds, nor whether this was an isolated incident or a routine practice during Mahmud's tenure as Karlieli's governor. In terms of proximity, Tripoli or Tunis would have been the most logical destination for the slaves, and so it may have been in the end, but the failure in the document to identify by name the site of the slave exchange in North Africa should give us pause. There are a number of possible, not mutually exclusive, reasons for these omissions: first, that the summary copy of the outgoing decree preserved in the register is incomplete—which was not uncommon—or includes an incomplete recapitulation of the salient details of the letter from Hasan that prompted it; second, that Hasan Bey did not know or did not report the answers to these questions; third, and most intriguing, that the site of the exchange in North Africa went unidentified because it took place in one of the small, temporary, and nameless shadow-slaving ports that cropped up periodically after the expulsion of the Moriscos from Spain in 1609 and operated geographically close to, but politically and legally outside of, the major cities like Tunis and Tripoli.[52] Such sites, which thrived on bulk captive exchange and re-export, seem to have been founded precisely to avoid official oversight and the substantial taxes owed to the authorities in the established corsairing ports. Wherever the villagers of Karlieli ended up, it appears the center was not prepared to pursue them there.

The measures the Ottoman central government took in response to the challenge of the illegal enslavement of its subjects varied drastically over time and space. On the empire's western frontier, there were limited resources available to combat the problem, and the occasional efforts to crack down on the consortia of naval irregulars, North African corsairs, and local officials that dealt in Ottoman, Venetian, and Ragusan captives sometimes ended in violence in the late sixteenth and early seventeenth centuries. *Levend*s and their local allies were not above murdering the Ottoman magistrates sent to investigate them, especially if they were not accompanied by a sizable military escort.[53]

This fact helps account for the typically vague orders to local officials—often people at least indirectly responsible for the offending action—to investigate and find and free the illegally enslaved. As opposed to instances of Venetian enslavement—wherein the bailo's continual petitioning, gift giving, and manipulation of extensive networks of consular agents and friendly Ottoman officials might eventually get results—there was rarely any obvious follow-through to such decrees. We usually have no way of knowing what efforts, if any, the recipients took to accomplish their mission. Whereas larger slaving ventures were harder for the center to ignore or forget, and higher-ranked officials with long careers and multiple postings ahead of them needed to insulate themselves from the worst accusations of malfeasance—thus Mahmud's attempt at slave laundering—it is clear that there was little to prevent either frontier forces or amphibious criminal gangs active along the coasts from opportunistically taking Ottoman subjects as slaves. And if they were content to keep them for themselves, there was little chance that the central government would find out or deploy scarce military resources to stop them.

For the Adriatic-Ionian coastal strongmen who established themselves on the outskirts of the main towns and were supported by gangs numbering in the teens to dozens, subterfuge of the sort practiced by the governor of Karlieli, Mahmud, was unnecessary—at least at first. For example, Avcı Oğlu, Kara Mustafa, Karaca Bali, and Aksak Hoca, pirates operating out of small skiffs (*kayık levendleri*) in the district of Albanian Iskenderiyye, were brazen enough to forgo selling their Ottoman Christian captives, the product of numerous coastal raids. Instead, they openly kept them as their personal slaves, even when they were living ashore. Such a state of affairs could occur only with a degree of willful ignorance on the part of local officials, though it is impossible for us to know whether this was due more to collusion with or intimidation by the pirates. Whether or not the center was similarly in the dark, it was careful to avoid an open breach with its governors. When the Porte ordered the *sancakbeyi*s of the surrounding districts—Avlonya (present-day Vlorë in Albania), Karlieli, Selanik (Salonica), and Ohri (Ohrid in present-day Macedonia)—to find and imprison the offending *levends* and free the slaves they had made in the summer of 1574, they were also instructed not to supply *levends* with grain, to warn the soldiery of the provinces not to give aid to such people, and to imprison those who did.[54] Alas, this was easier said than done, and there was no happy ending for these pirates' captives. In contrast, the administration could be incredibly tenacious in its pursuit of its subjects in areas more firmly under its control and could even be willing to stretch the evidentiary rules of the courts to secure their release.

That same summer, a pirate raid on Ottoman Naxos resulted in numerous Ottoman Greek subjects being sold off as slaves in various ports along the Anatolian coast. In each case, the Naxiotes were represented to buyers as legitimate enemy infidel captives. Certainly the *levend*s responsible might have questioned the "Ottoman-ness" of Naxos, if such a thing were a concern to them: Naxos had only been incorporated into the empire in 1566, and it had no Muslim settlement or permanent Ottoman administrative presence in 1574.[55] Moreover, control over Naxos, along with the other Cyclades Islands, had been temporarily lost during the recently concluded war with Venice, and accusations of the Cyclades islanders' infidelity to the sultan had led to state-sanctioned *levend* reprisals in the preceding years.[56] Nevertheless, from the point of view of Istanbul in 1574, the Naxiotes were unambiguously protected "tax-paying *reaya*," who were no different from those on the Anatolian mainland, and prior orders to that effect would have left no doubt of that fact in the *levend*s' minds.

During the pacification of the Cyclades two years earlier, the *levend*s and their commanders had been instructed to round up the traitors and treat them "as criminals." They could clap them in irons and put them to the oar, but they were warned repeatedly that they must not capture or sell the islanders "like captives who have been exported from the Abode of War."[57] The legal distinction was an important one; aiding the enemy was certainly considered reprehensible, a serious criminal act worthy of death or a very short life as an oarsman, but it did not meet the standard of rebellion or flight that would abrogate subjecthood.[58] Still, the *levend*s who raided Naxos in 1574 may have hoped that the short sea journey would suffice to obscure their Ottoman captives' subjecthood in the slave markets of western Anatolia. It evidently had in the past, and it very nearly did again.

Instead, the incident spurred a nine-month manhunt, in which the Ottoman central government dispatched a messenger (*çavuş*), Tahir, to coordinate the efforts of local officials to locate the slaves and take them from their owners.[59] Ottoman policy in these cases was that all illegally enslaved persons should be found and freed, but only those who had not converted to Islam were to be actively returned to their homes. The same policy applied in the event that Venetian, French, or other treaty-protected foreign subjects were enslaved in contravention of their treaties; the Ottoman government was unwilling to countenance apostasy, which would be the predictable consequence of returning new Muslims to Christian lands—including the Ottoman-ruled Cyclades Islands.[60] But even in the Naxos case, it proved difficult to establish the slaves' Ottoman subjecthood in the courts, for as we have already seen, Islamic law required the testimony of trustworthy Muslim witnesses, who could vouch for their identities, and there were none to be found in the almost exclusively Christian archipelago.

The fact that the western Anatolian region had been flooded with legally imported Cypriot Greek slaves after the conquest of that island in 1570–71 further complicated the situation. Indeed, the Naxos raiders may have hoped that their Greek captives, once sold, would be indistinguishable from the rest of the Greek slave population. The Naxos raid had garnered the attention of the center, but it was not the first of its kind, and as news spread of the Ottoman administration's efforts to free the Naxiotes, the courts were inundated with freedom suits from other Greek islanders claiming to have been illegally enslaved in the fog of the late war with Venice. The courts were overwhelmed.[61] Without the necessary witnesses, how was justice to be done?

The government's response was pragmatic and ultimately effective, but it made manifest the extent to which the Ottoman legal system was not equipped, in theory or practice, to deal with contested subjecthood. First, the Ottoman government dispatched a *zimmi* from Naxos named Marko to the districts where Naxiote slaves were suspected of being held to help its agent on the ground, Tahir *çavuş*, separate out the right Greeks from the wrong Greeks. Marko could identify

Naxiotes, but as a non-Muslim, his testimony could not prove the "free origin" of the Naxiote slaves over a Muslim master's objections. Instead, in the freedom suits pending before the courts in which Marko had indicated that the slave was a Naxiote, or in which the plaintiff was suspected of being another illegally enslaved Ottoman Greek subject, the government ordered Tahir and the Anatolian *kadi*s to require the owners of the contested slaves to present documentation showing that the *pencik* (one-fifth) tax on imported slaves had been paid.[62]

It is not at all certain that owners of all legal slaves would have normally possessed such papers, but the owners of the illegally enslaved certainly would not. It was an extraordinary gambit given that the courts typically refused to consider documents as evidence without supporting testimony, but here an owner's failure of the *pencik* papers test was interpreted as invalidating his ownership of the slave. It thus provided a convenient excuse for the government's agents to confiscate any slaves of questionable provenance, while completely sidestepping the effectively impossible task of legally proving that the slave was actually an Ottoman subject "of free origin." Once the government had done this, it could emancipate them without the need for further evidence and send home those who had not converted.

Notably, administrative intervention of this sort was both necessary and formally required to free foreigners enslaved in contravention of their *ahdname*. In the first half of the sixteenth century, the *ahdname* required that cases of suspected Venetian enslavement be brought before the Imperial Council in Istanbul for adjudication. Even this proved overly complicated, and by 1595, the procedural guidelines enshrined in the *ahdname* were changed so that the nearest representative of Venice—the bailo, or his agents or consuls—would be called on to verify Venetian subjecthood on the spot, upon which Ottoman officials would confiscate the slave and turn him over to Venetian custody.[63] The local Ottoman court might then be called on to certify the erstwhile slave's manumission, providing the legal documents (*itkname*) that would guarantee his freedom for the remainder of his sojourn in the empire, but it would not typically rule on the legality of his enslavement.[64] That was because the Ottoman central government and its foreign interlocutors recognized that Ottoman courts were not competent to judge foreign subjecthood. Certainly one could not expect to locate male, Muslim witnesses to attest to a foreign Christian's subjecthood. The fact that verifying Ottoman non-Muslims' subjecthood through Ottoman courts could be just as difficult did not change the fact that, absent direct administrative intervention, Ottoman-subject captives in Ottoman hands had recourse only to Ottoman courts and were bound by their often insurmountable evidentiary requirements.

Numerous amphibious slave raids like that at Naxos in 1574 were reported in the late sixteenth- and seventeenth-century Ottoman Mediterranean. Needless to say, the Ottoman government was not always as successful in finding and freeing illegally enslaved Ottoman subjects as it had been after the Naxos incident.

Between Anatolia and the Adriatic, its ability to project authority, to devote human and financial resources and exert continuing pressure to achieve its goals varied widely. Resolution for the Naxiotes in 1574–75 had been the product of months of close coordination among Istanbul, its agent on the ground, and its judges, with multiple decrees and letters passing back and forth, each one carried by messenger over long distances. The government's pragmatism enabled it to circumvent the legal hurdles involved in finding and freeing illegally enslaved Ottoman subjects, but its ability to rely on local officials to implement orders and overcome resistance was the decisive factor in its successful outcome. As we have seen, logistical constraints and entrenched interests meant that the administration, even if rapidly informed, could not always respond as aggressively in similar cases elsewhere. It typically had better luck in the Aegean districts, or even in Egypt, than in the Adriatic or North Africa. The stark divergence in capacity is best illustrated by the quartet of pirates discussed above, who appear again in our sources five years later.

Although they had not abandoned their Albanian stomping grounds, with time and continued success Avcı Oğlu, Kara Mustafa, Karaca Bali, and Aksak Hoca established slave-trading networks with Egypt and North Africa that enabled larger-scale human trafficking with less danger of interference from the government or rejection by suspicious buyers. In a foreshadowing of Mahmud Bey's trans-Mediterranean slave-laundering enterprise, it was reported in the summer of 1579 that they had disposed of cargoes of captives taken from villages near Shkodër in Albania in the markets of Alexandria, Egypt, and they were suspected of doing the same in Tripoli, in Tunis, and perhaps even in Algiers. Five years after the Porte's decree ordering that the pirate quartet be apprehended and their slaves freed, they were still able to operate with impunity in and around Ottoman Albania.[65] As with Mahmud nearly forty years later, the challenge was not in capturing or keeping Ottoman subject slaves—this they had done for years without repercussions—but in monetizing the commodity. The quartet's trans-Mediterranean slaving operation was intended to nullify the problems associated with selling Ottoman-subject captives too close to home, removing them to high-turnover markets where they could be rapidly sold in bulk as if they were legally enslaved enemy infidels.

This time, the Porte was not going to be satisfied by sending an angry letter to officials in Albania. Echoing the *çavuş* Tahir and Marko's mission to Anatolia in search of the Naxiotes, the Imperial Council dispatched a local *zimmi* named Irenc to Egypt to work with the *kadi*s in the district of Alexandria to locate the illegally captured Ottoman Albanians, arrange for their release through the courts, and escort them back to their homes.[66] But while the Porte was willing to send someone all the way to Egypt to hunt for illegally enslaved Ottoman Albanians, it was evidently unprepared to do so in the captives' backyard.[67]

Likewise, even as Istanbul sent slave-hunting agents to Anatolia and Egypt, it was more likely to rely on diplomacy—negotiating and cajoling—in Tunis, Tripoli, and Algiers. In 1577, for example, when news reached Istanbul that the treasurer (*defterdar*) of Tunis had seized a number of Ottoman Muslims and Christians and, claiming they were legal captives ("esirdir diyerek"), gifted them to his brother, the Imperial Council dispatched a decree ordering the governor and the *kadi* of Tunis to find and free them and enclosed a fatwa from the *şeyhülislam* condemning the abduction to help leverage compliance.[68] That these extraordinary efforts were necessary only a few years after the 1574 reconquest of the city gives some indication of the center's limited coercive capacity in North Africa. As a result, even though the quartet of pirates was suspected of selling Ottoman subjects in those cities as well, Irenc's mission was limited to Alexandria. Copies of the decree to Alexandria announcing Irenc's departure were sent to the *beylerbeyi*s of the three North African provinces—the center also probably suspected that the pirate quartet was now splitting its time between one or more of the North African regencies and its former base on the Albanian coast—but no comparable effort was made to locate any of their victims there, nor was any force dispatched to stop the trade at the source. Irenc's mission serves as a clear indicator of the unevenness of Ottoman control; bearing orders to free captives without compensation, he risked getting killed in consistently unruly Albania and would likely have been rebuffed in remote, increasingly independent North Africa.

It is well known that the corsairing leadership of Algiers, Tunis, and Tripoli disregarded the limitations imposed on them by the sultan's *ahdname*s with growing confidence in the late sixteenth and early seventeenth centuries and attacked and enslaved Venetians, Britons, French, and Dutch when it suited them. A logical, if unremarked on, corollary to this was that North African markets were equally receptive to captives who would not be welcome in the core Ottoman lands, regardless of who brought them there to sell. When English pirates captured a Venetian ship off the Morea in 1607, they did not bring their prize to the nearby Morean ports of Modon or Koron—neither of which were strangers to pirates—but to Tunis, where they sold the Venetian passengers and crew into slavery.[69] The trafficking of Ottoman subjects to North Africa described above indicates that Ottoman non-Muslims' subjecthood was no more an impediment to their sale there than that of the Venetians. At the same time, it underscores the economic, military, and personal ties that bound North Africa closely to the Ottoman Balkans. Cooperation between corsairs and frontier officials in pirating and illegal slaving ventures remained the norm through the first half of the seventeenth century.

The contrast between the two examples of slave-raiding governors of Karlieli—Mustafa in 1591 and Mahmud in 1617—is instructive. Both captured and enslaved large numbers of Ottoman subjects from the district, but whereas Mustafa employed them to build and row ships that he and his accomplices on Lefkada used to raid Venetian shipping, Mahmud exported them. Notably, neither of them attempted to sell their captives locally. What we have observed is that the Porte could not prevent the capture of Ottoman subjects—anywhere, really—and, in places like the Adriatic-Ionian-Morean region, could do little to free those held in thrall by powerful governors and amphibious strongmen. Yet neither could large groups of local captives easily be dispersed there, though Mahmud would have no trouble selling the captives of legal provenance he had imported from North Africa. Subjecthood, however tenuous its protections, however difficult it was to prove, did matter internally, even on the Adriatic edge of the empire. It could not prevent illegal capture, but it did complicate sale. The reach of Ottoman law was thus not coterminous with central authority throughout the empire.

In North Africa, however, neither reigned effectively. It is hard to imagine Ottoman subjects from the politically divided Balkans winning a freedom suit in Tunis, and, at the same time, the evidence suggests that Istanbul could not or would not do what it might elsewhere to arrange for their release. Completing the triangle, Tunis might as a consequence serve as a re-export point, with visiting Ottoman merchants and military personnel acquiring slaves in its bustling markets for service back in the core cities of the empire. As we have seen, after a brief sojourn in Tunis, an Ottoman-subject slave faced long odds in a suit for freedom, even in Istanbul's highest court. The relationship between the Ottoman Balkans and North Africa developed independently of Istanbul in the first half of the seventeenth century, which allowed for regular and progressively larger joint-corsairing expeditions that mostly targeted Venetian subjects and shores, to the dismay of both governments. But the processes that allowed for that sort of cooperation were, at the same time, employed to facilitate an irregular but not insignificant trade in Ottoman subjects, though not all were trafficked across the Mediterranean.

The total number of slaves taken and sold in this manner was, in proportion to the trade in licit captives in the Mediterranean, probably fairly small, and both were dwarfed by the traffic in slaves from beyond the Black Sea. The illegal enslavement of Ottoman subjects generally and slave laundering specifically worked only if shielded by the licit slave trade, with the illegally enslaved disappearing among and becoming virtually indistinguishable from the legal slaves surrounding them. The significance of the phenomenon is greater than the numbers might suggest, however, because of what it tells us about relations between the Ottoman center and periphery, tensions between religious and political identity, and the limits of subjecthood in theory and practice.

Above all, it should serve as a reminder of the dangers of relying on unqualified religious, political, or geographic binaries to understand the premodern Mediterranean: Christian versus Muslim, north versus south, or east versus west all presuppose internal unities and coherence where there was often fragmentation and sometimes chaos. By the late sixteenth century, Ottoman sovereignty blanketed the shores of the Mediterranean from the borders of Venice to the edge of Morocco, but the Ottoman, eastern half of the Mediterranean was a space divided as much as it was connected. If distance and difficult conditions were what permitted the capture of Ottoman subjects in the Adriatic-Ionian region, it was the sea itself that enabled them to be transported, laundered, and sold.

NOTES

1. Mühimme Defteri (hereafter MD) 82: 114/57 (9/L/1026), Başbakanlık Osmanlı Arşivi, Istanbul (hereafter BOA).

2. Alan Fisher, "The Sale of Slaves in the Ottoman Empire: Markets and State Taxes on Slave Sales, Some Preliminary Considerations," *Boğaziçi Üniversitesi Dergisi* 6 (1978): 149–74, esp. 157; Alan Fisher, "Studies in Ottoman Slavery and Slave Trade, II: Manumission," *Journal of Turkish Studies* 4 (1980): 49–56, esp. 50–51.

3. Mikhail Kizilov, "Slave Trade in the Early Modern Crimea from the Perspective of Christian, Muslim, and Jewish Sources," *Journal of Early Modern History* 11 (2007): 1–31; Halil Sahillioğlu, "Slaves in the Social and Economic Life of Bursa in the Late 15th and Early 16th Centuries," *Turcica* 17 (1985): 65–68. See also Hakan Erdem, *Slavery in the Ottoman Empire and Its Demise, 1800–1909* (New York: St. Martin's Press, 1996); and Ehud Toledano, *The Ottoman Slave Trade and its Suppression: 1840–1890* (Princeton, NJ: Princeton University Press, 1982). Tatar raiding was curtailed by treaty and then by the Russian occupation of the Crimea in the late eighteenth century; war as a source for slaves declined beginning in the seventeenth century, as Ottoman battlefield victories became less frequent, and diminished even further in the eighteenth century with the gradual emergence of a new prisoner-of-war system; see Will Smiley, *From Slaves to Prisoners of War: The Ottoman Empire, Russia, and International Law* (Oxford: Oxford University Press, 2018).

4. There is a vast literature on the *ahdnames*, better known in Europe as "capitulations," for the chapters (*capitulo*) into which they were divided. For an overview, see Alexander H. DeGroot, "The Historical Development of the Capitulatory Regime in the Ottoman Middle East from the Fifteenth to the Nineteenth Centuries," in *The Ottoman Capitulations: Text and Context*, ed. Maurits van den Boogert and Kate Fleet (Rome: Instituto per l'Oriente, 2003), 575–604; Dariusz Kołodziejczyk, *Ottoman-Polish Diplomatic Relations (15th–18th Century): An Annotated Edition of 'Ahdnames and Other Documents* (Leiden: Brill, 2000). On ransom slavery in Hungary, see the contributions in Geza David and Pal Fodor, eds., *Ransom Slavery along the Ottoman Borders* (Leiden: Brill, 2007).

5. Joshua M. White, *Piracy and Law in the Ottoman Mediterranean* (Stanford, CA: Stanford University Press, 2017); Suraiya Faroqhi, "The Venetian Presence in the Ottoman Empire (1600–1630)," *Journal of European Economic History* 15 (1985): 345–84.

6. He was not the first governor of Karlieli to enslave its residents; see Mühimme Zeyli Defteri (hereafter MZD) 4: 403/186 (20/ZA/999), BOA; and below.

7. White, *Piracy and Law*, 45, 49, 55–56; on the phenomenon of illegal enslavement more broadly, see Nicolas Vatin, "Une affaire interne: Le sort et la libération des personnes de condition libre illégalement retenues en esclavage sur le territoire Ottoman (XVIe siècle)," *Turcica* 33 (2001): 149–90.

8. For an example of this from 1594, see Rumeli Sadareti Mahkemesi 21, fol. 49a (28/ZA/1002), fol. 61b (15/M/1003), İslam Araştırmaları Merkezi, Istanbul, published in transliteration in Coşkun Yılmaz, ed., *İstanbul Kadı Sicilleri: Rumeli Sadareti Mahkemesi 21 Numaralı Sicil (H. 1002–1003/M. 1594–1595)* [Istanbul Court Registers: The Court of the Military Judge of Rumeli Register Number 21] (Istanbul: İSAM Yayınları, 2011), 202, 239–40; for examples of seventeenth-century suits lodged against slave dealers (*esirci*) after the emancipation of illegally enslaved Ottoman subjects that they had sold, see

Rumeli Sadareti Mahkemesi 60, fol. 81a (3/S/1046), İslam Araştırmaları Merkezi; and Rumeli Sadareti Mahkemesi 64, fol. 9a (9/N/1049), İslam Araştırmaları Merkezi.

9. MD 82: 114/57 (9/L/1026), BOA.

10. Vatin, "Une affaire interne; see also Leslie Peirce, "Abduction with (Dis)honor: Sovereigns, Brigands, and Heroes in the Ottoman World," *Journal of Early Modern History* 15 (2011): 311–29.

11. Daniel Vitkus and Nabil Matar, *Piracy, Slavery, and Redemption: Barbary Captivity Narratives from Early Modern England* (New York: Columbia University Press, 2001); Nabil Matar, *British Captives from the Mediterranean to the Atlantic, 1563–1760* (Leiden: Brill, 2014); Nabil Matar, *Britain and Barbary, 1589–1689* (Gainesville: University Press of Florida, 2005); Salvatore Bono, *Lumi e corsari: Europa e Maghreb nel Settecento* (Perugia: Morlacchi, 2005); Salvatore Bono, *I corsari barbareschi* (Turin: Edizion RAI, 1964); Godfrey Fisher, *Barbary Legend: War, Trade, and Piracy in North Africa, 1415–1830* (Oxford: Clarendon Press, 1957); Stanley Lane-Poole, *The Barbary Corsairs* (London: T. Fischer, 1890); Robert Davis, *Christian Slaves, Muslim Masters: White Slavery in the Mediterranean, the Barbary Coast, and Italy, 1500–1800* (Houndmills, UK: Palgrave Macmillan, 2003); Robert Davis, "Counting European Slaves on the Barbary Coast," *Past and Present* 172 (2001): 87–124; Ellen Friedman, *Spanish Captives in North Africa in the Early Modern Age* (Madison: University of Wisconsin Press, 1983); Daniel Hershenzon, *The Captive Sea: Slavery, Communication, and Commerce in Early Modern Spain and the Mediterranean* (Philadelphia: University of Pennsylvania Press, 2018). Gillian Weiss, *Captives and Corsairs: France and Slavery in the Early Modern Mediterranean* (Stanford, CA: Stanford University Press, 2011).

12. This is a central concern in White, *Piracy and Law.*

13. In addition to Vatin's examination of it in "Une affaire interne," illegal enslavement in the premodern Ottoman Empire has been briefly treated in Erdem, *Slavery,* 23–26; and Madeline Zilfi, *Women and Slavery in the Late Ottoman Empire: The Design of Difference* (Cambridge: Cambridge University Press, 2010), 206–12.

14. Molly Greene, *Catholic Pirates and Greek Merchants: A Maritime History of the Mediterranean* (Princeton, NJ: Princeton University Press, 2010); Michel Fontenay, *La Méditerranée entre la croix et le croissant: Navigation, commerce, course et piraterie, XVIe–XIXe siècle* (Paris: Classiques Garnier, 2010); Michel Fontenay, "La place de la course dans l'économie portuaire: l'Exemple de Malte et des ports barbaresques," *Annales: Économies, Sociétés, Civilisations* 43 (1988): 1321–47; Peter Earle, *Corsairs of Malta and Barbary* (London: Sidgwick and Jackson, 1970).

15. White, *Piracy and Law,* 128–56; see also Joshua M. White, "Shifting Winds: Piracy, Diplomacy, and Trade in the Ottoman Mediterranean, 1624–1626," in *The Well-Connected Domains: Towards an Entangled Ottoman History,* ed. Pascal Firges, Tobias Graf, Christian Roth, and Gülay Tulasoğlu (Leiden: Brill, 2014), 37–53.

16. Weiss, *Captives and Corsairs;* Weiss, "Infidels at the Oar: A Mediterranean Exception to France's Free Soil Principle," *Slavery and Abolition* 32 (2011): 397–412.

17. Earle, *Corsairs of Malta;* on North African diplomatic relations with European powers, see White, *Piracy and Law,* esp. 140–80; Guillaume Calafat, "Ottoman North Africa and *Ius Publicum Europaeum:* The Case of the Treaties of Peace and Trade (1600–1750)," in *War, Trade and Neutrality: Europe and the Mediterranean in the Seventeenth and Eighteenth Centuries,* ed. Antonella Alimento (Milan: Franco Angelli, 2011), 171–88; and Daniel Panzac, *Barbary Corsairs: The End of a Legend, 1800–1820* (Leiden: Brill, 2005), 25–40.

18. See Natalie Rothman, *Brokering Empire: Trans-imperial Subjects between Venice and Istanbul* (Ithaca, NY: Cornell University Press, 2012).

19. This legal "tension" is a major focus in Greene, *Catholic Pirates.*

20. Pal Fodor, "Piracy, Ransom Slavery and Trade: French Participation in the Liberation of Ottoman Slaves from Malta during the 1620s," *Turcica* 33 (2001): 119–34; Geza Palffy, "Ransom Slavery along the Ottoman-Hungarian Frontier in the Sixteenth and Seventeenth Centuries," in *Ransom Slavery*

along the Ottoman Borders: Early Fifteenth–Early Eighteenth Centuries, ed. Geza David and Pal Fodor (Leiden: Brill, 2007), 35–84.

21. Linda Colley, *Captives: Britain, Empire and the World, 1600–1850* (London: Jonathan Cape, 2002); Weiss, *Captives and Corsairs;* Friedman, *Spanish Captives.*

22. For a narrative overview of the period, see Caroline Finkel, *Osman's Dream* (New York: Basic Books, 2006), 200–223.

23. Emrah Safa Gürkan, "The Centre and the Frontier: Ottoman Cooperation with the North African Corsairs in the Sixteenth Century," *Turkish Historical Review* 1 (2010): 125–63; C. R. Pennell, "The Ottoman Empire in North Africa: A Question of Degree—Tripoli in the Seventeenth Century," *Studies on Ottoman Diplomatic History* 5 (1990): 35–55; Delenda Largueche, "The Mahalla: The Origins of Beylical Sovereignty in Ottoman Tunisia during the Early Modern Period," *Journal of North African Studies* 6 (2001): 105–16. Cf. Tal Shuval, "The Ottoman Algerian Elite and Its Ideology," *International Journal of Middle East Studies* 32 (2000): 323–44.

24. Maria Pia Pedani, "Beyond the Frontier: The Ottoman-Venetian Border in the Adriatic Context from the Sixteenth to the Eighteenth Centuries," in *Zones of Fracture in Modern Europe: The Baltic Countries, the Balkans, and Northern Italy*, ed. Almut Bues (Wiesbaden: Harrassowitz, 2005), 45–60.

25. Rothman, "Narrating Conversion and Subjecthood in the Venetian-Ottoman Borderlands," *The Turn of the Soul: Representations of Religious Conversion in Early Modern Art and Literature* (Leiden: Brill, 2012), 116.

26. On the unique, and complicated, position of the Adriatic city-state of Dubrovnik, an Ottoman tributary, which received an *ahdname* having much in common with the one granted to Venice but whose subjects often, if selectively, enjoyed the status of Ottoman subjects, see Nicolaas H. Biegman, *The Turco-Ragusan Relationship: According to the Firmans of Murad III (1575–1595) Extant in the State Archives of Dubrovnik* (The Hague: Mouton, 1967); Selma Zecevic, "Translating Ottoman Justice: Ragusan Dragomans as Interpreters of Ottoman Law," *Islamic Law and Society* 21, no. 4 (2014): 388–418.

27. Majid Khadduri, *The Islamic Law of Nations: Shaybani's Siyar* (Baltimore: Johns Hopkins University Press, 1966); Hilmar Kruger, *Fetwa und Siyar* (Wiesbaden: Harrossowitz, 1978). See also Biegman, *Turco-Ragusan Relationship.*

28. For example, MD 14: 1353/914 (17/N/978); MD 28: 265/109 (25/B/984); MD 35: 876/345 (8/N/986), BOA. For the application of this policy on a much larger scale in the eighteenth century, see Will Smiley, "Let Whose People Go? Subjecthood, Sovereignty, Liberation, and Legalism in Eighteenth-Century Russo-Ottoman Relations," *Turkish Historical Review* 3 (2012): 196–228; see also Erdem, *Slavery,* 23–26. For the treatment of this topic in early Hanafi legal theory, see Khadduri, *Islamic Law of Nations,* 218–22.

29. MD 36: 701/266 (21/RA/987), BOA.

30. MD 36: 139/46 (28/ZA/986), BOA.

31. Ebu Su'ud Efendi, "Fetava-yı Ebussuud" [The fatwas of Ebussuud], MS Ismihan Sultan 223, fol. 99a, Süleymaniye Kütüphanesi, Istanbul.

32. Such cases appear in Ottoman administrative documents, in which the officials responsible for detaining the individual are admonished not to interfere for example, MD 19: 20/8 (3/M/980), BOA, as well as in Ottoman court records. For example, a Mingrelian (from present-day Georgia) named Cafer ibn Abdallah sued for his freedom in the court of Galata in 1639, after he was arrested under suspicion of being a fugitive slave. Cafer claimed he had entered *darülislam* willingly to convert and was neither a fugitive nor an enslaveable infidel but a free Muslim; the court ordered his release after witnesses testified that he had in fact converted as described. Galata 62, fol. 79b (2/B/1049), İslam Araştırmaları Merkezi.

33. "Fetava-yı Ebussuud," MS Ismihan Sultan 226, fol. 152a, Süleymaniye Kütüphanesi.

34. Franz Rosenthal, *The Muslim Concept of Freedom* (Leiden: Brill, 1960), 32.

35. Çatalcalı Ali Efendi, *Fetava-yı Ali Efendi ma an-nükul* [The fatwas of Ali Efendi with the proof-texts] (Istanbul, H. 1289 [1872]), 207.

36. Dürrizade Mehmed Arif Efendi, "Neticetü'l-Fetava" [The summation of the fatwas], MS Esad Efendi 1080, fol. 311b, Süleymaniye Kütüphanesi.

37. Dürrizade Mehmed Arif Efendi, "Neticetü'l-Fetava," MS Nafiz Paşa 311, fol. 62a, Süleymaniye Kütüphanesi.

38. See White, *Piracy and Law*, 249–56.

39. Such manuals were known as *sakk*, or by its plural, *sukuk*, and proliferated around the turn of the seventeenth century. See, for example, the entry for proving and confirming the freedom of a slave in the early seventeenth-century "Sukuk-i Sâni Efendi" of Mehmed b. Derviş Mehmed es-Sâni el-Edirnevi, MS Supplement Turc 66, fol. 23a, Bibliothèque nationale de France. Most *sukuk* manuals of the seventeenth and eighteenth centuries contained similar entries in the chapter concerning manumission and related matters, as well as in the chapter on suits. For an introduction and survey of *sukuk* manuscripts in Turkey, see Süleyman Kaya, "Mahkeme Kayıtlarının Kılavuzu: Sakk Mecmuaları [The guide to court records: sakk compilations]," *Türkiye Araştırmaları Literatür Dergisi* 3, no. 5 (2005): 379–416.

40. Rumeli Sadareti Mahkemesi 56, fol. 59a (Evasıt/CA/1043), İslam Araştırmaları Merkezi; Yılmaz, ed., *İstanbul Kadı Sicilleri: Rumeli Sadareti Mahkemesi 56* [Istanbul court registers: the court of the military judge of Rumeli Register number 56], 270.

41. Rumeli Sadareti Mahkemesi 36, fol. 13a (Evail/M/1027), İslam Araştırmaları Merkezi. It is entirely possible that similar cases were brought in North Africa, but I am not aware of any research on the subject; if Cafer had previously tried to sue for his freedom in Tunis, it was not mentioned in the record. Rumeli *kazasker*s often heard cases relating to piracy and illegal enslavement in the seventeenth century, on which see White, *Piracy and Law*.

42. Distance and the sea were not always insuperable problems, but they posed serious logistical challenges, even when witnesses could be found. For example, Fatima, a woman from Kilis, an inland city wedged between the Anatolian plateau and northern Syria, successfully sued for her freedom in Egypt's highest court in June 1742, after being illegally enslaved the year before; witnesses from her neighborhood traveled to Egypt to testify to her free origin. No indication was given in the record as to how she had ended up in Egypt, how the witnesses were located, or who had arranged their passage; Al-Diwan al-ʿAli Sijill 1, #331 (5/R/1155), Egyptian National Archives. I am grateful to James Baldwin for sharing a facsimile of this case with me; on this court, see his *Islamic Law and Empire in Ottoman Cairo* (Edinburgh: Edinburgh University Press, 2017).

43. On piracy in the age of Süleyman, see Nicolas Vatin, "L'Empire ottoman et la piraterie en 1559–1560," in *The Kapudan Pasha: His office and His Domain: Halcyon Days in Crete IV, a Symposium Held in Rethymnon, 7–9 January 2000*, ed. Elizabeth Zachariadou et al. (Rethymnon: University of Crete Press, 2002), 371–408; on the meanings of *levend*, an ambiguous term that could be used to refer to irregular military forces on land and sea, pirates, bandits, and rebels, see Mustafa Cezar, *Osmanlı Tarihinde Levendler* (Istanbul: Çelikcilt Matbaası, 1965); Sophia Laiou, "The Levends of the Sea in the Second Half of the 16th Century: Some Considerations," *Archivum Ottomanicum* 23 (2005/6): 233–47.

44. White, *Piracy and Law*, esp. 35–54.

45. Mustafa Ali, *Mevāʾidüʾn-Nefāis fī ḳavāʿidiʾl-mecālis* [Tables of delicacies concerning the rules of salons], ed. Mehmet Şeker (Ankara: Türk Tarih Kurumu Basımevi, 1997), 288. Sixteenth- and seventeenth-century Ottoman and Venetian archival documents reveal the extent to which the *levends* of Aya Mavra were a serious problem for both powers and damaged relations between them; the island was lost to Venice in 1684. See White, *Piracy and Law*, 44–51.

46. MD 22: 30/12 (21/M/981), BOA.

47. MD 22: 332/172 (26/RA/981), BOA.

48. MZD 4: 403/186 (20/ZA/999), BOA.

49. MD 82: 114/57 (9/L/1026), BOA.

50. This too tested the limits of Istanbul's coercive capacity, especially in the troubled 1620s. For a discussion of Ottoman-Venetian efforts to win the release of Venetian captives taken in 1624 and held in Algiers and Tunis, see Joshua M. White, "Fetva Diplomacy: The Ottoman Şeyhülislam as Trans-Imperial Intermediary," *Journal of Early Modern History* 19, no. 2–3 (2015): 199–221.

51. MD 82: 114/57 (9/L/1026), BOA.

52. On the Moriscos of Tunis and their involvement in Mediterranean slaving, see Miguel de Epalza, "Moriscos y andalusíes en Túnez durante el siglo XVII," *Al-Andalus* 34 (1969): 247–327; and Luis Bernabé Pons, "Notas sobre la cohesión de la comunidad Morisca más allá de su expulsión de España," *Al-Qanṭara* 29 (2008): 307–32. On the establishment of a "pirate colony" by the Tunisian Moriscos at Capo Buon Andrea, near Tripoli in the 1630s, see Senato, Dispacci Costantinapoli, busta 116, fol. 486a-b, Archivio di Stato di Venezia. I thank Tijana Krstić for bringing this possibility to my attention and sharing these references. On the *mühimme defterleri,* their value and their limitations, see Geza David, "The Mühimme Defteri as a Source for Ottoman-Habsburg rivalry in the Sixteenth Century," *Archivum Ottomanicum* 20 (2002): 167–209.

53. White, *Piracy and Law,* 53, 135–36.

54. MD 26: 135/53 (8/RA/982), BOA.

55. The question of the "Ottoman"-ness of the Aegean Islands is a central concern of Nicolas Vatin: "Iles grecques? Iles ottomans?," in *Insularités ottomanes,* ed. Nicholas Vatin and Gilles Veinstein (Paris: Maisonneuve and Larose, 2004), 71–89. See also Colin Heywood's contribution to the same volume, "Ottoman Territoriality versus Maritime Usage," 145–73. For the history of Ottoman Naxos, see B. J. Slot, *Archipelagus Turbatus,* vol. 1 (Istanbul: Nederlands Historisch-Archaeologisch Instituut, 1982), passim, esp. 88–108.

56. MD 16: 305/156 (23/Z/979), 655/373 (1/B/979), BOA; MD 19: 5/2 (M/980), BOA.

57. MD 19: 196/90 (29/M/980), BOA.

58. On this subject, see Erdem, *Slavery,* 23, as well as the discussion earlier in this chapter.

59. MD 24: 744/277 (3/S/982); MD 26: 132/51 (5/RA/982), 133/52 (8/RA/982), 697/243 (13/C982), 713/248 (13/C/982); MZD 2: 52/21 (28/Ş/982), BOA.

60. MD 24: 744/277 (3/S/982), BOA; for the clause outlining this policy in the Venetian *ahdname,* formulated in 1521, see Hans Theunissen, "Ottoman-Venetian Diplomatics: The Ahd-names. The Historical Background and the Development of a Category of Political-Commercial Instruments Together with an Annotated Edition of a Corpus of Relevant Documents," *Electronic Journal of Oriental Studies* 1 (1998): 427–28.

61. MD 26: 697/243 (13/C982), 713/248 (13/C/982), BOA.

62. MD 26: 697/243 (13/C982), 713/248 (13/C/982), BOA.

63. Theunissen, "Ottoman-Venetian Diplomatics," 569–70.

64. See, for example, Galata 27, fol. 58a (1014), İslam Araştırmaları Merkezi, which is also published in transliteration in Timur Kuran, ed., *Mahkeme kayıtları ışığında 17: yüzyıl İstanbul'unda sosyo-ekonomik yaşam* [Social and economic life in seventeenth-century Istanbul: glimpses from court records], vol. 1 (Istanbul: Türkiye İş Bankası, 2010), 482–83. On *itkname,* see Joshua M. White, "Ottoman Slave Manumission Documents," in *Christian-Muslim Relations: A Bibliographical History,* vol. 12, *Asia, Africa and the Americas (1700–1800),* ed. David Thomas and John A. Chesworth (Leiden: Brill, 2018), 227–33.

65. MD 36: 722/274 (21/RA/987), BOA.

66. MD 36: 722/274 (21/RA/987), BOA..

67. Ottoman functionaries who interfered with the normal patterns of illicit coastal trade on the western frontier were risking their lives. In 1584, for example, Yaya Aşık, a *levend* captain who

commanded two frigates with fifty-to-sixty men, was implicated in the murder of Sinan, the *kadi* of Belgrade and treasury inspector in Avlonya, when Sinan began to investigate the *levend*'s activities in the Albanian port; see MD 53: 41/18 (7/CA/992), BOA.

68. MD 30: 844/358 (21/R/985), BOA. On the center's use of fatwas to bolster decrees to distant, frequently disobedient frontier officials, see White, "Fetva Diplomacy."

69. Bailo a Costantinopoli, Carte turche 250/2, fol. 112–3 (C/1016), Archivio di Stato di Venezia. This was a wise decision; a few years earlier, English pirates had brought a Venetian prize into Modon, only to be arrested by Ottoman port officials and handed over to the Venetian governor of Zante for execution. Horatio Brown, ed., *Calendar of State Papers Relating to English Affairs in the Archives of Venice,* vol. 10 (London: H. M. Stationary Office, 1900), 6–7, 13, 39, 60, 173, 181.

5

Piracy of the Eighteenth-Century Mediterranean

Navigating Laws and Legal Practices

Judith E. Tucker

The snow *Ermosa [sic] Rachel* was a chameleon. Originally a Portuguese ship, the *Ermosa Rachel* was captured in Mediterranean waters by corsairs from Algiers in 1767 and subsequently became the property of the ruling dey by virtue of his right to a share in his corsairs' prizes. The dey of Algiers then sold the ship to Demetrio Vidari, a Greek Ottoman subject from the island of Limos, who was residing in Algiers at the time. In 1768, Vidari in turn sent the ship to the port of Mahon on the British-controlled island of Minorca and sold it there in shares: half of the ship to Theodore Alexiano, the captain of the port and presumably a British subject; one-eighth to Jaymo Vidal, of unknown origin and identity; and the remaining three-eighths to David Busnach, a Tunisian Jew, who registered his shares in the name of his son Abraham Busnach. Then Alexiano and Vidal both sold their shares to Abraham Busnach, so that the ship, based in a British port, was owned in its entirety by a young Jewish subject of Tunis. At some point along the way, the *Ermosa Rachel* was issued a passport as a British ship. The British consul in Algiers, Archibald Campbell Fraser, who reported on the matter in 1772, was clearly disquieted by the whole affair for a mix of anti-Semitic and chauvinist reasons: how could a twenty-two-year-old Jew from Tunis, the "lowest, meanest and most abject of their subjects" be the sole owner of a ship with a British pass?[1] We might pose some questions of our own: How could a Portuguese vessel captured by corsairs from Algiers wash up as a lawfully registered ship sailing out of a British port under the British flag? And what does a story like this have to tell us about the mores of Mediterranean piracy, the complexities of life under the law in the twilight time of the early modern Mediterranean, and fundamental shifts in attitudes toward piracy as they unfolded in the late eighteenth century?

Peregrine Horden and Nicholas Purcell suggested in their now classic book *The Corrupting Sea* (2000) that piracy might hold one key to understanding the integration of the Mediterranean World in "the way in which it has served to wed the movement of materials and the mobility of people."[2] This suggestion has been fleshed out by David Coleman, whose research revealed that, even in a time of heightened and bitter conflict, in the fifty years after the Spanish conquest of the Iberian Peninsula and the expulsion of Muslims, the Alborán Sea served as a connecting space between Spain and North Africa, largely because of shared corsairing practices. He is less sanguine, however, about the longer term: he suspects that the Mediterranean after 1540 became the stage for a more clear-cut Christian-Muslim confrontation, one with less room for border crossing, by practices and personnel, in the *corso*.[3] In her reflections on the *corso* in the seventeenth century, Molly Greene also points to a religiously inflected discourse of difference among corsairs but notes the tension between this worldview and the pragmatic claims of state sovereignty when it came to the regulation of corsairing, an ambivalence that remained unresolved for much of the century.[4] I would like to follow this tension into the eighteenth century, to argue for the ongoing elaboration of a legal and institutional culture of piracy that was shared around the shores of the Mediterranean. At first blush it seems counterintuitive—how could a practice or set of practices that entailed violence, intimidation, and disruption and provoked such deep anxieties in travelers and coastal peoples alike be a force for diplomatic exchange, integration, and a meeting of the minds? It will become clear, however, that piracy worked in powerful ways to normalize relations and inform a common legal culture between and among Mediterranean shores for much of the eighteenth century. As the modern era then dawned in the region, this broad agreement on piracy was unsettled as the agendas and capacities of states active in the Mediterranean basin increasingly diverged.

These developments formed part of a wider phenomenon. Lauren Benton has explored how piracy on a global scale had produced a "new kind of regionalism" by the eighteenth century, as interimperial negotiations and pirate activities resulted in variegated patterns of regulation in different ocean spaces.[5] Her observations about the central role piracy played in the incubation and differentiation of maritime legal practices can be applied to the Mediterranean Sea and its shores. Local practices and customs, institutional and legal legacies, and pressures from powerful newcomers all combined to shape a common regulatory system for piracy in the early modern Mediterranean.

Did pirates resist or collude in the development of this system? Marcus Rediker has argued for the conscious defiance of convention and law on the part of pirates of the Atlantic: they challenged and even mocked the legal proceedings designed to bend them to the will of the state.[6] Benton, on the other hand, has emphasized the extent to which Atlantic pirates were "lawyers," who preferred to work within the legal order when possible and both shaped and reinforced its authority as a result.[7] There is little doubt that pirate activity and the responses it evoked helped shape the legal culture of the Mediterranean just as surely as in the Atlantic. As I argue below, pirates themselves, by both making and breaking the rules of the sea, played a key role in reinforcing and ultimately undermining a broad consensus among early modern states on the proper uses and practices of piracy.

PIRACY IN THE EARLY MODERN MEDITERRANEAN

In the early modern period, from the late sixteenth to the eighteenth centuries, states around the globe began to increase their powers and to acquire the arms, institutions, and organization that enabled them to impose their wills on growing numbers of people, whether they were their own subjects or were ones they encountered abroad. This was the age of the dramatic expansion of sea-based empires—the Spanish and Portuguese, followed by the Dutch, French, and British—that acquired wealth and power through sea trade and through the transport of goods to and from far-flung lands that they conquered or dominated through other means. The seas—in particular the Mediterranean Sea, the Atlantic Ocean, and the Indian Ocean, including the Arabian Gulf—came to be crisscrossed by corridors of navigation, trade routes plied by the ships of empire.

As a consequence, it was also the golden age of piracy: the seventeenth and eighteenth centuries were a good time for pirates. Piracy is by definition a parasitical activity—as the host flourishes, so does the parasite—and the valuable goods flowing into European ports enticed many to become pirates.[8] Most pirates of this era, however, were not simply opportunistic sea thieves. States also actively fostered piracy, as they sought to protect their shipping before the development of significant naval power by harnessing nonstate violence in the form of privateers and corsairs, who could be mobilized to attack their enemies while also swelling state coffers. State-sponsored pirates were a double-edged sword: pirates were never under full control and could easily slip into following their own interests at the expense of state priorities.[9] Until they developed alternatives, virtually all early modern states with seafaring capabilities sponsored pirates in some form.

Maritime violence, therefore, surged and piratical attacks on shipping—the armed boarding of ships, the confiscation of cargo, the capturing of crew and passengers, and the takeover of ships themselves—increased dramatically in number. Any merchant ship that took to the seas in this period faced the threat of predatory attack, and people of all backgrounds undertook sea voyages—whether on the Mediterranean, the Atlantic, or the Indian Ocean—with no small feelings of trepidation. The specter of falling into pirate hands haunted those who embarked: in the Mediterranean, for example, the anxieties surrounding sea travel were nurtured by a burgeoning literature of captivity narratives that exposed the sufferings of those who had been captured by pirates and enslaved on both southern and northern shores.[10] And, as would be expected, there were economic costs. At an extreme, pirate activity could ruin trade. We have the example of the city-state of Venice. In the late sixteenth and early seventeenth centuries, its sea trade, the lifeblood of its economy, was beset by pirate attacks, causing merchants to face mounting losses and expenditures. Merchants, who had to hire soldiers for their ships and pay their sailors more for hazardous voyages, faced escalating costs for insurance, when they could get it. The outcome was devastating for the city. Some historians attribute the decline of Venice to the dramatic reduction in the volume of sea trade and the consequent turn to less profitable land-based economic activities, all largely a result of the pirate factor.[11]

The Dutch, French, and British merchant and privateering ships that began to ply the Mediterranean in significant numbers in the late sixteenth and seventeenth centuries came prepared for pirate attacks or other forms of resistance to their intrusions. They were increasingly well armed and often well manned, ready to shoulder their way into the lucrative trade of the Mediterranean. In the absence of state naval forces, European traders often took it upon themselves to protect their ships and police their chosen routes as well as they could. As Pérotin-Dumon notes, the merchant ships of sixteenth-century Europe waged a low-level war against Spanish, Venetian, or Ottoman ships that appeared to contest their access to the Mediterranean, or simply proved to be lucrative targets.[12] Fernand Braudel had earlier taken a similar position, in viewing the appearance of aggressive northern European privateers in the Mediterranean as a sign that the English, French, and Dutch merchant empires were bent on establishing themselves in the area and were perfectly willing to employ whatever tactics were necessary, including piratical attacks.[13]

The view from the other shore reflects a distinct but intersecting trajectory. The scholarly consensus is that "Mediterranean piracy (*corso*) was the attempt of impoverished societies excluded from the mainstream of development to compensate themselves—at least in part—for the losses caused by the commercial ascendancy of the northerners."[14] The North African Ottoman provinces of Algiers, Tunis, and Tripoli, later known as regencies, increasingly came to rely on revenues from corsairing to fill state treasuries. The booty, ships, and captives brought into port by the corsairs, as well as the protection payments European powers made to shelter their ships from corsair attacks, were a significant source of income for these states from the late sixteenth through the eighteenth century.[15] The history of corsairing was an uneven one: trade patterns and alliances could shift over time, and the North African states adjusted their targets and tactics to the developing balance of power in the waters around them, as corsairing endured throughout the period as a vital source of goods, ships, captives, and the money that ransoms could bring in.

The ubiquity of pirate activity in an era of growing state ambition stimulated the development of legal discourses and practices aimed at defining, harnessing, and controlling piracy in accordance with the evolving interests of the early modern state. This is not a simple story of the suppression of piracy but rather a complex tale of assault, resistance, seduction, and discipline, in which pirates had a role to play. As subalterns, who operated on the fringes of power, both spatially and culturally, pirates did not leave many tracks of their own in the historical record, and so it is with difficulty that we follow their trail. In the world of law and diplomacy, however, they were not only objects and catalysts, they were also actors in a period of significant development of a regional legal culture, one that was deeply imbricated in the fashioning of laws and regulations on piracy, as well as in their unraveling. In the early modern period, this legal culture was being incubated in three related domains: first, the interplay of the legal discourses of Muslim jurists and their European counterparts; second, the local practices aimed at the regulation and control of pirates from many shores; and third, the treaties signed by seafaring states with a stake in Mediterranean trade.

LEGAL DISCOURSES OF PIRACY

In light of the growth of piracy, it should not surprise us that there was a flurry of legal activity, including the elaboration of legal discourses on piracy and the devising of rules and regulations aimed at defining, shaping, and controlling piracy and those who practiced it. Legal theorists working within the tradition of Islamic law had long engaged the issue of piracy, drawing on the work of their classical forebears. As Hassan Khalilieh has noted, the Islamic legal tradition did not develop a specialized law of the sea. Rather, Muslim jurists tended to deal with maritime topics by way of analogy to laws and cases on land, with particular reference to the desert as analogous to sea space and the camel as analogous to the ship.[16] In the early modern period, they employed such land-based analogies as they addressed a major legal concern in the Mediterranean, namely, how to tell the pirate outlaw from the licit privateer or corsair, a distinction that could not be made on the basis of simple observation: the ships, the crew, and the behavior of pirates and privateers were virtually indistinguishable.

Al-Wansharisi's collection of Maghribi and Andalusian legal opinions (*fatāwā*), which contains many of the extant fatwas delivered by followers of the legal school of Imam Malik, was assembled at the turn of the sixteenth century and was widely circulated and referenced. We find allusions to sea marauders in various fatwas, who are identified as "thieves of the sea" (*luṣūṣ al-baḥr*) in a straightforward analogy to thieves who operate on land. They are criminals, and if they are operating within Muslim territory, in rivers or coastal waters, it is the responsibility of the ruling authority to apprehend and punish them.[17] Another category of sea marauder, however, is treated with more legal nuance. These are referred to as *Rūm* (Roman, a fluid term being used for Christians) or *Naṣāra'* (Christians), who prey on Muslim ships, just as Muslim *ghuzāt* (warriors for the faith) capture Christian ships. In one telling fatwa from Ibn ʿImran, *Rūm* forcibly took a ship originally out of Alexandria, only to be later intercepted by *ghuzāt* from Sicily, who attacked and captured the prize, and then discovered that it was originally a Muslim ship. The *Rūm* and the *ghuzāt* in this case, although they both engaged in maritime violence, are not identified as *luṣūṣ*. And indeed, the Sicilians, as Muslims, are reminded that they are engaged in a form of jihad, and it is their responsibility as trustees to protect the ship and its cargo and restore it to the rightful owners.[18] We have a distinction being made here between pirates, who are simply thieves let loose on the sea, and corsairs and privateers, who are engaged in a public religious purpose and have rules to follow in their captures. It is a distinction overlaid with the Islamic religious discourse of jihad and ghazi, and it recognizes, at least indirectly by not eliding them with thieves, that the Christians have religious and public purposes of their own.

Most of the legal matters related to piracy in al-Wansharisi's collection—whether the pirates were simple thieves or commissioned warriors for faith or nation—are perhaps not surprisingly connected to property claims, insofar as piracy entailed the forcible seizure of a ship, cargo, or people, the last of which could be held for ransom or converted into property. Muslim legal theorists brought the richness of Islamic law on contracts to bear on questions arising in the aftermath of a piratical act. What were the rights and obligations of shipowners, investors, captains, and crew? Many of the legal questions raised in the context of the pirated ship out of Alexandria mentioned above, for example, focused on the need to disentangle the claims and obligations arising from the captures. In a long, detailed response, Ibn ʿImran sorted out a number of issues, including the responsibilities for costs incurred in restoring the ship to its rightful owners, the appropriate venue and acceptable testimony in a related court case, and the rights of the heirs of deceased passengers. Elsewhere he addressed an incident in which pirates boarded a ship and took the cargo but not the ship itself: could the shipowner still collect his fees for transporting the cargo? Ibn ʿImran used the analogy of the owner of a camel transporting a rider across the desert. If the rider were to die in the wilderness, the owner would not collect the transport fees. Similarly, the owner of the ship could not collect fees from the merchants who had shipped the cargo purloined by pirates.[19] In opining on these cases, Ibn ʿImran strove to apply Islamic legal rules and procedures as he understood them and to empower Islamic courts to adjudicate in questions related to pirate attacks, wherever they had occurred.

The strong connection in the Islamic legal tradition between discussions of piracy and legal issues pertaining to commercial arrangements, including business partnerships, investments, and debts, also emerges in the context of merchant voyages that were aborted by piracy. When the threat of a pirate raid at sea occasioned a return to port or aborted the journey before it even began, issues of liability arose. If the shipowner called off the voyage while at sea, and returned to port without the agreement of the merchants, he could not collect the transport fees; if the merchants agreed with his decision, however, they should pay their fees. There were also times when a captain might take a decision at sea to jettison cargo in the face of a threat of piracy, either to lighten the ship for a faster getaway or make it a less tempting target. Such a decision could be contested in court in order to hold the captain responsible for the losses, and the Muslim judge would rule on the basis of evidence collected from testimony and perhaps from the condition of the ship as well.[20]

European legal theorists also began to engage the issue of piracy actively in the late sixteenth century and continued to have animated discussions about definitions, legal categories, and sanctions throughout the early modern period. As Alfred Rubin, who wrote a classic and comprehensive study of the development of the law on piracy in British and early American legal circles, notes, the early modern jurists drew self-consciously if "inappropriately often" on classical legal theory, primarily Cicero and *The Digest of Justinian,* to formulate their doctrines about piracy.[21] The sparseness of the available material from the Roman tradition, however, encouraged these jurists to head in new directions, largely in response to the issue of piracy as it presented itself in their era. The development of this body of law is well-traversed territory, and most scholars focus on a handful of pivotal legal thinkers and their signal works, including among others Alberico Gentili and *Three Books on the Laws of War,* published in 1589; Hugo Grotius and *On the Law of War and Peace,* published in 1625; Emerich Vattel and *The Law of Nations,* published in 1758; William Blackstone and *Commentaries on the Laws of England,* published in 1765–69; and Richard Wooddeson and *A Systematical View of the Laws of England,* published in 1792–94.[22] Although these thinkers shared a concern with developing the conceptual tools to identify, regulate, and punish piracy where appropriate, and the general thrust of their work was to establish a legal framework that criminalized piracy in some novel ways and gave state power a free hand in its use of force against pirates, there were some significant differences among them.

Rubin usefully divides them into two broad categories: the "naturalists," who pursued the arguments of natural law to advocate for addressing piracy under an expansive law of nations, and the "positivists," who emphasized the responsibilities of sovereign states and their agents to protect the lives and property of their subjects as a matter of municipal law.[23] The proponents of natural law arguments, like Grotius and, later, Blackstone, adopted and adapted the classical concept of pirates as *hostis humani generis,* or enemies of all humankind, who act for private motives with the intention to steal *(animo furandi),* not for a political purpose There were objective criteria: pirates were those who banded together for wrongdoing, to pillage on or from the seas, and who did not discriminate as to place or target. As pirates were deemed to be in a perpetual state of enmity with all, they could be attacked with impunity, without a formal declaration of war. Pirates were under universal jurisdiction, in the sense that any person or state could attack them on the seas and punish them as a natural right of defense against an aggressor. Pirates were not protected under the laws of war: they had no legal title to what they captured or occupied, and they had no claim to fair treatment in defeat. Pirates did not have the rights of common criminals: they did not have a right to be tried in court, and they could be captured and killed at will. Pirates stood outside the law and, indeed, outside morality. Just as they did not recognize the laws and morals of humankind, they were not deserving of human treatment: one could unilaterally break any agreement made with them and could even renege on promises or sworn oaths without compunction. Daniel Heller-Roazen characterized this last position, as derived from Cicero's *De officiis:* "In speaking to a pirate, in dealing with a pirate, no matter one's acts, no matter one's word, and no matter one's faith . . . one becomes a pirate oneself."[24] Pirates lived, in the terms of Giorgio Agamben, in a "state of exception," excluded from political society and subject to sovereign violence at will.[25]

The positivists brought other considerations to bear. They agreed that state authorization made the difference between the bandit and the legitimate representative of a sovereign power. A corollary question immediately posed itself: which political entities were sovereign powers invested with the authority to sponsor pirates, to render them legitimate, if violent, actors in a public cause, who stood squarely within the law and the rules of war? Here the positivists disagreed with the naturalists. As a positivist, Gentili invested individual European rulers with this power; the corsairs of a North African state could be considered pirates if the ruling authority of the state were considered illegitimate by a European sovereign. Grotius and his successors disagreed on the basis that Algiers, Tripoli, and Tunis were organized states with established governments; European rulers could go to war against them, but they could not unilaterally deny them sovereign status and thus render their corsairs pirates.[26]

This disagreement carried into the eighteenth century. Vattel opined that there are nations that are "unjust plunderers," and "those who appear to relish the horrors of war, who wage it on all sides without reason or pretext, and even without other motive than their savage inclinations, are monsters, unworthy of the name of men. They should be regarded as the enemies of the human species."[27] And he later made explicit reference to the "maritime towns of Africa, those lairs of pirates,"[28] leaving no doubt as to which nations he deemed "unjust plunderers" and which, therefore, should be placed outside the boundaries of the rule of law and were deserving of the treatment reserved for pirates. Vattel's views, however, did not necessarily carry the day. The preponderance of opinion came down on the side of the followers of the Grotius line, including Richard Wooddeson, who emphasized the criteria by which one could recognize legitimate nations with the power to authorize corsairs and thus denied the sovereign the power to give or withhold recognition. Such nations "have a fixt domain, public revenue, and form of government." In addition, one could look to the precedent established by historical patterns of international relations. In the case of the North African states, European powers "sometimes carry on war, sometimes stipulate for peace, with them as with other nations."[29] At the end of the eighteenth century, then, most but not all European legal theorists concurred that similar to others, North African states could legitimately license privateers to pursue public purposes. The true pirate, the outlaw, was clearly established as a sea marauder, who acted for private motives and who lacked any commission from a sovereign power.

The jurisdictional issue also continued to arise over the course of the eighteenth century. The problem posed by the occurrence of piracy outside the territorial jurisdiction of any one state led to a wide range of questions about the who and how of prosecuting and punishing piracy. Was there universal jurisdiction over piracy, or should the sovereign who awards the commission be the party to hear the case? Did a state need to have a formal legal interest in a given case of piracy to try it? If pirates were apprehended outside the territorial jurisdiction of any state, could private justice be meted out? And if they were to be delivered for trial, should it be to the home nation of the pirate or that of the victim? As Rubin notes, "The relationship between municipal law and international law so central to an understanding of the conception that 'piracy' should be suppressed and that the normal jurisdiction of municipal law tribunals would not suffice to suppress it when foreigners and foreign commissions were involved, was never fully resolved in the 18th century."[30] And, as we shall see, as the nineteenth century progressed, the legal theorists were often asked to step aside when the interests of state and merchant demanded more decisive action than was allowed for by the finer points of legal discourse.

In brief, the North African and European legal cultures had ostensibly different points of departure for their discussions of piracy, as they laid claim to distinct legal legacies: Imam Malik was invoked in the south and Cicero in the north. They converged, however, in some significant areas, as they worked to apply the rules and regulations of their respective traditions to the many questions posed by this pervasive activity. They both wrestled with questions of jurisdiction and preferred the courts and the procedures that were familiar and close to home to settle the many property issues arising. And they both incorporated a moral discourse that distinguished piracy with a religious or public purpose from piracy that was plain thievery and was subject, as a result, to summary justice or criminal prosecution of pirates as outlaws.

PRACTICES

The convergence on matters of piracy was even more pronounced in a shared history of maritime practices found along the Mediterranean shores. Khalilieh, in his study of the ways in which maritime cultures of the Mediterranean interacted and influenced each other in the eighth to tenth centuries AD, views the region's maritime laws as a palimpsest with layers of Roman, Byzantine, and Islamic doctrines and practices.[31] In the early modern period, piracy came to play a leading role in the further development of maritime practices in the Mediterranean, through shared understandings of and approaches to the authorization of pirate activities, the adjudication of prizes, and the punishment of pirates who strayed from state control.

States operating in the Mediterranean developed a system of authorization of pirate activities that served to distinguish between the privateer, or corsair, and the pirate. European states used letters of marque or reprisal, which were formal commissions given to a ship and captain licensing the capture of ships belonging to specified enemies. Their terms could be generous. As Benton remarks, "The terms of commissions were often intentionally capacious, authorizing privateers to make captures of enemy ships and pirates, to strike in self-defense, and sometimes to intercept shipping in particular sea lanes."[32] They also operated prize courts, tribunals run by the admiralties, whose tasks included verification that ships captured and cargo taken were good prizes, that is to say that they fell within the bounds of the commission. The courts also existed, of course, to make sure that the state received its share of the prize.[33]

The Maghribi states of Algiers, Tunis, and Tripoli also employed corsairs, who sailed with the formal authorization of the state and were obliged to register their prizes upon their return to port. Daniel Panzac has documented how booty brought back by the corsairs was divided according to official formulas and strict accounting procedures. In the case of Algiers, for example, the ruling dey claimed any captured ship and roughly half of the rest of the booty—cargo and captives alike—and the type and distribution of the spoils were carefully recorded in prize registers.[34]

A key aspect of official control and surveillance of pirates was the passport, a document that came to be widely employed in the Mediterranean in the regulation and adjudication of piracy. By the mid-eighteenth century, the passport had become the chief measure of the legality of corsair or privateer operations. Countries whose merchants sailed the Mediterranean would supply their ships with passports attesting to the national identity of the ship and its claim to protection from attacks by the corsairs or privateers of allied countries. One study of such passports issued by Denmark in the eighteenth century illustrates the development of this genre of document into a sophisticated tool meant to ensure that treaty agreements were observed. An Algerian passport for a Danish ship, for example, would be composed in two languages, Danish and Arabic, and the document would be cut in half along an irregular line that allowed for later verification of the document by fitting the two pieces together. The Danish state would issue the Danish half of the passport to a Danish ship and send the other half to Algiers. If the Danish ship were approached by Algerian corsairs, the captain could then produce his half of the passport, and the corsairs should immediately withdraw. If the validity or any of the specifics of the document were disputed, it could be checked against the Arabic half, which would presumably have been stored in Algiers. Although passports were not mentioned as such in the treaties Denmark signed with various North African states, records of issuance were carefully kept in Denmark, and the system seemed to work; the Danish vice-consul in Morocco in the 1760s reported that the pass system was having very good results for Danish ships.[35]

Passports had also come to be an essential document for North African corsairing ships. According to Panzac, every corsairing captain in the Maghrib in the late eighteenth and early nineteenth centuries sailed with passports issued by European consuls representing treaty states. For example, 239 such passports were issued by the French consulate alone to Algerian corsairing captains between 1798 and 1816. The passes functioned to protect the corsairing ship from attack by the warships of treaty partners and obliged the corsairing captain to refrain from preying on their merchant ships in return.[36]

Passports did not always work to everyone's satisfaction, however. Corsairs and privateers were known to scrutinize the papers of ships they wanted to seize, looking for irregularities that could render the passport invalid. In 1749, a letter from the dey of Algiers to the king of England addressed one such incident:

> Dear faithful friends, One of Our Corsair Captains named Caroala [sic], in his Cruise, met with some English Ships, and it being Customary to Examine their Passports, he found, in his Opinion, Deficiencies in the Passports of some of them, whereupon he took on board his own Ship some Christians and put on board each of those Ships . . . some Turks to carry them to Algier for further Examination; Having finished his Cruise, he came to Algier, and I having been acquainted with what he had done, not giving any Credit to his Report, I made strict Examination myself, and found his proceedings were quite wrong, whereupon I immediately sent all the Christians he had to the English Consul in Order for their being returned to England.[37]

Captain Caroala, implicated in an attack on allied ships, sought to cover himself by acting like a bureaucrat, parsing documents and detecting irregularities. The dey, in his turn, claimed that he had fully intended to execute the captain for this transgression, but because the other corsair captains had intervened to ask for a pardon, he contented himself by removing him from his command. Legal proceedings were invoked all around. Pirates might also succeed in pressing a legal argument, as we see in the case of the capture of a ship with a British King's Packet Commission by corsairs from Algiers in the same year. They argued that the ship was not carrying a passport, and king's packets were not listed as exempt in the current treaty agreement between Britain and Algiers. In this case, the dey allowed corsairs to keep the prize, although he promised the British that the treaty would be amended to prevent the use of this loophole in the future.[38]

Such scrutiny might be well justified in other cases. The illegal distribution of passports was an issue of general concern. In 1769, the dey of Algiers complained to the French court that some of its consuls in Italy were issuing French passes to Genoese and other Italian ships that were not entitled to them.[39] Another thorny problem entailed the question of which ships qualified for a passport on the basis of the national identities of the owners, the question that had bedeviled Consul Fraser as he tracked the travels of the *Ermosa Rachel.* Elsewhere he provided an affidavit for a Catalan barque that had been purchased by a British subject, one John Caymaris of Minorca, from "Aly Hogia," a Turkish merchant and owner of privateering vessels in Algiers. Fraser had checked to make sure that Caymaris's registered co-owners were all British subjects from Mahon, that there were no owners unaccounted for, and that Caymaris understood that as long as he flew the British flag and held a British Mediterranean passport, no non-British subject could acquire a share in the vessel.[40]

The passport was part of a broader system of growing state control of pirates, in which European consuls came to play a central role. Most states preferred, or required, privateers to return to their homeport for adjudication of their prizes by state authorities in special admiralty courts, but there were often exceptions. In the French case, bad weather or an enemy presence could serve as an excuse for privateers to put ashore in a foreign port, where a resident French consul could oversee the adjudication of the prize, as well as its authentication, its sale, and the collection of the state's percentage. Distance led to abuses in the system: consuls were known to collude with captains and fail to report prizes in order to skim money from the sales and the state's shares.[41] The growing authority of the consuls, however, also signaled the states' intentions to keep closer account of their privateers' activities, and some consuls became watchdogs, ready to report not only on the misdeeds of foreign pirates but also on those of their own countrymen. The British consul Stanhope Aspinwall wrote to Sir William Pitt in 1757 from Algiers about an incident in which English privateers attacked a Swedish ship and killed a "Turk," who was on board, leading the dey to lodge a formal complaint. This evoked the following reflection on the part of Aspinwall:

> Indeed I hear of so many other Disorders, which our Privateers begin to commit with regard to Turks they meet with even on Neutral Vessels, that it is much to be wished they might be seasonably checked by some Severities, to nip these irregularities in the Bud, before Complaints of this kind multiply upon us, which may have bad consequences to all His Majesty's Consuls, settled in Barbary.[42]

The expanding system of courts and consuls was in part geared to bridling privateers, holding them to the terms of their commissions, and ensuring that they did not defraud the state.

North African states were also increasingly active in their attempts to assert control over the activities and the profits of their corsairs. Eric Staples has traced changes in the regulation and administration of corsairing out of Salé during the seventeenth century. In the earlier part of the century, letters of commission were issued by the local *dīwān,* a council with representatives drawn from the judiciary, the admiralty, the local governor, and local shaykhs. The vessel's captain and investors bore full responsibility for outfitting the ship and paying the crew, although the ship needed permission from the *dīwān,* as well as a formal commission, to sail. The *dīwān* was entitled to a rather modest one-tenth share in any prize. After the institution of ʿAlawi rule in 1666, the state took more direct control of corsairing and restructured distribution of the profits: the sultan claimed a half share in any captured vessel and 20 percent of all cargo and captives, while the local government retained its 10 percent share.[43]

In the eighteenth century, North African states continued to exert themselves to manage their corsairs, for motives born of politics and profit. As Panzac documents, states not only commissioned but also often acted as the main outfitters of corsairing ships; in Tripoli, the ruler monopolized the business, while in Algiers and Tunis, the head of state played the primary role and made the major investment in corsairing voyages. The North African states also deployed their soldiers to assist and, no doubt, to restrain corsairs when appropriate. In Algiers, for example, the dey routinely seconded Janissary troops to serve as guards and boarding parties on corsairing vessels. And once the ships returned to Algiers with their prizes, the state exercised tight surveillance of the process of valuation and distribution of the booty.[44]

There were other disciplinary measures that could be taken, including that of summary justice for corsairs who refused to stick to the terms of their commissions or otherwise misbehaved. Salvatore Bono recalls a legend about "el-Haggi Embarek," a corsair captain from Algiers, who enjoyed a successful twenty-year career in the 1740s and 1750s. The story has it that he and his crew once returned from a successful cruise and ran amuck on the streets of Algiers—getting into brawls, attacking women, and even killing city guards. The dey was irate and ordered severe punishment, which the captain and his crew eluded by fleeing to the sea, where they managed to capture a Spanish galleon and then obtain the dey's pardon by bringing home such a rich prize as a gift.[45] Even the most accomplished of corsairs could run afoul of authority, as we learn from the case of Raʾis Hamidou. A highly productive corsair in the late eighteenth and early nineteenth centuries, who was periodically recruited for Algerian naval service, Hamidou could still find himself under sentence of exile in 1808, although his value was such that he was recalled to Algiers shortly thereafter to resume his corsairing career.[46] North African rulers could also punish swiftly and severely when corsair activities threatened to disrupt political ties and agreements they valued: in 1767, the dey of

FIGURE 7. Rédha Chikh Bled, *Ra'is Hamidou.* Sculpture erected in Bab El-Oued, Algiers, 1987. Courtesy of Patriots on Fire.

Algiers reportedly ordered the strangling of a corsair captain, who had plundered a ship from Mahon, then a British port, that belonged to British subjects under treaty protection.[47]

As such incidents suggest, early modern states and empires could not always control the behavior of pirates they commissioned to act in their interests. It behooves us to remember that pirates, by definition, operated largely at sea, in spaces that were poorly regulated by the states of the time. Thus there were frequent violations of the terms of commissions. Recalcitrant privateers and corsairs had to be continuously reminded of the rules and brought to account before policing institutions. Still, it is important to recognize, as Lauren Benton and Molly Greene have both observed, that pirates often opted to adhere to legal norms and to cooperate with the emerging legal institutions that regulated piracy. Benton examines the case of William Kidd, the English corsair who mounted a vigorous albeit ultimately futile defense at his trial for piracy in London in 1701, claiming with some justification that he had been operating within the regulatory order.[48] Greene's study of the Tribunal of Malta, and its role in reviewing the legality of captures made by the Knights of Malta or their affiliates in light of claims made by Greek merchants, depicts the knights as somewhat restless but respectful subjects of the tribunal's authority. Faced with a ban on the capture of Christian ships, cargo, and persons, Maltese corsairs often tried to argue that Ottoman Greek captains and merchants might be Christians, but they were sailing Muslim ships and transporting Muslim cargo.[49]

The corsairs who sailed from North African shores often took equal care, as we have seen above, to adhere to the established rules and regulations; they carried passports, they inspected others' papers before attacks, and they usually brought their prizes back to their homeports for registration and distribution. In the Algerian court records, as studied by Fatiha Loualich, they appear as thoroughly integrated and law-abiding subjects, who buy or construct houses in the city, endow some of their property as *waqf*s, and leave inheritances for their descendants. Although Loualich notes that many lived lives cut short by the hazards of their profession, their business in court was not otherwise distinguished from that of their fellow urbanites. Indeed, some of the successful captains entered the ranks of the city's elite, building and occupying grand houses in the vicinity of the port.[50] This is not to suggest that corsairs could not and did not slip out of the state's control by violating the terms of their commissions or marketing their prizes in distant ports, issues that all of the commissioning authorities had to confront from time to time. Still, there were legalized systems of inducement and remuneration for those pirates all around the Mediterranean who operated on the right side of the law: they could reap tangible rewards in the form of shares of the prize, and their actions would be cloaked in legality.

The line between privateer, or corsair, and pirate no doubt wavered more than the rules suggest. In principle, the privateer and the pirate were distinct. The privateer served the state and the pirate served himself, but many of the captains and sailors on board these authorized ships had once been, and might again be, simple pirates. In practice, privateers and corsairs moved in and out of state service because their actions, after all—qua pirates or privateers—were virtually indistinguishable, and many had pirating backgrounds; they proved ready to take advantage of opportunities to attack unauthorized targets, and they were known to seek out the black markets that existed for the purpose of offloading captured goods away from the regulatory eyes of the admiralty court or the home port. The early modern states of the Mediterranean faced many similar issues of regulation of privateering and piracy, and came to handle them using strikingly similar methods.

TREATIES

Many of the practices regulating piracy in the early modern Mediterranean came to be undergirded by bilateral treaty agreements that formalized expectations on both sides about the behavior of privateers and corsairs, and the prohibition of other forms of piracy, drawing on the varied traditions of the region. Over the course of the period, as conflicts erupted and the balance of power shifted, these treaties were renewed and rewritten on numerous occasions. Between 1615 and 1830, a total of ninety-three such treaties were signed between the states of North Africa and European countries (and the United States after independence), fifty-one in the eighteenth century alone, when such diplomatic activity was at its peak.[51] The treaties were virtually all geared toward the protection and accommodation of each other's mercantile and corsairing activities, in keeping with the pragmatic tone of the times, as nicely enunciated by an anonymous English merchant in 1768:

> A trading nation doth not, nor cannot, enter into the Character of those they trade with. Mr. Wilkes was an Outlaw; but have the Taverns refused to draw wine for him? Or a Shoemaker or Draper to sell him Shoes or Cloth for his ready Money? The pope is a very sad Fellow, and we burn him along with the Devil once a Year, yet we trade to Civita-Vecchia. Tunis and Algiers are Pirate States, yet we keep Consuls, and trade with those Pirates and Infidels.[52]

The treaties that established peace and reciprocity between states operating in the Mediterranean had the practical aim of making that sea safe for "trading nations," despite bows to recognition of difference.

The North African treaties formed part of wider developments in diplomatic practices and instruments, in which the Mediterranean theater was a central setting. Historians who are writing the "new diplomatic history of the early modern Mediterranean" have begun to eschew a Eurocentric narrative of diplomatic history in favor of one that attends to the Ottomans as important players who made major contributions to innovations in diplomacy.[53] The Ottomans made it clear, for example, that part of the ruler's responsibility, as inscribed in many treaties, was to prevent or punish pirate attacks launched from his territorial domains against his subjects or his treaty partners. The first capitulation agreements, which were signed by Ottoman sultans with the French in 1569 and 1581, the English in 1579, and the Dutch in 1612, included clauses guaranteeing free passage to and protection for each other's ships, cargo, and people. These can be viewed as applications of the Islamic legal concept of *amān,* the Muslim ruler's grant of safe-conduct of person and goods to individuals or groups coming from outside his domains.[54]

It was not always easy, or even possible, for the Ottoman center to guarantee adherence to treaty terms on the part of its peripheral lands. Algiers, Tunis, and Tripoli launched attacks on Venetian shipping in the late sixteenth and early seventeenth centuries, in flagrant disregard of Ottoman-Venetian treaties, and neither the sultan nor reprimands by the highest religious authority could bring them to heel. Although, as Joshua White demonstrates, the Venetians continued to look to Istanbul for a remedy, other European states—the English, French, and Dutch—began to make treaties directly with the individual North African regencies.[55]

In the eighteenth century, many of these treaties went well beyond the provision of safe conduct to specify the services and accommodations that were to be made available to their respective corsairs and privateers. The English-Algiers Treaty of 1762, for example, contained three planks. First, the ships and subjects of both sides "shall not henceforward do to each other any harm offense or injury either in word or deed but shall treat one another with all possible respect and friendship." Second, "His Britannic Majesty's Ships or Vessels of War, or any English Privateers or Letters of Marque" were authorized to attack ships belonging to British enemies found off the coast of Algiers; bring the prizes to harbor in Algiers; and dispose of the ships, cargo, and crew and passengers as they wished. And third, if the British were at war with "any Mahometan Prince or State," they were to refrain from attack on the ships of that state if they were anywhere within sight of the coast of the Regency of Algiers.[56] The French-Algiers peace treaty signed in 1764 addressed some of the problems that might arise with corsairing. Article 2 specified that if Algerian corsairs clashed with French ships of any kind at sea, the incident should be thoroughly examined and the guilty party, if Algerian, should be harshly punished by the dey of Algiers, and, if French, by the resident French consul. Article 7 outlined the procedures to follow should Algerian corsairs arrive in port with a prize that had been abandoned by its crew out of fear of pirate attack. If the French consul had any reason to suspect it was a French ship, he could demand its sequestration and then take it into possession if information coming from France confirmed its identity.[57] Such treaties construe corsairing as a legitimate business, albeit one in need of joint regulation to ensure the peace.

The treaty terms that accommodated corsairing and privateering were to be upheld, at least in theory, in naval practice. Sir Henry Penrice, who served as judge of the Admiralty from 1715 to 1751, responded to a question posed in 1716 about whether a British admiral should sanction the retaking of ships of other nations that had been captured previously by North African corsairs:

> The question being so very general, to consider it in its full extent may seem too tedious; for some nations are at peace with the Moors, others are at war; and with some of the Moors we are in amity, with whom our allies are at war, as the Dutch with the

> Algerines; in which case I presume, we are not to assist a friend against a friend. For the Algerines being at war with the Dutch may make lawfull prize of their ships; but it would look like a breach of amity between us and that country, if we should retake any Dutch ship from the Algerines taken by them as prize. On the contrary pyrates and sea rovers, and such as have no lawfull commission to take ships, cannot acquire a just property in them, and if any ships belonging to other nations should be taken by such persons, and retaken by Admiral Cornwall, I am humbly of opinion, upon due proof of property, such ships ought to be restored to their lawfull owners.[58]

Penrice is describing the Mediterranean world that had been created by the interplay of maritime practices and diplomacy, and it was a world of flux and reciprocity. Some European states were allies and some were enemies; some European states had treaties with some North African states and were in conflict with others. Each situation has to be read in its own moment, but the overall thrust of his remarks is clear: under the terms of the treaties, corsair captures established property rights and could not be interfered with, even if an allied nation were the victim. He is also careful, however, to remind the petitioner that pirate outlaws who lacked recognized authorization enjoyed no such protection.

As European maritime empires gained ever-greater ascendency in the Mediterranean and came to monopolize the carrying trade, diplomatic relations between European and North African states acquired some distinguishing features. First, North African rulers came to demand and receive gifts and financial contributions in return for refraining from attacks, an agreement that appears to be much in keeping with the ethos of tribal customary law in the region, which treated the right of passage free of attack through tribal territory as a valuable resource that could be bartered.[59] The money procured through these treaty arrangements contributed to state coffers as North African merchant activities shrank with rising European dominance of the sea. Some treaty partners, particularly Sweden, the Netherlands, and Denmark, were also willing to provide scarce and much coveted munitions and materials for the outfitting of ships, as demonstrated by the following list of items delivered by Sweden to Algiers in 1767: ten twenty-four-pound cannons with carriages, five thousand cannon balls, five hundred quintals of powder, one hundred barrels of pitch, two hundred pieces of canvas, and five hundred fir planks, each two inches thick and fifteen feet in length.[60] During the same period, the Netherlands and Denmark presented the dey of Algiers with similar items, including cannons, cannon balls, and gunpowder, as well as naval supplies.[61] The pattern of tribute payments and gifts was fundamentally an asymmetrical exchange, with European states paying for peace and protection from attack from North African shores as part of a calculation of the costs of hostilities to their trading activities. The Maghribi states, therefore, moved increasingly into a position of dependence and vulnerability vis-à-vis their European allies. The flow of money the Maghribi states required to meet their financial obligations, and their ability to maintain and arm their ships in order to sustain corsairing activities, rested ever more on retention of the good will of their European treaty partners; when conflicts arose, the spigot could be turned off.

Asymmetry also arose in the area of diplomatic representation. Many treaties reiterated the rights of states to appoint resident consuls, which in the case of North African states was a one-way street. European consuls increasingly came to play an active role in representing their respective countries by making and receiving complaints about the violations of treaty agreements; interceding for countrymen, both merchants and captives; and reporting on the movements of corsairs and privateers in the area.[62] The North African regencies did not appoint resident consuls in return, but, over the course of the eighteenth century, they did send ambassadorial envoys to Europe to resolve problems that arose from corsairing and to negotiate ransoms and the renewal of treaties. Tripoli, for example, sent visiting ambassadors to Paris in 1719, to the Netherlands in 1735, to Sweden in 1756, to Venice in 1764, and to London in 1765 and 1773, to sign treaties or to represent the bey on state occasions. In doing so, the North African states followed a longstanding practice of statecraft on the eastern and southern shores. Although we lack a comprehensive list of diplomatic missions sent to Europe in the early modern period by the Ottomans and the Maghribis, the available evidence suggests that they were a frequent and standard practice. According to Mathieu Grenet, between forty and fifty diplomatic missions from the Ottoman Empire, North Africa (including Morocco), and Persia reached the French court between 1581 and 1825, and untold others were no doubt sent but either failed to arrive or were directed elsewhere in France. And France was only one destination out of many: diplomatic missions were sent to the Italians, English, Spanish, Dutch, Hapsburgs, Swedes, and Danes.[63] This practice only intensified in the second half of the eighteenth century, when, as Panzac has observed, the age of gunboat diplomacy had given way by and large to a regime of treaties and peaceful representations.[64] Although the Maghribi states did have substantial diplomatic representation, temporary embassies were by definition bound to be less effective, particularly in the areas of intelligence gathering and the ability of ambassadors to maneuver within the European system and work with local power brokers.

Despite growing disparities in power and spurts of hostility, the treaties of the eighteenth century did seem to inform an era in which the signatories took some pains to live up to their agreements. In 1745, the Senate of Hamburg complained that one of its merchant ships had been captured by Algerian corsairs, who had then been allowed to sell the ship and cargo in the British port of Gibraltar, where they could obtain higher prices than in Algiers; the Senate asked for a ban on the sales of prizes in British ports that had been taken from allies. Dr. Paul, the

Admiralty advocate asked to report on the complaint, cited the renewal in 1716 of the treaty of 1686 between Great Britain and Algiers and the addition of articles that allowed Great Britain and Algiers to sell prizes in each other's ports. He further cautioned that the prohibition of prize sales by Algerian corsairs in Gibraltar could result in the prohibition of prize sales by British privateers in Algiers.[65] Paul stressed the clear legal commitment to honoring the terms of the treaty and added the pragmatic observation that violation of its terms could result in retaliation injurious to British operations in the Mediterranean.

There were times, however, when immediate needs overrode treaty commitments. Although the dey of Algiers repeatedly signaled his commitment to treaty terms by reining in his corsairs, by confiscating prizes and returning them to treaty partners, and by punishing egregious violations with exile or even death, as we have seen above, the temptations could be great. The gunpowder, gold, and cotton carried by a French prize brought into Algiers in 1767 proved irresistible and were off-loaded before the dey released the ship to his French allies, much to their displeasure.[66] The ruler's share of the prize had long been an important if variable source of state revenue in the Maghrib, and such violations of protection agreements illustrate how difficult it was for them to abstain from prohibited corsairing altogether. The North African states were caught on the horns of a dilemma: protection payments collected from European states under the treaty regime could not compensate fully for the total loss of revenue from corsairing, and, in any case, they could get paid for protection only if they retained the ability and demonstrated the will to launch corsair attacks.[67]

Many treaties of the eighteenth-century Mediterranean pivoted around the issue of piracy, and the outcome of this "pirate diplomacy" included the implicit recognition of the North African states as sovereign nations that had the right to use corsairing against their enemies but not their treaty partners. They also established multiple means and channels to address conflicts that arose over the disruption of shipping. Treaty terms integrated many of the understandings and practices of the region at the time, including the legitimacy of authorized piracy, the acceptance of agreements that bartered protection for goods and money, and the principle of free market access to captured goods. The treaties stood as documents of reference for the rulers, jurists, and diplomats, as well as for the pirates themselves, who were the primary players in the maritime activities of the Mediterranean. All was not necessarily harmonious, as a result; disagreement and armed clashes between the North African states and their European treaty partners could and did erupt upon occasion. As Pennell points out, it would have been very difficult for the North African states to make ends meet if they had to refrain from attacks on English, French, and Dutch ships all at the same time.[68] The North African states could not always afford to comply with the terms of the treaties they signed. As the century wore on, the practices of the treaty regime also worked to develop a relationship of growing dependence, as the Maghribis came to rely on the maintenance of good relations for their survival.

Let us return to the voyage of the *Ermosa Rachel* and our disgruntled Consul Fraser's report of 1772. A Portuguese ship was captured at sea by Algerian corsairs, acquired by the dey as his perquisite, sold to a Christian Ottoman intermediary, sailed to a British port, passed through the part ownership of a British subject, and resold to a Tunisian Jew. The ship's owners were, in turn, Portuguese, Algerian, Greek Ottoman, Minorcan British, and finally Tunisian Jewish. Within a period of not more than five years, the ship could have been flagged as Portuguese, Algerian, Ottoman, and finally British. The cast of characters and countries testifies to the ways in which a captured vessel could voyage through the connected legal spaces of the Mediterranean and come the full distance from Algerian prize to documented and protected British ship. The maritime laws and practices of the early modern Mediterranean undergirded such voyages, and the corsairs and privateers could not but benefit from the web of state and business interests that facilitated such ship laundering, as they used knowledge of the rules to capture and market their prizes. Weighing the identities of a ship's owner, port of record, captain and crew, and cargo in the determination of not only the issuance of passports but also the legality of the taking was commonplace. Ships were by definition mobile, with crews of mixed ethnicity and nationality seeking ports of call and markets on the basis of profit and convenience, not patriotism; they could not always be called to account simply they belonged to state or empire.

The discomfort of Consul Fraser draws our attention, however, to change on the horizon. Firmer forms of distinction were being made. The consul was dealing in national and racial essence: how could a lowly Tunisian Jew own a British ship? Here and elsewhere the consul was very clear on the point that a British passport could be issued only to a ship owned in its entirety by British subjects. It was not only the tightening of the rules for passports that was at stake here, however, but also a sense of outrage that a British passport could fall into the hands of such an unworthy recipient. This was the beginning of a new order in the Mediterranean, one that would harden the fluid and permeable boundaries of territory and identity in Mediterranean space. The pirates of the early modern period had crossed these boundaries at will, as the Mediterranean seemed to shrink and the shores drew closer. Intersecting legal cultures, widespread agreement on maritime practices, and numerous treaties that spelled out the basis for cooperation on the regulation of piracy had shaped a sea space of shared understandings, if not always tranquility. In the latter part of the eighteenth century, however, growing disparities in power began to be manifest in the development of diplomatic relations of dependence. And by the 1770s, we sense a shift was

FIGURE 8. Edouard DuBufe, *Le congrès de Paris, 25 février au 30 mars 1856*. Chateau de Versailles. Courtesy of Wikimedia Commons.

underway, with the possibility that things were moving in another direction, toward a heightened sense of a fractured territorial identity and relations of dominance that would contest the free movement of pirates and ships from the southern shores.[69]

The intensification of piracy in the early modern period helped give rise to a Mediterranean in which maritime laws and practices became familiar from one end of the sea to the other, mingling people in ways that can be credited with leading to various levels of cooperation and at least some mutual comprehension. As modern European states continued to expand their navies in the nineteenth century and increased their capacity to police their sea routes, however, privateers became more of a liability than an asset. They suppressed their own pirates, and they launched relentless campaigns against the pirates of the southern shores and their redoubts. They also finally agreed to ban privateering and corsairing altogether as legitimate practices. In the Paris Declaration Respecting Maritime Law, the plenipotentiaries representing their countries in the signing of the Treaty of Paris in 1856—from the Ottoman, British, French, Austrian, and Russian Empires, along with the Kingdom of Italy—outlawed the authorization of pirates by sovereign states, and this practice virtually came to an end.[70] The modern Mediterranean thereafter would be a very different place indeed, a theater of unabashed European dominion in pursuit of imperial interests, a place with shrinking space for pirates.

NOTES

1. Public Record Office, SP 71/10/747–750, National Archives of the United Kingdom.

2. Peregrine Horden and Nicholas Purcell, *The Corrupting Sea: A Study of Mediterranean History* (Oxford: Blackwell, 2000), 388.

3. David Coleman, "Of Corsairs, Converts, and Renegades: Forms and Functions of Coastal Raiding on Both Sides of the Far Western Mediterranean, 1490–1540" in *Spanning the Strait: Studies in Unity in the Western Mediterranean,* ed. Yuen-Gen Liang, Abigail Krasner Balbale, Andrew Devereux, and Camilla Gómez-Rivas (Leiden: Brill, 2013), 167–92.

4. Molly Greene, "Beyond the Northern Invasion: The Mediterranean in the Seventeenth Century," *Past and Present,* no. 174 (February 2002): 58–63.

5. Lauren Benton, "Legal Spaces of Empire: Piracy and the Origins of Ocean Regionalism," *Comparative Studies in Society and History* 47 (2005): 722.

6. See chapter 8 of Marcus Rediker, *Villains of All Nations: Atlantic Pirates in the Golden Age* (Boston: Beacon Press, 2004).

7. Lauren Benton, *A Search for Sovereignty: Law and Geography in European Empires, 1400–1900* (Cambridge: Cambridge University Press, 2010), 112–20.

8. See J. L. Anderson, "Piracy and World History: An Economic Perspective on Maritime Predation," *Journal of World History* 6, no. 2 (Fall 1995): 182. Anderson also points out the limits of the simple parasite analogy.

9. See Janice Thomson, *Mercenaries, Pirates, and Sovereigns: State-Building and Extraterritorial Violence in Early Modern Europe* (Princeton, NJ: Princeton University Press, 1994), 22–26.

10. See Daniel J. Vitkus, ed. *Piracy, Slavery, and Redemption: Barbary Captivity Narratives from Early Modern England* (New York: Columbia University Press, 2001); and Khalid Bekkaoui, *White Women Captives in North Africa: Narratives of Enslavement, 1735–1830* (London: Palgrave Macmillan, 2011), for European narratives of captivity. See also Nabil Matar, "Piracy and Captivity in the Early Modern Mediterranean: The Perspective from Barbary," in *Pirates? The Politics of Plunder, 1550–1650,* ed. Claire Jowitt (London: Palgrave Macmillan, 2007), 56–73, for a discussion of captivity narratives written by North Africans.

11. As argued by Alberto Tenenti, *Piracy and the Decline of Venice: 1580–1615* (Berkeley: University of California Press, 1967).

12. Anne Pérotin-Dumont, "The Pirate and the Emperor: Power and the Law on the Seas, 1450–1850," in *Bandits at Sea: A Pirates Reader,* ed. C. R. Pennell (New York: New York University Press, 2001), 26.

13. Fernand Braudel, *The Mediterranean and the Mediterranean World in the Age of Philip II,* vol. 1 (Berkeley: University of California Press, 1996), 629, 634–35.

14. Pal Fodor, "Piracy, Ransom Slavery and Trade: French Participation in the Liberation of Ottoman Slaves from Malta during the 1620s," *Turcica* 33 (2001): 121.

15. See Daniel Panzac, *Les corsaires barbaresques: La fin d'une épopée 1800–1820* [The barbary corsairs: the end of an epic] (Paris: CNRS Éditions, 1999), 24–35.

16. Hassan Salih Khalilieh, *Admiralty and Maritime Laws in the Mediterranean Sea (ca. 800–1050): The Kitāb Akriyat al-Sufun vis-à-vis the Nomos Rhodion Nautikos* (Leiden: Brill, 2006), 252–54.

17. See Ahmad ibn Yahya al-Wansharisi, *al-Mi'yar al-mu'rib wa-al-jami' al-mughrib 'an fatawa ahl Ifriqiyah wa-al-Andalus wa-al-Maghrib* [The clear measure and the extraordinary collection of the judicial opinions of the scholars of Ifriqiya, al-Andalus, and the Maghrib], vol. 8 (Rabat: Wizarat al-awqaf, 1981–83), 302–5.

18. Al-Washarisi, *al-Mi'yar,* 8:302–5.

19. Al-Wansharisi, *al-Mi'yar,* 8:302.

20. See Hassan Salih Khalilieh, *Islamic Maritime Law: An Introduction* (Leiden: Brill, 1998), 70–71, 87–93. Khalilieh notes that the three basic legal questions raised about pirate raids on ships all dealt with the apportioning of fiscal liability.

21. Alfred P. Rubin, *The Law of Piracy* (Newport, RI: Naval War College Press, 1988), 10.

22. See Benton, *Search for Sovereignty,* 120–48; Daniel Heller-Roazen, *The Enemy of All: Piracy and the Law of Nations* (New York: Zone Books, 2009), 119–31; and Rubin, *Law of Piracy,* 66, 109–11, for discussions of these and a number of other significant European legal theorists.

23. Rubin, *Law of Piracy,* 90–92.

24. Heller-Roazen, *Enemy of All,* 21.

25. See chapter 1 of Giorgio Agamben, *State of Exception,* trans. Kevin Attell (Chicago: University of Chicago Press, 2005).

26. Heller-Roazen, *Enemy of All,* 105–11. See also Guillaume Calafat, "Ottoman North Africa and *ius publicum europaeum:* The Case of the Treaties of Peace and Trade (1600–1750)," in *War, Trade and Neutrality: Europe and the Mediterranean in the Seventeenth and Eighteenth Centuries,* ed. Antonella Alimento (Milan: FrancoAngeli Storia, 2011), 171–86, for a discussion of the evolution of European legal thought on the question of the sovereignty of North African states.

27. Emerich de Vattel, *The Law of Nations, or the Principles of Natural Law Applied to the Conduct and to the Affairs of Nations and Sovereigns,* trans. Charles G. Fenwick (Washington, DC: Carnegie Institute of Washington, 1916), 3.3, no. 34, 246, as cited in Heller-Roazen, 117.

28. Vattel, *Law of Nations,* 3.4, no.68, 258, as cited in Heller-Roazen, 118.

29. Richard Wooddeson, *A Systematical View of the Laws of England,* 423–24 (Dublin: E. Lynch, 1792–94), 423–24, as quoted in Rubin, *Law of Piracy,* 111.

30. Rubin, *Law of Piracy,* 105.

31. See Khalilieh, *Admiralty and Maritime Laws,* 250–55.

32. Benton, *Search for Sovereignty,* 140.

33. See Benton, *Search for Sovereignty,* 145–48, for a discussion of changes in the English courts' jurisdiction in the seventeenth century.

34. For a discussion of the distribution of corsairing booty, see Daniel Panzac, *Barbary Corsairs: The End of a Legend* (Leiden: Brill, 2005), 121–31.

35. Eric Gøbel, "The Danish 'Algerian Sea Passes', 1747–1838: An Example of Extraterritorial Production of 'Human Security'." *Historical Social Research* 35, no. 4, issue 134 (2010): 176–78.

36. Panzac, *Les corsaires,* 51–52.

37. Public Record Office, SP 71/11/258–59, National Archives of the United Kingdom.

38. Public Record Office, SP 71/11/260–61, National Archives of the United Kingdom.

39. *Independent Chronicle* or *Freeholders Evening Post,* October 9, 1769–October 11, 1769, issue 6, Burney Collection, British Library.

40. Public Record Office, SP 71/11/157, National Archives of the United Kingdom.

41. See Halvard Leira and Benjamin de Carvalho, "Privateers of the North Sea: At Worlds End—French Privateers in Norwegian Waters," in *Mercenaries, Pirates, Bandits and Empires: Private Violence in Historical Context,* ed. Alejandro Colás and Bryan Mabee (New York: Columbia University Press, 2010), 55–82.

42. Public Record Office, SP 71/10/207–09, National Archives of the United Kingdom.

43. Eric Staples, "Intersections: Power, Religion and Technology in Seventeenth Century Salé-Rabat" (PhD diss., University of California, Santa Barbara, September 2008), 91, 118–19.

44. Panzac, *Les corsaires,* 51, 59–60. See also chapter 4 for a detailed discussion of the Algiers' register of prizes, which reflects the results of state supervision.

45. Salvatore Bono, *Les corsairs en méditerranée,* trans. Ahmed Somaï (Paris: Éditions Paris-Méditerranée, 1998), 152–53.

46. See Panzac, *Les corsaires,* 54–55, for more details of Hamidou's career.

47. According to letters from Gibraltar to the *London Evening Post,* September 15, 1767–September 17, 1767, Burney Collection, British Library.

48. Benton, "Legal Spaces of Empire," 707–9.

49. Molly Greene, *Catholic Pirates and Greek Merchants: A Maritime History of the Mediterranean* (Princeton, NJ: Princeton University Press, 2010), 154–66, 179–88.

50. See Fatiha Loualich, "In the Regency of Algiers: The Human Side of the Algerian Corso," in *Trade and Cultural Exchange in the Early Modern Mediterranean,* ed. Mohamed Saleh Omri, Colin Heywood, and Maria Fusaro (London: I. B. Tauris, 2010), 69–96.

51. See the appendix in Panzac, *Les corsaires,* 279–81, for a list of all treaties signed between the Maghrib and the West from 1605 to 1830.

52. *Public Advertiser,* Friday, May 26, 1768, Burney Collection, British Library.

53. See Maatuje van Gleder and Tijana Krstić, "Introduction: Cross-Confessional Diplomacy and Diplomatic Intermediaries in the Early Modern Mediterranean," *Journal of Early Modern History* 19, nos. 2–3 (2015): 101–3, for a discussion of the elements of the new diplomatic history in the context of the Mediterranean. Other features of this approach include attention to the interactions on the ground that forged new concepts and practices and, in keeping with new diplomatic history elsewhere, investigation of the many individuals who engaged in diplomatic or intermediary activities outside the realm of ambassadorial circles.

54. See Hasan Khalilieh, "Amān," in *Encyclopaedia of Islam,* ed. Gudrun Krämer, Denis Matringe, John Nawas, and Everett Rowson, accessed November 24, 2018, dx.doi.org/10.1163/1573-3912_ei3_SIM_0048.

55. See Joshua M. White, "Fetva Diplomacy: The Ottoman Şeyhülislam as Trans-imperial Intermediary," *Journal of Early Modern History* 19, nos. 2–3 (2015): 199–221, for an intriguing discussion of diplomatic interventions made by the Ottoman şeyhülislam on behalf of Ottoman and European treaty partners.

56. Public Record Office, FO 95/510/46–49, National Archives of the United Kingdom.

57. For the text of this treaty, see E. Rouard de Card, *Traités de la France avec les pays de l'Afrique du Nord* (Paris: Libraire de la cour d'appel et de l'ordre de avocats, 1906), 79–80.

58. R. G. Marsden, ed., *Documents Related to the Law and Custom of the Sea,* vol. 2 (n.p.: Publications of the Navy Records Society, 1916), 239–40.

59. See Franklin H. Stewart, "Customary Law among the Bedouin of the Middle East and North Africa, in *Nomadic Societies in the Middle East and North Africa,* ed. Dawn Chatty (Leiden: Brill, 2006), 249.

60. *London Gazette,* Wednesday, February 18, 1767, Burney Collection, British Library.

61. *Lloyd's Evening Post,* March 20–23, 1767; *Public Advertiser,* Wednesday, January 6, 1768; *London Chronicle,* October 5, 1769–October 7, 1769, all from the Burney Collection, British Library.

62. The Public Record Office, consular correspondence FO 71/10, 353–489, National Archives of the United Kingdom, reports on these kinds of activities.

63. Mathieu Grenet, "Muslim Missions to Early Modern France, c. 1610-c.1780: Notes for a Social History of Cross-Cultural Diplomacy," *Journal of Early Modern History* 19, no. 2–3 (2015), 228–30.

64. Panzac, *Les corsaires,* 35. Calafat further emphasizes that the series of treaties made between European and North African regencies implicitly recognized the North African states as sovereign entities with a right of legation, and shaped diplomatic relations between Europe and North Africa right up to the colonial period. See Calafat, "Ottoman North Africa," 186.

65. Marsden, *Documents,* 2:316–18.

66. *London Evening Post,* September 10–12, 1767, Burney Collection, British Library.

67. As Panzac notes, protection payments were also an unpredictable form of revenue, since the European powers tended to make them upon the signing of a new treaty or with the arrival of a new consul, rather than on a regular annual basis. See Panzac, *Les corsaires,* 110–12, for estimates of the contributions of corsairing to state revenues.

68. C. R. Pennell, *Piracy and Diplomacy in Seventeenth-Century North Africa: The Journal of Thomas Baker, English Consul in Tripoli, 1677–1685* (Madison, NJ: Fairleigh Dickinson University Press, 1989), 51.

69. For a discussion of the shift in gendered discourse on Mediterranean pirates in this period, see Judith E. Tucker, "She Would Rather Perish: Piracy and Gendered Violence in the Mediterranean," *Journal of Middle East Women's Studies* 10, no. 3 (Fall 2014): 8–39.

70. This is not to suggest that piracy disappeared altogether from the Mediterranean. On the contrary, Leonidas Mylonakis makes a convincing case for the persistence and even occasional surges in piratical activity in the eastern Mediterranean in the nineteenth century. While piracy had lost its legal cover, harsh economic conditions could produce pirates in significant numbers intermittently over the course of the century. See Leonidas Mylonakis, "Transnational Piracy in the Eastern Mediterranean, 1821–1897" (PhD diss., University of California San Diego, 2018).

6

The Mediterranean in Saint-Simonian Imagination

The "Nuptial Bed"

Osama Abi-Mershed

In early 1832, Michel Chevalier (1806–79), Saint-Simonian doctrinaire, engineer, and political economist, authored a series of articles for his society's official broadsheet, *Le Globe: Journal de la religion saint-simonienne*. Labeled collectively as *Système de la Méditerranée*,[1] the articles introduced Chevalier's philosophical prescriptions for bridging the historical fault lines between Christendom and Islam in the Mediterranean basin. The future "peaceful association" between "Occident" and "Orient," he proclaimed, was to be cemented in the connectivities made newly possible by the industrial and scientific achievements of the young nineteenth century. More specifically, Chevalier professed his unshakable faith in the capacity of technological breakthroughs in the fields of mechanization and steam power—combined with recent innovations in infrastructural and telegraphic networks of communication—to multiply and enhance commercial and cultural interactions between the two shores of the internal sea. Transregional networks of finance and credit, railway and steamship routes, electromagnetic telegraph lines, and optical semaphore systems, among other inventions, Chevalier believed, would intensify economic cooperation and integration across the Mediterranean lands and transform the long-divided sea into "the nuptial bed," in which to reconcile Orient and Occident. Ultimately, Chevalier concluded that the Orient's deepening communion with European science, industry, commerce, and banking would bring about its intellectual reawakening and sociopolitical rejuvenation.

Today, Chevalier's *Système de la Méditerranée* is widely regarded as an emblematic Saint-Simonian scripture: utopian, if not naïve, in its political and strategic calculations, it is yet remarkably discerning and prescient in its attention to the transformative impact of industry and technology on socioeconomic structures and relations. True to the Saint-Simonian canon, Chevalier prophesied the reorganization of human society according to individual aptitude and merit, and extolled scientific and technological prowess as the main catalyst for the perfectibility of humankind, the elimination of class conflict, and the definitive resolution of international discords. Appropriately, his statements concerning the effects of technological modernization on economic integration and international cooperation have garnered much attention from political scientists and economists, who have detected in *Système de la Méditerranée* the earliest advocacy for securing peace in Europe through continental unification and, therefore, a far-sighted prediction of the rise in the 1950s of the European Economic Community. In the light of such analyses, Chevalier, and the Saint-Simonians more generally, appear as harbingers of the state-making "techno-politics" of the late nineteenth century, with their grandiose geospatial plans to modernize national infrastructures, urban centers, and human relations.[2]

Seen through the lens of political theory, *Système de la Méditerranée* reads indeed like a youthful speculative expression of the ambitious engineering schemes that were beginning to entertain the imaginary of French elites in the early nineteenth century.[3] It is important to note, however, that Chevalier's blueprint for modernizing the economic landscape of France was rooted in actual (and profitable) rationalities made possible by industrialism, capitalism, and the maturation of a national technocratic elite. By the time he drafted his articles for *Le Globe,* Chevalier was intimately familiar with the Becquey Plan of 1822, which launched the post-Napoleonic phase of "national-economic" infrastructural improvements.[4] In his duties as *Ingénieur du corps des mines* in 1829–30, he oversaw the implementation of partial elements of the plan in northern France.[5] Finally, as his subsequent writings demonstrate, Chevalier clearly understood that material improvements fell short of their stated purpose when restricted to the production apparatus of the state, or limited to feats of physical engineering and public works. As did his fellow Saint-Simonians, he recognized that the postrevolutionary state's mandatory preoccupation with public welfare implicated it in nationwide projects of moral edification, and necessarily projected its activities into domains heretofore under the purview of private or religious agencies. Such vital concerns invited government elites to reconfigure public institutions as facilities in which to forge the required political and socioeconomic solidarities of the "economy-nation." Not surprisingly, Chevalier earmarked specifically these sites and solidarities for penetration by Saint-Simonian know-how and ideals. *Système de la Méditerranée*—and many an article in *Le Globe,* for that matter—held as its most basic premise that, in order to realize the social and moral vision of Saint-Simon, the "will of the people" had to be reoriented away from individual pursuits and channeled toward activities that unified all social classes under the leadership of the nation's capable and forward-looking technocrats.

In this respect, the more engaging intellectual facet of *Système de la Méditerranée* is its acute sensitivity to how the industrial configuration of inhabited territorial spaces might bring about or consolidate a particular socio-moral order. To introduce and explain the "social engineering" scope of his vision, Chevalier eschewed conventional climatic, ecological, or geological definitions of the Mediterranean region, presenting it instead as a uniquely "socio-physiological" entity, sustained by the historical interplay between "living systems" (human cultures) and "scientific functions" (industrial applications). Stated more plainly, Chevalier regarded the future unity of the Mediterranean World as the inevitable outcome of intensifying circulation by capital, commodities, and ideas along "artificial" (constructed) regional axes of communication. With the help of modern modes and networks of transport, he expected the sociocultural priorities and routines of the economy-nation to radiate throughout the geographic surface of France, and beyond to the other civilizations bordering the Mediterranean Sea. To be sure, the Saint-Simonian genealogy and globalist dimension of *Système de la Méditerranée* cannot be ignored. Chevalier's initiatives aimed to return France to its former international economic and cultural primacy, peaceably and without brutality, as decreed by the principles of harmonious progress. By the same token, his prescriptions for trans-Mediterranean association invariably cast the "living systems" of the Orient as territorial markets and social laboratories for the "industrial functions" of the mother country.

Indeed, despite its unmistakable intellectual sophistication and ingenuity, *Système de la Méditerranée* remained firmly tethered to the philosophical orthodoxy of French Enlightenment thinking, especially in its representations of Oriental decay and lethargy, its confidence in the curative benefits of rational sciences and modern technologies, and its emphasis on the moral duty of France's savants and engineers to harness the powers of nature in the service of humanity. In practical terms, such ideological contours imposed a utilitarian logic on the Saint-Simonian ideal of association, whereby French norms and experiences served as standards for gauging the merits of foreign cultures and societies. In the end, for all its professed pacifism and antimilitarism, *Système de la Méditerranée* still offered compelling arguments for an expansive "civilizing mission" under the dual stimulus of French industrialism and state-run programs of modernization. Few studies of Chevalier's texts—or of the entire Saint-Simonian anthology to this effect—have noted the colonialist essence of their premises and their propensity to validate imperial civilizational designs.[6]

THE LEARNED PRIESTHOOD

The Saint-Simonian movement developed in France as an elitist doctrinal response to the violent revolutionary upheavals of the late eighteenth century. The political volatility that followed the fierce destruction of the traditional order (ancien régime) in 1789 set the stage for a protracted struggle among brokers competing to dominate the postrevolutionary polity and devise new social contracts with which to reinstate stability and prosperity. The impressive concentration of powers in the hands of Napoleon Bonaparte (1769–1821) after the Eighteenth Brumaire spelled a return to social and political security but at the expense of many constitutional rights and liberties that had been gained since 1789. Thus, in its initial impulse, Saint-Simonian political philosophy aimed to carve out a middle ground between the belligerent authoritarian administration of Napoleon I and the unpredictability of government by and for the people. Saint-Simonian commitments to the libertarian and meritocratic legacies of 1789 were always mitigated by the movement's manifest hostility toward democratic populism, and were stamped with its pronounced and often-voiced aversion to the first hint of social turmoil.[7]

In his first pamphlet, *Letters from an Inhabitant of Geneva to His Contemporaries,* published in 1802, the founder of the movement, Claude-Henri de Saint-Simon (1760–1825), outlined his program for mollifying postrevolutionary conflicts of interest with a more legitimate and conciliatory sociopolitical hierarchy dominated by individuals who were distinguished by their *industry.* He used this term to designate any productive activity—"theoretical and practical, intellectual as well as manual"—that prioritized the social emancipation and organic unity of humankind.[8] The society of the future, Saint-Simon claimed, was to be nourished with principles of productivity and cooperation and governed by a "learned priesthood" (*clergé de savants*) comprising the nation's leading industrialists, financiers, scholars, and artists. In contrast to the old propertied nobles and ruling aristocrats, who had idled by on the backs of the lowborn, the Saint-Simonian priesthood toiled for the rational and harmonious reorganization of its nation, as well as for a new "secular association" between its distinct social classes. Saint-Simon thus presaged the end of class struggles in the coming Industrial Age, and the subsequent emergence of a modern society, differentiated yet united by the productive associations among its different strata: "All privileges of birth, without exception, shall be abolished: To each according to one's capacity; to each capacity according to its labor." In time, Saint-Simon's dictum caught on as the society's motto, and Socialist and Communist unions later adopted versions of it as their spirited battle cry.

Social tensions, for Saint-Simon, resulted from pairing individuals with vocations that did not square with their intellectual or moral aptitudes. The revolution had compounded social dysfunction when it imposed an idealized equality on unequal individuals. He pointed to France's recent history of "horrifying atrocities that ensued naturally from the application of the principle of equality, which amounts to placing power in the hands of ignorami."[9] Consequently, by valorizing the native and acquired differences between people, the industrial society of the future would complete the true promise of 1789 and dispose, finally, of the lingering discordant institutions of the ancien régime:

> We exaggerate when we declare that the French Revolution destroyed ecclesiastical and feudal power completely. It did not do away with them; it merely diminished confidence in their basic principles to the extent that today they no longer retain sufficient strength and credibility to bind society together. What [alternative] ideas can provide this [missing] vital and organic binding force? It is to industrial ideas, and to them alone, that we should look for our salvation and the end of the revolution.[10]

In April 1825, as Saint-Simon lay on his deathbed, his disciples gathered to publish his fragmentary dissertation on the core articles of the society's creed. Published under the title *Le nouveau christianisme,* Saint-Simon's posthumous pamphlet is considered the definitive enunciation of the "natural faith" he intended for the industrial society of the future.[11] Its hurried composition was motivated in part by the accession of ultraroyalist Charles X (r. 1824–30) to the Bourbon throne. The restored king's reactionary measures to resurrect the rites and institutions of the ancien régime, and reinculcate nationwide dedication to the traditions of inherited or spiritual authority, awakened Saint-Simon's determination to spare his countrymen renewed rounds of class warfare.[12] While critical of the monarchy's efforts to roll back or sanitize republican institutions, the author also seized the opportunity to remind his readers of the dangers of a politicized social underclass. To avert this scenario, Saint-Simon proposed raising the new Christian temple on the material and spiritual solidarities forged in the crucible of industrialism. Such associations, Saint-Simon asserted, would shield "the wealthy and the governments" from acts of violence perpetrated by the poorer classes, while simultaneously inhibiting the propensity of industrial leaders to disenfranchise their workers. As an organic entity that transcended its individual members, industrial society was subject to its own laws and freed from the tyranny of generic individuals seeking to satisfy their senses. Rather, all members labored interdependently toward a collective rational ideal, creating in the process mutual and synergistic associations between classes. The proletariat was uplifted through its contacts with the unified elites, while the industrial commitments of the latter prevented them from regressing to the idle or predatory tendencies of the old aristocracy. "The new Christian organization," Saint-Simon explained, "will develop temporal as well as spiritual institutions from the one principle that all men should act as brothers toward one another."[13]

Saint-Simon expected his universalist faith to transcend the idiosyncratic convictions and beliefs of old, thus cementing human interactions with the new rational and spiritual associations of the Industrial Age.[14] It was not long, however, before events in North Africa and the Levant afforded his disciples the occasion to extrapolate his views on the proletarian classes and apply them to the "lesser" peoples of the Mediterranean World. In October 1827, the French navy triumphed decisively in two engagements against Muslim adversaries: the first, in support of the military blockade of the Ottoman Regency of Algiers (October 4–5); and the second to sink the Ottoman-Egyptian fleet in Navarino Bay (October 20). These international developments led several Saint-Simonians to ponder the viability of nonviolent association with Arabs and Turks. If, as Saint-Simon had professed, the lower classes of French society were perfectible through their "association" with the industrial elite, then so too were subordinate races or nationalities redeemed through contact with technologically advanced cultures. Already in *De la réorganisation de la société européenne,* co-authored in 1814 with his "student" Augustin Thierry (1795–1856), Saint-Simon had augmented the historical mission of Europe's industrial vanguard to include a humanist interest in "advancing the well-being of all peoples" and "emancipat[ing] all nations subject to absolute monarchy . . . , without wars, without disasters, without political revolutions."[15]

Saint-Simon's model for civilizational development—deeply indebted to Condorcet's notion of the "indefinite perfectibility of the human mind,"[16] and later reworked by Auguste Comte (1798–1857) as the Law of the Three Estates (*loi des trois états*)[17]—catalogued societies according to three linear stages of progress, each representing a distinct succession in intellectual and industrial maturity. Human thought, according to this historical diagram, had proceeded at unequal pace through theological, metaphysical, and scientific (positive) phases. Europe began to part ways with the Orient, when it renounced metaphysical speculation in the seventeenth century, and positivism came to govern its abstract sciences by the late eighteenth. Similarly, as he makes repeatedly clear in *Système de la Méditerranée,* Chevalier understood the advancement of Oriental societies in terms of their deliverance from the archaic certainties of the theological and metaphysical eras. Echoing the prevailing civilizational paradigm of the time, he and other Saint-Simonians professed that the cumulative progress of humankind stipulated the thorough modernization of primitive organizations and idiosyncratic mentalities through their association with the best-equipped European polity: "All physical circumstances being equal, the best organized species or race civilizes itself first, and henceforth decrees the development of inferior races and species until general association is understood and accepted by all."[18]

Saint-Simon's writings had an especially pronounced impact on the mindset of young Frenchmen, reared on imperial nostalgia and sensitized to the homeland's precipitous fall from the ranks of the powerful in 1815. His visionary theories for national rejuvenation appealed especially to the students enlisted in the premier academies of the state, notably, the School of Bridges and Roadways (École des Ponts et Chaussées, founded in 1747), School of Engineering (École du Génie, 1748), School of Mines (École des Mines, 1783), and Polytechnical School (École Polytechnique, 1794). Confident in their superior erudition and faculty, yet starved of appropriate opportunities for social mobility by the conformist Bourbon regime, the cadets of the celebrated *grandes écoles* heard Saint-Simon speak directly about their frustrated destiny with patriotic greatness.

Saint-Simon's personal connection to the elites of the academic world was made through his acquaintance with the founding fathers of École Polytechnique, Antoine de Fourcroy (1755–1809) and Gaspard Monge (1746–1818), the latter a veteran of the Napoleonic expedition to Egypt and former director of the Institut d'Égypte. Saint-Simon's fascination with the rarefied atmosphere of the school was such that, in 1798, he relocated to an apartment opposite its walls in order to mingle more readily with its polytechniciens faculty and students and rekindle his own scientific edification. Holding court in his philosophical salon, Saint-Simon captivated his gifted and restive guests with predictions of a dawning society of industrialism and science, seducing them with accounts of their pride of place in cementing the corporate interest and welfare of the nation. Over the course of the 1820s, Saint-Simon's academic standing grew exponentially as his political theories were taken up by eminent polytechniciens, talented men of letters and science, and financial luminaries, such as Jean-Baptiste Biot (1774–1862), Edme-François Jomard (1777–1862), François Arago (1786–1853), Augustin Fresnel (1788–1827), Augustin Thierry, Prosper Enfantin (1796–1864), Auguste Comte, Hippolyte Carnot (1801–88), and Michel Chevalier, the foremost exponent of the Saint-Simonian movement's Mediterranean dream.

Chevalier was attending the Polytechnical School (1823–25) as the doctrine began to dominate the political conversations of faculty and students.[19] He participated in the colleges of Saint-Simonian friends, who debated ways to amplify their message through academic and journalistic channels. After the master's untimely disappearance in May 1825, polytechniciens and liberal opponents of the reactionary monarchy rallied around Prosper Enfantin and Saint-Amand Bazard (1791–1832), the charismatic, self-styled "supreme fathers" of the Saint-Simonian Society. Enfantin and Bazard soon founded the biweekly periodical, *Le Producteur: Journal philosophique de l'industrie, des sciences et des beaux-arts* (1825–26), in order to distill the "prophetic passions and theories" of Saint-Simon and publicize his ideas through the important filiations of the Polytechnique: "It is the milk that we have suckled at our dear École that must nourish the generations to come," Enfantin admitted to Bazard in 1827.[20]

Le Producteur militated for supplanting the archaic and venal hierarchies of Restoration France with a new politic based on scientific and technical competence. In August 1829, the new periodical *L'Organisateur: Journal des progrès de la science générale* (1829–31) picked up the banner from its defunct precursor and prolonged its appeals to the government to invest the young technicians and engineers of the *grandes écoles* with the mission to serve the public weal, modernize the economic infrastructures and institutions of the land, and lift the nation from its deepening stagnation.[21] Like many of his polytechniciens peers, Chevalier saw his personal vexations brought to public light in the editorials of *Le Producteur* and *L'Organisateur.* By the time he graduated from École des Mines in 1829, to assume his post as *Ingénieur du corps des mines,* he was firmly convinced that his art was key to France's regeneration. Accordingly, during his time at the helm of *Le Globe,* he redacted stentorian articles by Enfantin, Comte, and Bazard that equated social renewal with the political empowerment of France's men of learning, and for the remainder of his life, he kept faith in the capacity of public applications of science to uplift the condition of his countrymen and pacify international relations.[22]

Chevalier's Saint-Simonian commitments intensified in the weeks after the traumatic events of July 28–30, 1830. He resigned his post to join the society formally and was serving as editing director of *Le Globe* by January 1831. He sharpened the paper's focus on questions of political economy and industrial growth and authored articles that advocated for largesse in spending on manufacturing and public works, arguing that these sectors provided the most fruitful investment of government funds in the social capital of the nation. He also appealed to private entrepreneurs by foretelling the massive profits to be made in harnessing the energies of mechanization, especially in the technologies and infrastructures of transportation. However, the paper's continued denunciations of the nation's antiquated institutions and mores incurred civic outcry and legal injunctions against Enfantin's circle. In April 1832, the authorities seized the assets and premises of *Le Globe* and, in August, sentenced the Enfantinistes to prison terms of up to one year.[23] Upon their release from Sainte-Pélagie Prison, the surviving supreme father and some followers set their sights upon more welcoming lands, namely, Egypt and the Ottoman Empire. The ongoing reforms of the "industrial pasha" Mehmet Ali of Egypt suggested to Enfantin that association with French technology and learning had prompted even "a barbarous despot . . . [to] improvise suddenly and in the midst of ruins, the marvels of modern civilization."[24] There, with the patronage of local reform-minded potentates like Mehmet Ali, the Enfantinistes hoped to cut their teeth on grand modernizing projects of infrastructure, industry, and public education before returning home fully vindicated by their Oriental triumph.

Chevalier, on the other hand, was dispatched in October 1833, by then-minister of the interior Adolphe Thiers, to report on the state of industrial development in the United States and Mexico. Chevalier found in the "industrial autocracy" of the United States partial embodiment of the original Saint-Simonian vision: "the absence of hereditary nobility and customs; women who enjoyed the respect of men; . . . labor as the primary [economic] engine; employment, the universal rule."[25] At the same time, he perceived in America's "hive-like laborious activity" and "prodigious spirit" an "[industrial] development that threatened to overwhelm Europe." Upon his return to Paris in November 1835, Chevalier was appointed State Counselor (*maître des requêtes*) and tasked with drafting a report on his American journey. The resulting study, *Des intérêts matériels en France* (1837), would solidify his credentials as France's foremost advocate of economic liberalism and free trade.[26] More importantly, his American experience had further substantiated his belief in

FIGURE 9. Émile Barrault, Michel Chevalier, and Charles Duveyrier during the trial of the Enfantinistes, Paris, August 27–28, 1832. Courtesy of Bibliothèque nationale de France.

the potential of mechanization (*machines motrices*) to revolutionize the circulation of labor, credit, and commodities. Steam engines and railways, for Chevalier, augured the concentration of disparate commercial and financial networks, the reinvigoration of infrastructural improvements on the national scale, and the redistribution of rents and wealth along new private and public circuits.[27]

In 1838, Chevalier was rewarded for his service to the nation with the Legion of Honor and appointed counselor of state in extraordinary service. In 1841, he was named chair in political economy at Collège de France, and four years later he was elected to public office as deputy of Aveyron. However, his meteoric professional rise was interrupted by the outbreak of the Revolutions of 1848, when he joined the opposition to the government and authored dissenting opinion pieces in the critical *Journal des débats*. The government retaliated by unseating him from his post at Collège de France and revoking his title of *Ingénieur en chef des mines*.

Chevalier returned to political activism in December 1851, when he spoke in support of the coup d'état of (the Saint-Simonian) Louis-Napoleon Bonaparte (later, Emperor Napoleon III). Louis-Napoleon (1808–73) was especially captivated by Chevalier, with whom he shared the experience of persecution and imprisonment for political opinions. The emperor restored Chevalier to the post of counselor of state in extraordinary service and, in time, came to consider him among his most reliable economic advisors. He entrusted him with drafting a study of the benefits of free trade to counter the antagonism of local industrialists and their parliamentary lobby. In the course of the 1850s, Chevalier joined forces with notable Saint-Simonians, such as the Lyonnais industrialist and railway pioneer François Barthélemy Arlès-Dufour (1797–1872), to negotiate, along with the British liberal statesmen Richard Cobden (1804–65) and John Bright (1811–1889), the seminal Anglo-French Free Trade Agreement of 1860, known as the Cobden-Chevalier Treaty (January 23). In the same year, he was elected senator, only to withdraw from public life and resume his teaching at Collège de France after the fall of the Second Empire in 1870. In the last decade of his life, Chevalier explored the prospects for building a tunnel across the English Channel and founded a research firm to develop its engineering plan.[28] The firm was granted a government concession in 1880, mere months after Chevalier's death. Without his leadership, the initial excavations for the Channel tunnel near the commune of Sangatte were soon abandoned.[29]

In light of his extraordinary career, Chevalier is an appropriate figure by which to assess Edmund Burke's description of the Mediterranean World as "the first recipient of the nineteenth century liberal reform project in its political and economic forms, [and] a good site from which to begin the process of rethinking European modernities (in the plural)."[30] Indeed, in his brief time directing *Le Globe,* Chevalier outlined a thoroughly modern rendering of a Mediterranean World unified by the linkages between technological innovation and sociopolitical development. Written at a time when learned and public opinion was largely dismissive of the value of railways, *Système de la Méditerranée* is an unconventional and visionary analysis of the "complex set of relations" between scientific methods, social theory, and imperial designs, which combined to produce new understandings of state power, socioeconomic relations, and spatial organization. With professional experiences straddling, and in fact joining, the realms of governance, academia, and economics, Chevalier seemed to presage the emergence of a new form of statecraft, in which the exercise of sovereign power over populations and territories grew increasingly reliant on the authority of technocratic know-how and expertise.

SYSTÈME DE LA MÉDITERRANÉE

Schematically, Chevalier's Mediterranean system is a living organism. Like any physiological entity, it comprises various subsystems, joined in a complex network of organs of varying scale that work together to execute distinct vital functions. The larger organism or body system in this case is humankind, while the subsystems are, in the words of Chevalier, Europe's "most natural zones of industry," the landscapes of which have been deeply configured by the historical development of manufacturing activities.[31] Each zone of industry performs a specific productive function and is integrated into the corporal system by networks of communication and credit that facilitate large-scale traffic in products, capital, and laborers. For this reason, zones of industry are generally situated in large river basins and are connected to maritime outlets and port cities. In Chevalier's imagery, port cities are the pulsating heart in the international circulation of men and merchandise, and their movements over roads, canals, waterways, and, increasingly, telegraph and railway lines, act like the system's "blood veins and arteries carrying the flow of a rousing civilization."[32] Thus, the general system is complete when Europe's disparate, partial hubs of industry are linked together by a constructed grid of railway lines, waterways, and trunk routes. And in his articles Chevalier urges the governments of Europe to invest in the emerging technologies, especially steam-powered engines and electromagnetic telegraph cables, to link the continent's various zones of industry, and thus bring about the integrated Mediterranean system.

Recent scientific advances, Chevalier argued, were poised to overhaul the material conditions of human existence. In his periodization of the history of France, his country's modernity commenced with industrial mechanization in the 1780s, following the transformative invention of the steam engine and discovery of electromagnetic currents. Specifically, the improvements made to the original Newcomen steam engine by James Watt (1736–1819) and Claude de Jouffroy (1751–1832) promised to revolutionize communication across territories and seas, respectively.[33] Innovations in interconnected technologies accelerated in subsequent decades. In 1794, John Fitch (1743–98) unveiled the first working model of a steam-rail locomotive, and, in 1804, an engine designed by Richard Trevithick (1771–1833) hauled the first train and inaugurated the development of railway networks. Similarly, semaphore telegraphs, first conceived by Claude Chappe (1763–1805) in 1802, were greatly perfected in 1820–21, with the invention of the galvanometer and the discovery of electromagnetic fields.[34] Throughout *Système de la Méditerranée,* Chevalier predicts future progress in these scientific fields, and underlines the exponential impact of such inventions on the productivity and prosperity of European industry, manufacturing, mineral exploitation, infrastructure, and agriculture.[35]

However, in Saint-Simonian fashion, Chevalier also insisted on highlighting the "political and moral" dimensions of this industrial revolution, for while transport and telegraph lines may establish physical links between the partial systems, he suggested an equally significant "spiritual" corollary to growing contacts between human societies.[36] Steam engines were not be appreciated for their technical wizardry alone, nor valued merely for their economic utility, for such perspectives overlook the capacity of rail transport, by its sheer velocity, to multiply contacts between regions and mediate between the material progress and moral improvement of human communities. Railways, for Chevalier, were the very embodiment of the technological spirit of the positive age, and "the most perfect" vehicle for universal association, which he claimed, "is only possible between peoples who can materially pour into one another, and really live the lives of each other."[37] With average speeds approaching the "prodigious" rate of forty kilometers per hour in 1832,[38] the new locomotives were bound to hasten the integration of Europe's various industrial hubs and renew their societies in definitive ways. "Railways," he predicted, "will transform the conditions of human existence":

> The introduction, on a grand scale, of railways on the continents, and steamboats on the seas, will constitute an industrial, as well as a political, revolution. By their means, and with the help of other modern discoveries like the telegraph, it will become easy to govern the major part of the continents that border the Mediterranean with the same unity, the same instantaneity, that exist today in France.[39]

By connecting the factory to its labor markets, the city to its countryside, the region to its hinterlands, the nation to its neighbors, and the European "self" to its Oriental "other," railway lines would reorganize the Mediterranean space to suit the economic and political imperatives of industrialism and forge new transnational associations on the basis of mutual interests, common legal codes, and shared circuits of rent and wealth production.

The graph (fig. 10) calculates the aggregate volume of merchandise by mode of transport in France between 1820 and 1880.[40] The statistics report proportional volumes over four modes of transport: roadways (practicable pavements over land and bridges), waterways (navigable rivers and canals), railways (steam-powered carriages only), and cabotage (shipping along coastal routes, usually port to port). The trendlines bolster the accuracy of Chevalier's predictions and illustrate the exponential increase in the volume of goods circulating by rail from a share of 3 percent in 1832, as he composed *Système de la Méditerranée,* to 63 percent in 1879, the year of his death. The graph also reveals the negative impact of railways on competing modes of transport, the commercial volumes of which declined noticeably after 1850. The most precipitous effect was felt in transportation over roadways, where the proportional rate of ferried merchandise dropped from 55 percent of total volume in 1820 to 18 percent in 1880. Likewise, the improving trend for merchandise transported over riverways and canals after 1830 was suddenly reversed, declining from a share of 27 percent to 13 percent by 1880. The expansion of merchandise traffic by rail continued unabated until the mass production of the automobile and the completion of high-speed roadway systems after 1945.

In practical terms, Chevalier divided the spiritual and moral transformation of the Mediterranean into two programs of action. The first aims to achieve the political federation of European states through industrial connectivity, with nothing less than perpetual peace as the main dividend to be gained from the industrial integration of Europe. Indeed, *Système de la Méditerranée* delivers a sustained and adamant antiwar message, as its author notes repeatedly that economic invest-

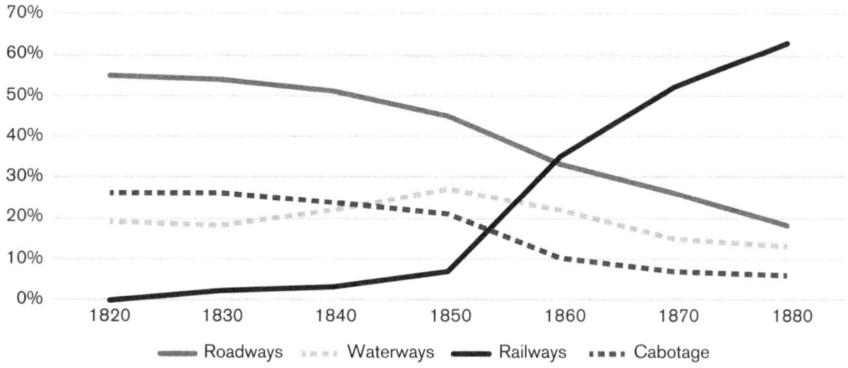

FIGURE 10. Graph showing merchandise by mode of transport in France, 1820–80. From Didier Rouchaud and Alain Sauvant, "Volume et partage modal du transport de marchandises en France de 1845 à nos jours" (Paris: Commissariat Général au Développement Durable, May 2011).

ments in industry, credit, and communication will enhance international cooperation and moderate the political temperament of European states:

> Industry is eminently pacific. It instinctively rejects war. What creates cannot reconcile with what kills. At the first sound of the drums of war, credit will be suspended; a declaration of war would annihilate it. But eliminate credit, and only ruin and misery will rain upon this immense army of industrialists, who fifty years ago came out of this earth to inseminate and embellish it. . . . Thereafter, war becomes the destruction of one of the branches of civilization; war becomes degeneration; war, instead of emancipating populations, would turn them into herds of starving proletarians. . . . It would mean the reconstitution of feudalism.[41]

Moreover, peace in Europe is expressly desirable for France which, by the revolutionary passions of its people, had been led down the via dolorosa of nations:

> And what? Is it not enough that generous France has suffered on its own the cataclysm of a terrible revolution? Is it not enough that it received the baptism of fire, and plunged itself audaciously in the ensuing bloodbath? Why, dear God, should not its merits and its accomplishments be for the benefit of all humanity? France drank the revolutionary chalice, it swallowed it in one swig; France climbed upon the cross; France has been the Christ of nations. It purchased the world's peace and progress with its treasures, its sorrows, and the lives of its sons strewn upon every battlefield.[42]

Clearly, Chevalier was not disavowing his country's revolutionary credentials but, rather, criticizing the lingering notion that the principles of 1789 could propagate across Europe only in the wake of marching armies.[43] The Revolutionary and Napoleonic Wars had shown the futility in trying to change the nature of a people by defeating and occupying it. Railways and telegraph lines were the new vectors for the peaceful enlightenment and emancipation of human societies, and, among all nations, France, the historical custodian of the ideals of liberty, equality, and freedom, was best suited to serve as "pacifier of the world." In conformity with the Saint-Simonian "law of the three estates," Chevalier asserted his nation's historical entitlement, even obligation, to extend its hand to all peoples and invite them to join the parade (*carrière*) of civilized nations:

> The pacifier will welcome all: to all—peoples, classes, and individuals—he will assign, according to their [particular] vocation, a distinct place, a distinct assignment in the common *œuvre*. . . . He will make grow every individuality—race, people, class or man—according to its proper laws, by teaching it to rely on all and to help all, by connecting it to all. Through [the pacifier], the entire world, led in procession through the pomp of industry, the brilliance of science, [and] the pleasures of the arts, will gravitate towards universal association.
>
> I say "the entire world" because it is not a question of including in our most immediate plans for pacification only the peoples who were once part of the European Catholic collective. It is not only the members of this outdated (*ci-devant*) Christianity that we propose to reconcile and associate.[44]

In other words, any prospect for perpetual peace lacked practicality so long as it did not rest on the association of Orient and Occident. Indeed, the lion's share of *Système de la Méditerranée* is devoted to extolling the rewards to be reaped from reconciling two civilizations that had been in conflict for thirty centuries: from the Trojan War to the recent naval engagement at Navarino. For Chevalier, the millennial war between Islam and Christianity, with the Mediterranean as its main battleground, was the most devastating, the "most colossal, the most sweeping, and the most deeply-rooted."[45] In comparison, European conflicts were internecine squabbles, mere conjugal tussles.

Thus, the second movement in the *Système de la Méditerranée* orchestrates the material and spiritual union of cross and crescent, first, through the usual medium of railways, steamships, and telegraph cables, and then by reawakening and reassigning the productive capacities of the Orient. In the words of Chevalier, the consummation of this "intimate communion" between the divided peoples of the Mediterranean "will be the first step towards UNIVERSAL ASSOCIATION,"[46] and he offers three justifications for his proposed *Pax Mediterranea*.

In the first instance, Chevalier explains to his readers that the clash between Orient and Occident is not a religious contest. It is the result rather of the "conflicting dualism" between spirit and matter. When the Arabs turned away from rationalism and science, they inhibited their technical and material development. Their ensuing overcommitment to spirituality retarded their historical progress. The Orient as a whole fell into a profound, unworldly torpor; its ruling classes became complacent; and its peoples became downtrodden.[47] The representation of the conflict between Orient and Occident as the manifestation of disequilibrium between spirit and matter was an article of faith for the followers of Enfantin, supreme father of the Saint-Simonian sect and Chevalier's mentor. For Enfantin, the hallmark of the age of industry was, in effect, its resolution of all opposing dichotomies: "The law is the unceasing progress of harmony between flesh and spirit, between industry and science, between Orient and Occident, between woman and man."[48]

Similarly, Chevalier assures his readers that the historical discrepancies between Orient and Occident were temporary and bound to melt away in the heat of trans-Mediterranean communion. The hyphen—or in this case the more appropriate French term *trait d'union*—in trans-Mediterranean association will be provided by the deepening intercourse across the body of water:

> The Mediterranean has been forever crisscrossed by enemy fleets. The Mediterranean has been an arena, a combat zone where, for thirty centuries, the Orient and the Occident waged war against each other. Henceforth, the Mediterranean must be like a vast forum, on all points of which hitherto divided peoples will commune. The Mediterranean will become the nuptial bed of the Orient and the Occident.[49]

Appropriately, Chevalier's second rationale is that the current cultural differences between Orient and Occident were necessary for the mutual regeneration of each. The Saint-Simonian notion of universal association, it bears repeating, is predicated on the coexistence of asynchronic civilizations and is made possible, in effect, by the unique capacity of Europe's modernity to harness developmentally and morally dissimilar societies to the march of its own totalizing historical progress. Indeed, for Chevalier, the only heresy was "the immobile fanaticism of the Muslims."[50] Consequently, he embraced the "otherness" of the Orient to the extent that it conformed to industry's need for essentialized aptitudes, as summarized in the Saint-Simonian motto, "To each according to one's capacity":

> A project founded on the annihilation, the expulsion, the extermination or the ruin of certain peoples or certain classes within each population, is a backwards plan. . . . Every people, every class has its own genius, its particular destiny. The humanitarian task is at once one and multiple. All peoples are members of humanity, and humanity will not be happy until all its members are free, until every people occupies in the workshop, in the laboratory, in the temple, the place that nature assigns it.[51]

As mentioned earlier, a recurring feature in *Système de la Méditerranée* is Chevalier's juxtaposition of discerning premonitions with unaffected utopian simplicity. Its proponent is surely far-sighted in recognizing the capability of rapid and regular circulation by capital, machines, and men to anchor disparate regions in shared political-economic interests and unifying codes and customs. He is also accurate in regarding urban networks as vital in modulating regional economic and cultural development. Yet he displays little appreciation for the potential asymmetries within his proposed trans-Mediterranean structures and offers no arguments against the likelihood that the increase in wealth, opportunity, and social mobility should dramatically favor the lands of the European rim. In the end, it may be argued that *Système de la Méditerranée* is but a refashioned, if pacifist, rationalization for Europe's ancient objective of extending its political and cultural reach into the dominions of Islam, and securing it with economic clout.

Indeed, Chevalier's advocacy for peaceful association is squarely situated within what Henry Laurens has labeled the "geopolitics of the Enlightenment," or the set of ideological parameters that had delineated French dispositions and policies toward the Orient since the mid-eighteenth century.[52] These parameters, initially folkloric and construed from France's lengthy commercial presence in Muslim Mediterranean lands, were progressively formalized after 1750, to gratify the internal necessities of the Enlightenment movement. Factual or intelligible observations about the Orient were increasingly laced with normative historico-philosophical reflections to produce instrumentalized Eurocentric narratives. It is in light of Europe's orientalist myths that one must take full stock of *Système de la Méditerranée.*

GEOPOLITICS OF THE ENLIGHTENMENT

In the 1750s, the philosophers and chroniclers of the French Enlightenment began to advance a civilizational notion and history of "reason" as a means to explain Europe's newfound advantages over "despotic" oriental societies. According to the narrative, the Arabs by the twelfth century had largely disavowed reason, which they had inherited from the Greco-Romans, but not before it had migrated through Latin translations to Renaissance Europe, where it found its amplest, most perfect expression. The contemporaneous Arab world was perceived as a distorted image of its previous self; a land of monstrosities unleashed by the "sleep of reason."[53] Europe, however, was indebted to the Arabs for their continuation of Greco-Roman Reason, and according to some imperial imaginings, France's destiny in the Mediterranean was to restore ancient grandeur to the region by repatriating reason to its birthplace (Egypt) and the larger Orient, where Muslim custodians had once elevated it to most august summits.

Such imperial ruminations certainly found traction in the geopolitical context of the time, especially as France's global stature eroded significantly after its defeats in the Seven Years Wars (1756–63). Its mercantile position in the Levant continued to decline through the 1770s, as the Ottoman economy weakened and rivals Britain and Russia made important regional inroads.[54] State counselors advised their king to reinforce commercial interests in the Orient with material and cultural commitments. Finally, with the Revolution of 1789, the nation's universal imperatives became more insistent still, and as illustrated by *Système de la Méditerranée,* the pages of orientalist narratives grew thick with images of a decomposing

Ottoman body and an archaic Islamic civilization, nostalgic for its past glories and awaiting release from its current depredations:

> I turn [my attention] now to Turkish Asia, to this poetic land traversed by so many famous peoples, and whose earth is layered with the debris of so many great empires. It is there that the imagination of our fathers situated earthly paradise with its infinite delights. . . . It is there [that] the caliphs, successors to Muhammad, cultivated the sciences and the arts. . . . And all this is no more. Of all these thrones and all these dynasties there remains but dust, and this dust has not fertilized the soil. . . . Today, cities are scattered, populations are rare; the Euphrates and Tigris flow amidst ruins and uncultivated fields.[55]

The geopolitical parameters of the Enlightenment were decisive in mobilizing Napoleon's expedition to the Orient in 1798. The military-scientific conquest of Egypt was an unprecedented venture, singular in its conflation of imperial and civilizational ambitions.[56] Besides undermining Britain's position in the eastern Mediterranean, the objective of the Oriental campaign was to liberate Egyptians from the "tyranny of the Mamluks."[57] To this end, Napoleon endorsed the use of military force to disseminate the achievements of 1789 to Arab societies and thus reawaken their political and cultural interests. The scholars, scientists, and artists attached to the expeditionary corps embodied the synthesis of humanism and militarism in France's emerging mission to civilize, and continued to inspire Chevalier's peers in the post-Napoleonic age.

The notion of the universal civilizing mission was arguably the sole Napoleonic legacy to be adopted with less-than-usual trepidation by the resurrected Bourbon monarchy, which was struggling to contend with the residual populist politics of the revolution and the ascendance of British influence in the Mediterranean. In the 1820s, the economic and strategic importance of the broad area encompassing the sea swelled as Ottoman control waned, and the warships and trading vessels of the English, Dutch, and Americans—Protestant powers, all—began to arrive in force. The Mediterranean, moreover, remained the arena where France could safely resurrect the former Napoleonic project. While "empire" was unequivocally banished at home and in Europe, the French monarchy was able to pursue military glory on the fringes of the sea: in Spain (1823), Greece (1826–27), and North Africa (1827–29). Likewise, scholars and cadets in the *grandes écoles* had reason to revel in the legacies of their revolutionary and Napoleonic forefathers.[58] Many among them, Saint-Simonians primarily, looked for opportunities to revisit the nation's former glories without risking war or invasion. Technological advances, capital accumulation, and modern communications made available new prospects for "moral" conquests. Accordingly, Chevalier remained adamant that his nation's meritocratic revolution was best served through scientific and cultural partnerships, rather than futile military feats: "Had it been possible to *be done* with the feudal forces [of Europe] by means of war, then the giant of battles, Napoleon, *would have been done* with them. . . . This is why wars today are without purpose and must not occur."[59]

Yet, Chevalier also makes clear that his "Orient" is territorially indispensable to the realization of France's industrial ambitions. Industrial growth and financial prosperity at home demanded the material improvement (*mise en valeur*) of Oriental lands and resources. This trans-Mediterranean equation bound France and the Orient in a logic of mutual development: association with the Orient could unfold only in tandem with the making of the post-1830 industrial regime. The same technological and scientific capabilities that had enabled the conquest of the national space provided Chevalier with the rationale for the territorial administration of the Orient, which became a reality with the French invasion of the Ottoman Regency of Algiers in July 1830. For this reason, one may look upon *Système de la méditerranée* as a document connecting, at one end of the spectrum, with the revolutionary and humanitarian impulses of 1798, and, at the other end, with explicit colonial practices in French Algeria after 1830. In this regard, Chevalier's utter silence throughout *Système de la méditerranée* on the military action of July 1830, despite its imperial connotations, is perhaps more telling than peculiar.

The invasion of Ottoman North Africa in 1830 reverberated with echoes from the Napoleonic mission to Egypt in 1798. Algiers evoked memories of Alexandria or Cairo, and of a young general exhorting his soldiers to realize the nation's manifest destiny in the shadow of the pyramids. Similarly, the commanders of the Army of Africa hoped to replicate the military and scientific feats of their Napoleonic forebears and galvanize their troops with summons to return civilization and enlightenment to the darkened recesses of Africa. Colonial officials took up posts in Algiers to resume the "crusade against Oriental futility" and spearhead the dissemination of Europe's cultural and intellectual standards to local Arabs and Kabyles. The events of the summer of 1830 prompted a critical discussion among the Saint-Simonians concerning the rightfulness of the invasion. The group opted eventually to excuse France's return to military adventurism by seeing in the "improvident conquest" the opportunity to vindicate the teachings of Saint-Simon:

> If we could make Algeria the testing grounds (*lieu d'essai*) for [the Saint-Simonian] organization; if we could carry out such invaluable innovation in this country where all remains to be done, and realize it far from the obstacles that would be raised to it in France by the archaic laws of our old society or the exaggerated pretenses of our youthful dreams for the future, what acts of grace would we not owe God for this happy outcome to our improvident conquest![60]

Moribund, aimless France was to be revived in its association with Algeria, and the breach of peace was justified by the upcoming economic and moral improvement of the conquered. From the coupling of spirit (Orient/Algeria) and matter (Occident/France), a modern society would spring forth: technological and industrial in its economic enterprises and peaceful and spiritual in its sociopolitical relations.

In 1839, Enfantin, the supreme father, sailed to Algiers to join the commission for scientific exploration. There, he relied on a supporting cast of Saint-Simonian admirers, superimposed on a larger partisan community of polytechnicien officers and public servants, to channel the essence of the doctrine to the inner sanctum of colonial decision making. For Enfantin, the colonization of Algeria was the obverse facet to the modernization of France, and, in his reports, he called for invigorating the local economy with extensive capital investments in communications, industrial infrastructures, and agriculture. Accordingly, in *Colonisation de l'Algérie,* compiled and edited in 1843, he clarified his blueprint for the experimental development and modernization of the colony by demarcating and juxtaposing two domains of primary economic interests that worked in conjunction, with each suited to the respective essentialized abilities of the European and Arab races. To the "modern" settlers or *colons,* Enfantin allotted industrial, commercial, and infrastructural developments, while the "traditional" natives were to engage in fieldwork and pastoral agriculture, farming, or the breeding of livestock.[61]

"To each according to his capacity." In Algeria, Chevalier's theories of Mediterranean association were about to be put into practice. The social engineering project implied grafting a French cultivar onto native hosts, animating them with its unique spirit, ethics, and habits, and fusing with them to create a more vigorous mutual civilization. With Saint-Simon's disciples at the helm of the colonial administration by the late 1840s, the indigenous populations of Algeria were increasingly governed as the colonial foil to the proletariat of France, and the same "technocratic" schemes that were designed to obviate class conflict at home, were also expected to pacify and rationalize the archaic economies and primitive impulses of North Africans.[62]

In his lectures and seminars on "governmentality," Michel Foucault observed that the end of feudalism in Europe was attended by "the birth of new forms of economic and social relations and new political structurations in which the behavior of a set of individuals became involved, more and more markedly, in the exercise of sovereign power."[63] These transformations, in turn, became the bases for the emergence of a new art of governing, the rationality (raison d'état) of which aimed to ensure the security of the state from without (diplomatic-military technology), while increasing its powers from within (policy).[64] The growth of the state, according to Foucault, depended on its ability,

> to mark out and improve its position in the game of rivalry and competition between European states, and to guarantee internal order by ensuring the "welfare"

> of individuals. Development of the competitive state (economically and militarily), development of the *Wohlfahrt* state (wealth-tranquility-happiness): it is these two principles that "policy," understood as the art of governing, must be able to coordinate.[65]

Here Foucault has rearticulated the primary concerns of Michel Chevalier in 1832, and has echoed his guidelines for enhancing the capacities of the French state (i.e., bolstering economic competitiveness, fiscal health, and political security) through European integration and Oriental association. On both fronts, the rationalities of state-making were to be channeled through industrial and technological applications; specifically, comprehensive engineering schemes to redesign the national infrastructure and landscape in artful and instrumental ways. In undertaking such ventures, the state mobilized elements of governance, science, and capital, and rationalized them with technocratic expertise.

In this regard, Chevalier's intellectual formation and vocational itinerary, especially when considered in conjunction with the broader experiences of his Saint-Simonian peers, herald the birth of "techno-politics" in France, and exemplify the "personification" of the force of capital by the mid-nineteenth century.[66] The rapid institutional maturation of this new technocratic elite in the decades since Saint-Simon imprudently baptized it as his "learned priesthood," was in large part due to the rapid standardization of the modern scientific curriculum of the *grandes écoles,* with its emphasis on mastering the advanced sciences, calculus, analytical geometry, mechanics, physics, and chemistry. By the 1820s, the profession of engineering had become a state-run enterprise, as attested to by the sizeable number of Saint-Simonian bankers, economists, and private entrepreneurs that served in governmental posts after their formation as state engineers (*ingénieurs d'état*).

Yet equally important for the instrumentalities of techno-politics is the capacity of infrastructural projects and public works to nurture links between physical and social engineering. According to Antoine Picon, the enduring connection between engineering and social preoccupations in France is "probably stronger than in other countries," and begins to manifest itself with the emancipation of the profession of engineering from its military roots, and its meritocratization with the founding of the royal *écoles d'état* in the late eighteenth century.[67] In this domain, too, the influence of Saint-Simonian technocrats in academic and policy circles facilitated the application of scientific principles to the world of social facts. While positivist experiments in social engineering figured prominently in the modernization of France, the Saint-Simonian blueprint did not preclude more romantic notions of social reform "as a culturally specific moral project of social uplift."[68] Ultimately, the various scientific and social commitments of French techno-politics would come together in a colonialist venture in Algeria.

NOTES

1. The four articles that compose *Système de la Méditerranée* appeared in *Le Globe*, in January and February 1832, under the following rubrics: *La paix considérée sous le rapport des intérêts* (January 20), *Impossibilité de fonder un équilibre européen par la guerre* (January 31), *La paix définitive doit être fondée par l'association de l'Orient et de l'Occident* (February 5), and *Exposition du Système de la Méditerranée: Politique nouvelle* (February 12). The articles formed the introduction to the series entitled, *Politique industrielle et Système de la Méditerranée*, published through April 1832 as follows: *Organisation industrielle de l'armée* (March 8), *Notre politique en présence des partis et en particulier des Légitimistes* (March 21), *Politique d'association: Politique de déplacement* (March 30), *Le choléra-morbus* (April 9), and *Aux hommes politiques* (April 21). For a recent compilation of the four articles, see Michel Chevalier, *Système de la Méditerranée*, ed. Philippe Dugot (Paris: Fayard/Mille et une nuits, 2006).

2. For example, Timothy Mitchell, *Rule of Experts: Egypt, Techno-politics, Modernity* (Berkeley: University of California Press, 2002); Pierre Musso, *Le Saint-Simonisme, l'Europe et la Méditerranée* (Paris: Manucius, 2008); and Antoine Picon, *L'invention de l'ingénieur moderne: L'École des ponts et chaussées, 1747–1851* (Paris: Presses de l'École nationale des ponts et chaussées, 1992).

3. Antoine Picon, "French Engineers and Social Thought, 18th–20th Centuries: An Archaeology of Technocratic Ideals," *History and Technology* 23, no. 3 (September 2007), 197–208.

4. Named after Francois-Louis Becquey (1760–1849), director general of Ponts et Chaussées under the restoration, the plan aimed to endow France with a nationwide network of navigable waterways (rivers and canals), modernized and integrated into the national transportation system. Becquey's hope was to rationalize transportation over riverways and canals and revive industrial growth and commerce. Reed Geiger, "Planning the French Canals: The 'Becquey Plan' of 1820–1822," *Journal of Economic History* 44, no.2 (June 1984): 329–39.

5. École Polytechnique, *Livre du Centennaire, 1794–1894* (Paris: Gauthier Villard et Fils, 1895), 509–10. In the course of the 1830s, Chevalier was a decisive player in securing public funding for the improvement of roadways and harbors, and for the inauguration of the first state-owned rail lines. In the 1850s through the 1860s, he was closely associated with the innermost circle of Napoleon III, as the infrastructural reforms of the emperor culminated in the massive renovation and embellishment of the French capital and other important urban centers under Georges-Eugène Haussmann (1809–91), prefect of the Department of the Seine from 1853 to 1870. Patrice de Moncan, *Le Paris d'Haussmann* (Paris: Éditions du Mécène, 2012).

6. This paper draws substantively from my earlier study of the role of Saint-Simonian officials and policy makers in the colonization and administration of Algeria. See Osama Abi-Mershed, *Apostles of Modernity: Saint-Simonians and the Civilizing Mission in Algeria* (Palo Alto, CA: Stanford University Press, 2010).

7. In the days after the revolution of July 1830, some Saint-Simonian leaders did not hesitate to call for an autocratic government to restore social order. Jean Walch, *Michel Chevalier, économiste saint-simonien (1806–1879)* (Paris: J. Vrin, 1975), 16–17.

8. See Marcel Emerit, *Les Saint-Simoniens en Algérie* (Alger: Les Belles Lettres, 1941), 26–27; and Georg Iggers, *The Cult of Authority: The Political Philosophy of the Saint-Simonians* (The Hague: Nijhof, 1970), xxxviii.

9. Olinde Rodrigues, *Saint-Simon: Son premier écrit; Lettres d'un habitant de Genève à ses contemporains* (Paris: Librairie Saint-Simonienne, 1802); *sa Parabole politique, 1819; Le nouveau Christianisme, 1825; précédés de Fragmens de l'histoire de sa vie écrite par lui-même publiés par Olinde Rodrigues, son disciple, Chef de la religion Saint-Simonienne* (Paris: Librairie Saint-simonienne, 1832), 46.

10. Claude-Henri de Saint-Simon, *Œuvres de Saint-Simon et d'Enfantin publiées par les membres du conseil institué par Enfantin pour l'exécution de ses dernières volontés; et précédées de deux notices historiques*, 47 vols. (Paris: E. Dentu, 1865–78), 18: 165.

11. Claude-Henri de Saint-Simon, *Nouveau Christianisme—Dialogues entre un conservateur et un novateur—Premier dialogue* (Paris: Bossange Père, A. Sautelet et Cie, 1825).

12. Within weeks of his enthronement, Charles announced his intention to be anointed at the cathedral of Reims, the traditional site of consecration of French kings. He declared his full allegiance to the institutions of the Roman Catholic Church and embraced a proposal to indemnify members of the nobility and aristocracy, whose estates had been nationalized during the revolution.

13. Saint-Simon, *Nouveau Christianisme,* 113. See also, Henri Desroche, *Henri de Saint-Simon: Le Nouveau Christianisme et les écrits sur la religion: Textes choisis et présentés par Henri Desroche* (Paris: Seuil, 1969); and Jean Dautry, "Nouveau Christianisme ou Nouvelle Théophilanthropie? Contribution à une sociologie religieuse de Saint-Simon," *Archives de sociologie des religions* 20, no. 1 (1965): 7–29.

14. Desroche describes Saint-Simon's New Christianity as "Christianity without religion ... perhaps even without God" (*Henri de Saint-Simon,* 41).

15. Here Saint-Simon and Thierry are advocating for the political union of the nations of England and France, based on their superior parliamentary systems and industrial capacities, as the first step toward reorganizing and peacefully unifying the rest of Europe under one common government: "Que les Anglais et les Français entrant en société établissent entre eux un parlement commun; que le but principal de cette société soit de s'agrandir en attirant à soi les autres peuples; que par conséquent le Gouvernement anglo-français favorise chez toutes les nations les partisans de la constitution représentative; qu'il les soutienne de tout son pouvoir, afin que des parlemens s'établissent chez tous les peuples soumis à des monarchies absolues; que toute nation dès l'instant qu'elle aura adopté la forme de gouvernement représentatif, puisse s'unir à la société et députer au parlement commun des membres pris parmi elle, et l'organisation de l'Europe s'achèvera insensiblement sans guerres, sans catastrophes, sans révolutions politiques," in *De la réorganisation de la société européenne, ou De la nécessité et des moyens de rassembler les peuples de l'Europe en un seul corps politique, en conservant à chacun son indépendance nationale, par M. le comte de Saint-Simon et par A. Thierry, son élève* (Paris: A. Égron, Delaunay, 1814); Let the English and the French join together to establish among themselves a common parliament; let the chief aim of this association be to grow by attracting to it the other peoples [of Europe]; let the Anglo-French Government subsequently favor among all nations the partisans of representative constitutionalism; let it support them with all its power, so that parliaments may be instituted among all peoples subjected to absolute monarchies; so that every nation, from the moment it has adopted the form of representative government, may unite with this society and delegate to the common parliament members chosen from its own population, and the organization of Europe will be accomplished imperceptibly without wars, without catastrophes, without political revolutions.), 80.

16. Condorcet (1743–1794) identified ten stages in the general progress of the human spirit in the domains of science, morality, and politics. The perfectibility of humankind in the tenth stage was to be made possible by the progress of social equality in society, the elimination of inequalities between nations, and finally the real improvement of man. See Jean-Antoine-Nicolas de Caritat, *Esquisse d'un tableau historique des progrès de l'esprit humain* (Paris: Agasse, 1795).

17. Though it is generally attributed to Comte, Arthur John Booth makes a compelling argument in support of Saint-Simon's paternity for the "law of three estates." See his *Saint-Simon and Saint-Simonism: A Chapter in the History of Socialism in France* (London: Longmans, Green, Reader and Dyer, 1871). See also, Auguste Comte, "Considérations philosophiques sur les sciences et sur les savants," *Le Producteur: Journal de l'industrie, des sciences et des beaux-arts* 1 (1825): 289–305, 349–74, 450–69; and Dominique Bagge, *Les idées politiques en France sous la Restauration* (Paris: Presses Universitaires de France, 1952), 408–17.

18. "Note du Père Enfantin sur la civilisation de l'Asie, 19 Août 1827," in Saint-Simon, *Œuvres de Saint-Simon et d'Enfantin,* 13:167–68.

19. Walch, *Michel Chevalier, économiste saint-simonien;* École Polytechnique, *Livre du Centennaire,* 509–16.

20. Quoted in Sébastien Charléty, *Histoire du Saint-Simonisme, 1825–1864* (Paris: P. Hartmann, 1931), 45.

21. John C. Eckalbar, "The Saint-Simonians in Industry and Economic Development," *American Journal of Economics and Sociology* 38, no. 1 (January 1979): 83–96.

22. *Le Globe,* "Organisation Scientifique," June 1–3, 1831. See also Auguste Comte, "Considérations sur le pouvoir spirituel," *Le Producteur: Journal philosophique de l'industrie, des sciences et des beaux-arts* 1 (1825): 596–616.

23. For the transcript of the trial proceedings, see Religion Saint-Simonienne, *Procès en la Cour d'assises de la Seine les 27 et 28 août 1832* (Paris: Librairie Saint-simonienne, 1832).

24. Auguste Blanqui, quoted in Saint-Simon, *Œuvres de Saint-Simon et d'Enfantin,* 1: 316. See also Philippe Régnier, "Le mythe oriental des saint-simoniens," in *Les Saint-Simoniens et l'orient: Vers la modernité,* ed. Magali Morsy (Aix-en-Provence: Édisud, 1989), 31.

25. École Polytechnique, *Livre du Centennaire,* 510–11. See also, Tangi Villebru, *La conquête de l'Ouest: Le récit français de la nation américaine au XIXème siècle* (Rennes: Presses Universitaires de Rennes, 2007), 206–9.

26. Chevalier published three voluminous accounts of his mission to America: *Lettres sur l'Amérique du Nord* (Paris: Gosselin, 1836); *Des intérêts matériels en France: Travaux publics, routes, canaux, chemins de fer* (Paris: Gosselin et Coquebert, 1837); and *Histoire et description des voies de communication aux Etats-Unis et des travaux d'art qui en dépendent* (Paris: Gosselin, 1840–41).

27. Walch, *Michel Chevalier, économiste saint-simonien,* 39–46.

28. Walch, *Michel Chevalier, économiste saint-simonien,* 39–46; Christopher H. Johnson, *The Life and Death of Industrial Languedoc, 1700–1920* (Oxford: Oxford University Press, 1995).

29. Sangatte is currently the French endpoint for the Eurotunnel (completed in 1994) and the high voltage direct current interconnectors between the continental European and British electricity grids (completed in 1986).

30. Edmund Burke III, "Toward a Comparative History of the Modern Mediterranean, 1750–1919," *Journal of World History* 23, no.4 (2013): 907–39, 909.

31. *Système de la Méditerranée,* 49–51.

32. Chevalier's explication of the different territories that make up his "general system" is reminiscent of Henri Lefèbvre's definition of modernity as the transformation of "natural" into "abstract" space. See Henri Lefèbvre, *The Production of Space* (Oxford: Wiley-Blackwell, 1992).

33. Thomas Newcomen (1654–1729) in 1712 created the first practical steam engine for pumping water, the precursor of the model introduced by Watt after 1763 and standardized by 1775. In 1774, Jouffroy applied the Newcomen steam engine in designing the first steamboat, Le Palmipède.

34. The galvanometer, invented by Johann Schweigger (1779–1857), consists of a coil of wire around a compass, used as a sensitive indicator for an electric current. Hans Christian Ørsted (1777–1851) discovered that electric currents produce a magnetic field that will deflect a compass needle. In 1821, the polytechnicien (and, later, professor at Collège de France), André-Marie Ampère (1775–1836) introduced a telegraph that was based on the principles of electromagnetism.

35. Within months of the publication of *Système de la Méditerranée,* Pavel Schilling (1786–1837) created an electromagnetic telegraph, which was followed in 1833 by Carl Friedrich Gauss (1777–1855) and Wilhelm Weber's (1804–1891) development of a code to communicate over a distance of twelve hundred meters. In 1838, the first electric telegraph was built by Charles Wheatstone (1802–75).

36. *Système de la Méditerranée,* 44–45.

37. *Système de la Méditerranée,* 50.

38. Chevalier based his estimate on the duration (75 minutes) of travel by rail between Liverpool and Manchester (52 kilometers), *Système de la Méditerranée,* 46n5.

39. *Système de la Méditerranée,* 47.

40. Alain Sauvant and Didier Rouchaud, "Volume et partage modal du transport de marchandises en France de 1845 à nos jours," *Dossiers des notes de synthèse OEST-SES-SESP: Modèles économiques dans les domaines des transports et du logement, 1988–2008* (Paris: Commissariat Général au Développement Durable, Centre de Ressources Documentaires, Ministère de l'Écologie, du Développement Durable, des Transports et du Logement, May 2011).

41. *Système de la Méditerranée,* 12.

42. *Système de la Méditerranée,* 31–32.

43. "We believed that in order to penetrate, progress had to engrave its passport into a cannonball," *Système de la Méditerranée,* 7.

44. *Système de la Méditerranée,* 33.

45. *Système de la Méditerranée,* 36.

46. *Système de la Méditerranée,* 43 (emphasis in original): "The pacifist policies of the future will aim, in their most immediate application, to constitute to the state of association around the Mediterranean, the two massifs of peoples who have been clashing for 3000 years as representatives of Orient and Occident."

47. *Système de la Méditerranée,* 42–43.

48. Saint-Simon, *Œuvres de Saint-Simon et d'Enfantin,* 5:130n4. See also, Nathalie Coilly and Philippe Régnier, *Le Siècle des Saint-Simoniens: Du Nouveau Christianisme au canal de Suez* (Paris: Bibliothèque Nationale de France, 2007), 101.

49. *Système de la Méditerranée,* 38.

50. Edmond de Cadalvène and Émile Barrault, *Deux années de l'histoire d'Orient 1839–1840, faisant suite à l'Histoire de la guerre de Méhémed-Ali en Syrie et en Asie-mineure 1832–1833* (Paris: Delloye, 1840), 2:65.

51. *Système de la Méditerranée,* 30.

52. Henry Laurens, *L'expédition d'Égypte, 1798–1801* (Paris: Seuil, 1997), 17–18.

53. I have in mind Francisco de Goya's contemporaneous painting *The Sleep of Reason Produces Monsters (El sueño de la razón produce monstruos),* completed between 1797 and 1799.

54. Laurens, *L'expédition d'Égypte,* 20–26.

55. *Système de la Méditerranée,* 60–61. Also, "Christian peoples are not alone today in their thirst for progress. If you doubt this, ask yourselves who is this sultan who has tamed the undisciplined janissary *ortas,* . . . who today in Istanbul publishes a Moniteur in the French language, who surrounds himself with the civilization of the Occident; and more, ask yourselves to what end is Mehmet Ali, the industrial pasha, now invading the lands of the Phoenicians and bringing his laws to the littoral coast of Sidon and Tyre," (34).

56. Henry Laurens, *Le royaume impossible: La France et la genèse du monde arabe, 1990* (Paris: Armand Colin, 1990), 11.

57. Vivant Denon, *Voyage dans la Basse et la Haute Égypte, pendant les campagnes du général Bonaparte,* vol. 1 (London: M. Peltier, 1802), 136.

58. Napoleon's scholars produced ethnographic and historical surveys of Egypt to buttress imperial domination with scientific certainty. The intelligence and expertise they gathered were instrumental in institutionalizing the academic disciplines of Egyptology and orientalism, and thereafter would serve as points of reference for conceptualizing and interacting with the Muslim world. Indeed, for Edmund Burke III, the "French tradition of the empirical study of Muslim societies" was born between the military expeditions to Cairo and Algiers, as its central paradigms were "laid down in the volumes of the *Déscription de l'Égypte,* and the work of the first generation of Frenchmen in Algeria." See "The Sociology of Islam: The French Tradition," in *Islamic Studies: A Tradition and Its Problems,* ed. Malcolm H. Kerr (Malibu, CA: Udena, 1980), 73–88. For a distinctive treatise on the epistemological legacy of French orientalism in the field of North African studies, see Jean-Claude Vatin, "Le Maghreb de la

méconnaissance à la reconnaissance," in *Connaissances du Maghreb: Sciences sociales et colonisation,* ed. Jean-Claude Vatin (Paris: Centre National de la Recherche Scientifique, 1984), 11–21.

59. *Système de la Méditerranée,* 24–25 (emphasis in original).

60. Prosper Enfantin, *Colonisation de l'Algérie* (Paris: P. Bertrand, 1843), 116–17 (emphasis in original).

61. Enfantin, *Colonisation de l'Algérie,* 146. See also, Philippe Régnier, "Enfantin et la 'Colonisation de l'Algérie,'" in *L'Orientalisme des Saint-simoniens,* ed. Michel Levallois and Sarga Moussa (Paris: Maisonneuve et Larose, 2006), 131–55.

62. The techno-economic improvement of French Algeria was integral to the modernization of the French polity proper. During the reforms of the Second Empire in the 1860s, the government's treatment of Algerian rights paralleled metropolitan policies aiming to ameliorate the conditions of the working classes of France. The project to secure indigenous rights of property in Algeria was fashioned in tandem with imperial legislative campaigns to grant workers the right to strike and associate. Such reforms also found their spatial corollaries when, between 1860 and 1867, Algiers, similar to Haussmann's Paris, was refurbished into a modern European city.

63. Michel Foucault, "Security, Territory, and Population," in *The Essential Foucault: Selections from the Essential Works of Foucault, 1954–1984,* ed. Paul Rabinow and Nikolas Rose (New York: New Press, 2003), 260.

64. "Thus, the reason of state . . . takes shape in two great ensembles of political knowledge and technology: a diplomatic-military technology that consists in ensuring and developing the forces of a state through a system of alliances, and the organizing of an armed apparatus. . . . The second is constituted by "policy" *(police),* in the sense given to the word then: that is, the set of means necessary to make the forces of state increase from within. At the juncture of these two great technologies, and as a shared instrument, one must place commerce and monetary circulation between the states: enrichment through commerce offers the possibility of increasing the population, the manpower, production, and export, and of endowing oneself with large, powerful armies" (Foucault, "Security, Territory, and Population," 261).

65. Foucault, "Security, Territory, and Population," 262.

66. Mitchell, *Rule of Experts,* 27–31.

67. Antoine Picon, "French Engineers," 197–208. For histories of the French corps of engineers, see Anne Blanchard, *Les ingénieurs du "Roy" de Louis XIV à Louis XVI: Étude du corps des fortifications* (Montpellier: Université Paul Valéry, 1979); André Brunot and Roger Coquand, *Le corps des Ponts et Chaussées* (Paris: Centre National de la Recherche Scientifique, 1982); Jean Petot, *Histoire de l'administration des Ponts et Chaussées* 1599–1815 (Paris: M. Rivière, 1958); Antoine Picon, *L'invention de l'ingénieur moderne L'École des Ponts et Chaussées 1747–1851* (Paris: Presses de l'École Nationale des Ponts et Chaussées, 1992); and Antoine Picon, "Le Corps des Ponts et Chaussées: De la conquête de l'espace national à l'aménagement du territoire," in *Ingenieure in Frankreich, 1747–1990,* ed. André Grelon and Heiner Stück (Frankfurt: Campus, 1994), 77–99.

68. Omnia El Shakry, *The Great Social Laboratory: Subjects of Knowledge in Colonial and Postcolonial Egypt* (Palo Alto, CA: Stanford University Press, 2018), 11.

7

The Mediterranean in Colonial North African Literature

Contesting Views

William Granara

The history of and scholarship on modern North African literature, especially during the colonial period (1830–1962) but to a significant degree extending into the [postcolonial] present day, have been kept conveniently apart, both linguistically and academically, bearing the seemingly innocuous labels *la litterature d'expression francaise* or *d'expression arabe,* to draw a clear distinction between what has long been billed as two different corpuses of literary production. The extensive list of literary anthologies on North African literature, the by-products of both academic and publishing institutions working in unison to manufacture knowledge, have drawn and safeguarded epistemological boundaries that have been in existence since the early years of French colonial history. Departments of French Studies and Near Eastern Studies kept to their own side of the divide for a long time, and it is only recently, by way of translations and the persistent pushiness of postcolonial studies in academe, that the institutional walls have begun to crumble. The once-dominant dividing line that separated North African literature in French from that in Arabic has given way to new subdivisions and categories—women's, Berber, Beur, Jewish, and so on. But apart from the occasional anthology that cautiously crosses the linguistic divide, the literature of North Africa (Morocco, Algeria, and Tunisia) continues to be written, read, and taught with its bilingual expressions hovering in the paratext. With that comes all the cross-cultural baggage—perceptions, judgments, reader expectations, and academic criticism—that keep the two neatly separated.

My chapter attempts to study *a* North African literature, situated at a specific time and space in literary and political history, focusing on the early stages of modern Arabic Tunisian literature. In the decades of the 1930s and 40s, Arabic literature was at a more advanced stage of development in Tunisia than in Morocco and Algeria for a host of reasons—a relatively higher level of Arabic literacy enhanced by traditional Islamic institutions and a greater degree of contact with Egyptian and Syrian literature, to mention two obvious examples.[1] My contention is that this literature is at once Arabic *and* Mediterranean. It is to a significant degree the product of bonding among a small group of artists, journalists, and intellectuals, who penned their seminal works in the decades of the 1930s and 1940s, and who survive in contemporary Tunisian culture as the founding members of the Taḥt al-Sūr Club (*jamāʿat taḥt al-sūr*).[2] These men, at this early, colonial stage, were polymaths (*mutafanninīn*), were politically engaged, and were aggressively committed to this national literary project. The literature is Arabic in language and temperament, in literary heritage and influence, and in political stances. It is Mediterranean in historical consciousness, in geographical setting and outlook, and in its expansive aesthetic, ethnic, and cross-cultural attitude.

My focus is on three literary works by a single figure, Zīn al-ʿAbidīn al-Sanūsī (henceforth Sanūsī) (1899–1965), which were penned between 1936 and 1948. My primary strategy for reading these works is to establish a direct interface between them and between the French *pied-noir* epic novel by Louis Bertrand, *Le Sang des Races* (1899).[3] Both figures stood at the forefront of intellectual movements that defined the colonial era of North Africa. The Latinist movement of Bertrand was inspired as much by the "wave of neoclassical architecture and ideology in many parts of the world at the end of the 19th and beginning of the 20th century,"[4] as it was inspired by the theories of Compte de Gobineau (1816–82) concerning white racial supremacy and European expansion. As a cultural force, it sought to situate and justify France's imperial project and "civilizing mission" within the continuum of Latin (read: European) sovereignty over the Mediterranean, which dates back to the Roman Empire.[5] I argue that the novel is, above all, a clear reflection of the *declensionist* narrative, meticulously studied by Diana Davis,[6] which posits the thesis that the spread of Islam in the seventh century, and the later Arabian Banī Hilāl invasions of the eleventh century, wreaked havoc on the environmental fertility of North Africa and destroyed the great Roman civilization that arose from it. The Latinist movement's embrace of this narrative, Davis argues, sought justification in the French colonial mission to civilize the savage by social control and appropriation of land and resources.[7]

Sanūsī's fictional works are embedded in the reality of a colonized Tunisia. They are best read—but need not be exclusively read—as direct responses to or stances toward French imperialism and its presumptuous cultural hegemony. His fiction draws from the weapons of Mediterranean history, the rise and ascendancy of Islam, and a deeply entrenched Arabic literary heritage (*al-turāth*), all combined to produce a master narrative that sets in relief Tunisia's existence as a Mediterranean civilization, fortified by the Arab conquest of North Africa read as Islam's own liberation (civilizing?) mission. Sanūsī situates this conquest within a long historical continuum of Semitic, Near Eastern, and Arab settlements along the Mediterranean rim. I argue that all of my proof texts, French and Arabic alike, are grounded in their own contemporary political contexts as much as they are in the authors' understanding, at once literal and mythical, of European and Islamic histories. This contestation over the Mediterranean as an indigenous, rightful, and historically legitimate space is central to the ways in which all of these literary texts sought to construct their national character.

In juxtaposing Bertrand's novel with Sanūsī's fictional pieces, my reading admittedly carries with it a certain imbalance on both the aesthetic and political fronts. Generically, Louis Bertrand's *Sang des Races,* widely distributed and well known throughout the French North African colonies, is a three-hundred-page epic novel that draws from a Western literary canon that was, by the time of its publication, multifaceted, fully matured, and popularly received. Its canonical stature among Franco-European novels penned in the early decades of the twentieth century in Algeria and Tunisia articulated, according to Peter Dunwoodie, "a historical narrative which displaced and relativized the indigenous Islamic culture relegating it to the status of simple hiatus in the history of the 'Latin race' in North Africa."[8]

The Tunisian pieces, amounting to less than a hundred pages in combination, are experimental, hybrid, and penned in an intermediate phase of generic development, when North African Arab writers were still navigating their way through the complex of Western generic strictures, on the one hand, and Arabic modes of creative writing still dictated by the classical tradition, on the other. Politically and linguistically, Bertrand was writing from a position of power—literary and political—at a time and place in which French occupational governments maintained a firm control over most of the means of communication, which obviously included the publication of literary works, in the areas they occupied. On the academic and critical fronts, one need look only at contemporary literary histories and anthologies to see how French, or Francophone, literary production was privileged and deemed worthy of critical study,[9] while its Arabic counterpart was restrained by what Ian Coller has recently called "the closely guarded bastions of academic Orientalism."[10] Sanūsī wrote from behind the lines of defense, constantly subjected to colonial as well as domestic censorship, as most Tunisian intellectuals found themselves wrestling with the French authorities over licenses to print and publish. Here, as much as the *literarity* of these texts draws my attention, so does their contribution to the political debates and national cultural formation processes that they subsumed. The imbalance in my interface may be more apparent in the fact that Bertrand's Latinist movement represents what may be labeled as the "'right wing" faction of European colonialism, aggressive and exclusionist in comparison to the tolerant and multicultural outlook of the Saint-Simonian movement of the nineteenth century, the impact of which could be felt, as Neil Foxlee reminds us, in the sympathetic views of Albert Camus in 1937.[11] Sanūsī, however, represented the moderate, secular humanist faction of "reformist" Islamic discourse and Tunisian Arabic nationalism, situated between the old-guard religious and political conservatives, on the one hand, and the more radical thinking, secular-reformist neo-Destourians of the other.[12]

My justification for reading these authors and their work in juxtaposition rests, however, precisely on the oddly similar ways in which both writers use history to construct national identity, and on the centrality of the Mediterranean as an "indigenous homeland" and legitimate historical space to which each author stakes his literary claim. I also argue that the pairing of these two nationalist-oriented literatures leads to further lines of inquiry into how the Arab (Muslim, Eastern) and European (Christian, Western) continue to this day to interconnect textually, vacillating between mutual attraction and disdain. For that matter, the pairing also makes sense of the persistence of a residual Franco-Arabic divide in the way we write, read, and critique modern novels from the Maghrib that continues to permeate modern Mediterranean literatures to this day.[13]

Additionally, I read these two authors within the long-standing battle between French and Arabic for supremacy as the sole legitimate language of erudition, high culture, and popular national expression in North Africa from the colonial period until today. The literatures of Sanūsī and Bertrand, which represent two histories in conflict, are consciously written in a high register of these imperial languages to attract and persuade the educated and literate masses to their causes. This is not to say that other languages and language registers did not exist within this contestation. Sanūsī's choice to write in modern standard Arabic and Bertrand's in French, for that matter, are equal expressions of a linguistic chauvinism, especially when viewed against other choices available to them at the time.

First, especially for Sanūsī, there was French itself, which was the language of choice for many young Algerian and, to a lesser degree, Tunisian writers, who aspired to careers as poets and writers of fiction. Francophone writing, especially that penned by Algerian and Tunisian *evolués,* was often subversive and almost always critical, but in the end it was a willing participant in the French civilizing mission. Second, there was colloquial Arabic, disdained by the religious and cultural elites as a medium of written expression, which emerged nonetheless in short stories, picaresque narratives *(maqāmāt),* songs, anthems, poetry, and theater that enjoyed wide popular appeal. Third, languages such as Italian, Greek, Maltese, Spanish, and Judeo-Arabic could be seen and heard, particularly among the mixed neighborhoods of *pieds-noirs* and other minority communities. And fourth, there was the lingua franca of franco-arabe. This playful mixture of European languages with Arabic, so derisively described by Bertrand as "the cacophony of languages and dialects," filled the ports, train stations, bathhouses, and marketplaces and at times made its way brazenly into art forms. The vernacular of *pataouète,* a medium of expression in the colonial Algerian Cagayous *feuilletons,*[14] and the franco-arabe of Maḥmūd Bayram's Tunisian *maqāmāt* provide two examples of linguistic choices taken by creative writers.[15] Sanūsī's choice of standard Arabic was a political one, given that the historical, cultural, and literary gravitas of "classical" Arabic was to him and his like-minded cohort the only effective weapon to use against the mighty French language.

Finally, I read these texts, and the affinities I see within them, with an eye on the current debates in the contemporary cultural theories of postcoloniality and Mediterraneanism. The emergence and persistence of postcolonial theory since the 1980s have provided a wide technical vocabulary and new critical tools that allow us to read more expansively on Tunisian literature in its early formation: 1) the concern with place and displacement; 2) the complexity and hybridity of generic forms and strategies; and 3) the dialectic of self and other, indigene and exile, language and place, slave and free, which is "the matrix of post-colonial literatures."[16] The recent round of debates on Mediterraneanism that followed the publication of Horden and Purcell's *Corrupting Sea* (2000),[17] the depth and breadth of which span far beyond the contours of my essay, nevertheless proffers the idea of connectivity as a way of understanding the series of connections and fragmentations that has replaced the more traditionally held view of a united, monolithic Mediterranean basin. It is precisely this binary of connectedness and fragmentation that lies at the heart of the fictional cosmos of Sanūsī, as well as of others among his Tunisian cohort. For in their contestation of the French imperial project concerning Tunisia's place in the world, temporally and spatially, lurks the constant reminder that Tunisia, as Phoenician, Greek, Roman, Carthaginian, Byzantine, Arab-Muslim, Ottoman, and modern, has always been there alongside Europe, then and now.

In juxtaposing these works, I consider three areas on which to base my comparisons: geography, race, and gender. By geography I mean the physical borders and interior spaces that delineate the world of the texts. Assuming that the Mediterranean is situated at the center of the fictional cosmos, and is constructed as an area of contested space, what are the temporal and spatial circumferential points that give it its centrality? In considering race, I examine the people(s) who populate the fictional cosmos and interrogate the texts' positions on human agency, identity, and essentialism, which inform civilizational and political rivalries and contestations. Finally, by considering gender, I show how these texts deal with those shifts from tradition to modernity that dominated much of early modern Mediterranean literature. Areas of gender include notions of power and patriarchy (familial authority and political sovereignty) and sexuality (family and other human relationships), highly significant social markers that allow us to decode the political and social messages of the texts. I am especially interested in the contrast between the female characters of each author, given that the depiction of Muslim women, as either traditionally veiled or Western clothed, was equally paramount, and obsessively so, in (European) colonial and (Arab-Islamic) indigenous reformist discourses. The writings of the Egyptian Qāsim Amīn (1863–1908) and the Tunisian al-Ṭāhir al-Ḥaddād (1899–1935) stand out as pioneering works on the subject of liberating women in Arabic intellectual history,[18] while Frantz Fanon was among the first to draw serious scholarly attention to the French colonial obsession with unveiling the Algerian woman as a strategy to achieve France's ultimate goal of wrestling Algerians from the grip of Islamic tradition and integrating Algeria into the French Empire. Fifty years after the publication of Fanon's essay "Algeria Unveiled,"[19] the contentious issue of the Muslim veil erupted in a suburban Parisian high school and emerged as a bitterly contested national issue concerning the role of *laicité* in modern French identity.[20] This one issue, a powerfully significant marker in both colonial and postcolonial relations between France and North Africa—long lasting, deeply divisive, and unresolved—was, I argue, at the heart of French Latinist and Tunisian Arabic contestations over the Mediterranean, as reflected in the texts under discussion here. Whether read as "national allegory" or as a criterion for "progress" and assimilation, or the lack thereof, the Arab/Muslim woman has enjoyed—or suffered—inordinate attention since colonial times.

SANG DES RACES: A PIED-NOIR EPIC

Bertrand's *Sang des Races* is an epic novel about Algeria's European settler community (pieds-noirs) at the turn of the century. It may be read as the generation of the grandfathers of Camus's *The Stranger* (1942), a time of unabashed aggressive and confident colonization. Its physical world recognizes two realms: the countries that border the western European Mediterranean (Spain, France, and Italy) and Algeria. There are no references to Morocco or Tunisia as consanguineous neighbors. In keeping with the French colonial practice of "divide and conquer," Algeria stands alone in its binary opposition to Europe, stripped of linguistic, historical, religious, and cultural ties to the wider Arabo-Berber North Africa and to the Arab-Muslim east.

The Algerian landscape includes both the urban and rural (i.e., desert, farmland), with the cities of Algiers and Lagouat as central points. Algiers, located on the Mediterranean, is a bustling cosmopolitan city, described with a natural beauty enhanced by its proximity to both mountain and sea. Its thriving ports are depicted as receptacles to imported food, wine, furniture, and other luxury goods from Europe and as depositories for a hybrid population of mixed peoples and races speaking in a cacophony of languages and dialects. The city of Constantine shares with Algiers the mongrel quality, a world the author held in disdain for its commotion and diversity.[21]

The city of Lagouat (al-Aghwāṭ), located two hundred miles south of Algiers and serving as a gateway to the Algerian Sahara, stands in sharp contrast to the cosmopolitan cities that dot the Mediterranean coast. As an oasis town, a colonial military headquarters for the Sahara, and a thriving trade center, Laghouat is valorized as authentic "homeland" for pied-noir Algeria. It functions as a starting point for European manifest destiny, expanding the frontiers of France's conquest far beyond the porous, effeminate, and impure port cities, in order to reclaim, or reimagine, an indigenous landscape of the Roman Empire's African province (*Ifrīqiyā*). The pied-noir settlers, the heroes of Bertrand's *Sang*, brutal, masculine, and headstrong, explore and subdue the wild terrain in wagon trains and horse carriages that cut across the Algerian desert, pillaging its natural resources and whipping savage indigenes into submission and civilization.

The Europe of *Le Sang des Races*' cartography includes France, Spain, and Italy, actual places of origin for the majority of the Algerian pied-noir population. The novel maps them into one geography that traces its roots to Roman imperial history.[22] Highly significant in this mapping is a clear distinction between France—and more specifically Paris as metropole—and Spain (and, to a lesser extent, Italy). Put another way, the distinction is between the political and cultural French elite, who inhabit the cities and reap the fruits of conquest, and the Spaniards (and, by extension, the Italians), who man the docks, work in the factories, till the soil, and traverse the desert. The Italian province of Piedmont and the cities of Turin, Naples, and Bari, major sites of mass emigration in the latter years of the nineteenth century, are constantly evoked through character traits, dialects, and personal habits that reinforce the novel's racial essentialism. However, it is the binary of France and Spain that defines most significantly the Europe of Algerian colonization. The France of *Le Sang des Races* is constantly evoked by the force of political and cultural sovereignty, articulated through images of its institutions, language, refined manners, and luxury goods, deftly played against the rugged earthiness of pied-noir society. Spain, by contrast, is drawn in most graphically by the continuity of the extended family that emigrates from Valencia to Algeria shortly after the establishment of the French protectorate in 1860, giving the novel its strong family-saga quality. Rafael's grandfather is introduced by way of family anecdotes, while his father, Ramon, a powerful patriarch and the quintessence of the true colonial European spirit, dies early in the novel, bequeathing to Rafael his settler legacy. The linking of Spain to pied-noir Algeria, in keeping with Bertrand's idealization of the Spaniard as the true pioneer of the Latinist movement, is taken one step further with Rafael's journey back to the mother country to visit relatives in Valencia. The journey is fraught with cross-cultural conflict, as Rafael reacts like the consummate outsider to the ways of the "Old World" of the Spanish motherland.

He is shocked by the antiquated customs and primitiveness of the Spanish countryside and its poor roads and stunned by the family's ritual of saying the evening rosary in Latin. He finds himself uncomfortable with the table manners of his uncle, who scoops paella with a piece of bread and tears pieces of meat with his fingers instead of a fork, and of family members, who all drink wine from a common goblet—habits that disturb the French customs he has internalized in Algeria. It is through Bertrand's journey back to Spain that we can best understand his vision of colonized Algeria as the way toward the European future.

Race and nationality are also significant markers in the novel. The continental divide between European and indigenous Algeria is reinforced with a stark polarization between Europeans, on the one hand, and native (Arab, Berber, and Jewish) Algerians on the other. Italians and French, "othered" by their strange dialects and quirky personality traits, are nevertheless counted among the novel's pied-noir, colonizing Algerians. Whatever differences they may bear from the dominant Spaniards pale in comparison to the depiction of Bertrand's non-European cast of characters. Racial distinctions are constantly reinforced, and the novel provides no major characters with mixed European/Arabic Jewish lineage.

Algeria's indigenous population remains faceless and voiceless throughout the novel, a hallmark of French colonial literature in North Africa and a narrative strategy that Bertrand's novel ironically shares with the later fictional works of the more liberal-minded Albert Camus.[23] In Bertrand's grand epic, we see sporadic references to an Arab gardener, a Kabylie soothsayer, and a young Jewish housekeeper, as well as a smattering of references to Arab and Jewish businessmen. The character Rebecca, a wealthy Jewish woman and early love interest of Rafael, is the sole exception. Her passion for Rafael brings her to finance his business ventures, which he accepts readily, but in the end he abandons her, since it is unthinkable that he marry a Jew. Arabs are evoked through their loud weddings, the guttural and ear-piercing trilling of their women, and the hordes of bodies that pollute the ports and marketplaces. Echoing loudly Latinity's "declensionist narrative" mentioned above, and in keeping with his conviction that "Arabs bring only misery, anarchy and barbarity to Algeria," Bertrand provides us with a colorful scene:

> What disgusted [Rafael] above all else was the mongrelism of the docks with which he was forced to mix. The natives were particularly repugnant because they were dirty and servile. Their clothes were tattered and filthy, and to him they felt like vermin crawling all over his body. Their smell sickened him. Their food, installed in every corner, emitted odors of oil, butter and grease, splattering and burning from their hot-plates and frying pans. Chunks of bloody liver sat on dirty dishes, and fried sardines piled up on the meat stalls. Water melon and prickly pear rinds were thrown on top of heaps of garbage all around the vendors. The stench of what they called "sea dogs," a kind of fish the lowest of them eat, was especially offensive to Rafael. There were piles of them, skinned and beheaded, hideous to look at. All these revolting foods were

> mixed together with wedges of lemons and oranges, bars of chocolate, and wheels of cheese. What strange people rushed to do business with this den of thieves! Rafael recalled the beauty and refined manners of the Arabs of the South[ern desert] and could only hold this riffraff in the greatest contempt. In the midst of all this muck, two or three hooligans would stand out. Usually French, some of mixed Spanish blood, Maltese and Neapolitans. Dressed in rags, with acned and scarred complexions, they exuded something much more sinister than your average Parisian low-life. Not one of them dared to approach Rafael, who reacted to them with hostile looks. He abhorred them to the point of resentment and wanting to beat them up (my translation).[24]

Gender constructions, and here I focus primarily on the novel's female characters, convey much of the Latinist movement's political and social conservatism. Male and female characters are unequivocally delineated, with Bertrand's women assuming minor roles and falling strictly within the mother/lover or virgin/whore dichotomy. The sole female character with any agency is Rafael's mother, Mama Rosa, who staunchly defends the traditional family structure after her husband, Ramon, dies, leaving her to raise a young family. Her matriarchal strength lies in her rigid adherence to the patriarchal order: her place is in the home, pleasing her husband in bed, bearing children, performing domestic chores, maintaining religious observances (prayers, Sunday mass), and even taking secret pride in and offering tacit approval of her son Rafael's brutish interference in his sister's engagement.

Outside the home, life in *Le Sang des Races* escapes the matriarchal grip as hard drinking, brawling, and whoring rule the public spaces of the small towns. Women appear as saloon girls, cigarette and food vendors, prostitutes, and charwomen. Rafael inherits his father's wanderlust, swaggering from saloon to saloon in quest of money, power, and sex. He falls for a cigarette vendor from Malaga but in the end leaves her to pursue his financial interests. His brief affair with Rebecca, the wealthy Jewish women (discussed above), also calls attention to the cavalier and dismissive treatment of women that permeates Bertrand's fictional cosmos. The character of Thérèse, the long-suffering wife of Rafael's roguish and hard-drinking friend Alfonse, remains perhaps the most textured of the novel's female characters. Rafael's attraction to her underlines all the tensions between "province" and "métropole." White skinned, stylishly dressed, haughty, and intelligent, Thérèse remains faithful to her roguish and drunkard husband, despite his failure to give her children and despite her secret love for Rafael. In turn, Rafael finds himself drawn to her despite his ostensible resentment of French high culture and sophistication. She keeps her modest house clean and is skilled in cooking, knitting, and household economizing.[25] Drawn from models similar to nineteenth-century American prairie wives, Thérèse remains obedient and faithful, refraining from female gossip and other frivolous behavior. Her refined manners contrast sharply with Rafael's brutish character and uncouth habits, binding them into a mutual attraction of opposites, which underlines the sexual undertones of colonial encounters.

The image of an *Afrique Latine* as projected in the novels of Louis Bertrand, as well as of authors writing in a similar vein, finds its counterpart in the construction of North Africa as indigenous space throughout a Near Eastern, Semitic, Arab, and Islamic historical continuum, as illustrated in contemporary Arabic literature that sought to contest French imperial sovereignty and to stake its own claims to the Mediterranean. The three fictional works of Sanūsī discussed below illustrate some of the narrative strategies he and other Arab writers used to make such claims. Two distinguishing features in these texts are worthy of mention: the persistent and liberal use of history and historical periods in crafting the fictional cosmos and the direct interface between Arab and European characters throughout the texts. I discuss the following works not in the chronological order of their composition but in the chronological order of their narrated worlds: first, the Muslim conquest of North Africa in the late seventh century; second, the Arabian Banī Hilāl integration into North Africa and the concurrent end of indigenous Christianity in Ifrīqiyā in the eleventh century; and finally, the beginning of French colonial rule in the nineteenth century.

FATH IFRĪQIYĀ: THE CHRISTIAN-MUSLIM BINARY

On December 15, 1938, Zīn al-ʿAbidīn al-Sanūsī's *Fatḥ Ifrīqiyā* opened at the Municipal Theater (*al-masraḥ al-baladī*) in downtown Tunis and was performed by the National Theater Union troupe. Sanūsī began writing the "script" for this piece in February of that year, after the French authorities temporarily closed down his newspaper, *Tūnis,* which, ironically, he had founded two years earlier upon the July 1936 decree by the protectorate government lifting restrictions on the Tunisian press. It was particularly Sanūsī's editorials, printed in a weekly column he entitled "Tunisia First and Foremost" (Tūnis qabla kulli shayʾ) and replete with his biting criticisms of the colonial government, that angered the French authorities. All of the timing, venue, form, and subject matter of this play fit neatly into the political and artistic nexus that was the hallmark of Sanūsī's literary project.[26]

The Municipal Theater, situated in the heart of the Tunisian capital, is a magnificent art nouveau building erected in 1902 and may well be viewed as the crown jewel of the imperial French civilizing mission in Tunisia. It showcased operas, ballets, symphonic concerts, and plays—all the imports of a high European culture. Theater, in the modern sense of the term, was unknown in premodern Arab culture yet was enthusiastically embraced by both Arab intellectuals and wide swathes of the population throughout North Africa and much of the Arab East (Egypt and greater Syria). Like the printing press, theater was a "western" commodity that was quickly imported and imitated and effectively appropriated to create new forms of indigenous expression to articulate powerful national sentiments at the expense of the European colonial project. Sanūsī could make no stronger statement against the French reneging on its commitment to freedom of the press than to author and stage this work, in Arabic and about Arab history, through perhaps the most French of contemporary arts and in a most conspicuous symbol of France's civilizing mission.

Although Sanūsī describes his *Conquest of North Africa* as a historical novel (*riwāya tārīkhiyya*), reflective of an arbitrary critical vocabulary of the time, it reads very much like a royal court drama in the tradition of seventeenth-century French theater, with echoes of Racine's and Corneille's famous reworkings of classical Greco-Roman theater to treat the philosophical issues and political obsessions and tensions of their own times. Sanūsī's novel, a short piece in three acts, narrates the story of an Arab general, who pays a visit to the Byzantine warlord of Ifrīiqiyā with an appeal that he end his fractious rule and submit peacefully to the inevitable Muslim conquest of North Africa.[27] The play even adheres to the seventeenth-century French reworking of the classical Greek theatrical stricture of the "three unities"—time, space, and action.[28] All the action takes place in one timeframe, in one palace, and over the course of one storyline: to convince the Byzantine court to accept the inevitable triumph of Islam. Moreover, the adaptation of Greco-Roman characters and themes continues well into twentieth-century French theater, first with such playwrights as Jean Giraudoux (*La Guerre de Troie n'aura pas lieu,* November 22, 1935, and *Electre,* May 13, 1937) and Jean Anouilh (*Eurydice,* 1941, and *Antigone,* 1942)[29] and later with Sartre and Camus and their more familiar works. For this reason, we are safe in assuming a considerable degree of intertextuality between colonial and metropolitan (i.e., Arabic and French) literatures, especially given how much North African Arabophone scholars, artists, and intellectuals kept abreast of and were artistically influenced by French culture. And this is not even to mention the modern Arab fascination with theater, as previously discussed.[30] It is not a rejection of French intellectualism and art forms that lies at the heart of Sanūsī's fictional and political worlds but of its arrogant dismissal of Arabs and Arabic language and culture and its view of Islam as belonging to a *passé barbare.* In fact, modern Tunisian's first universally acclaimed novel, Maḥmūd al-Masʿadī's *al-Sudd* (*The Dam,* 1940; published in 1955), draws heavily in form and content from both the classical Greek tradition and contemporary European existentialist thought.[31]

The story takes place in the late classical provincial town of Sbeitla, which was located on the outskirts of Kairouan (al-Qayrawān) and was the capital city of the rebellious Byzantine governor Gregory, on the eve of the Muslim conquest of central North Africa in the mid-seventh century. Although Constantinople, Arabia, and other points east are evoked in the play, the locus of the story remains exclusively inside the Sbeitla Palace, contested space between the imperial armies. More than faraway places, distant eras are evoked throughout the narrative as markers for the Arab claim to their Mediterranean roots.

The self/other opposition is drawn on the surface along East-West lines: Greeks (Byzantines), Romans, and Vandals on the one side and Arabs, Berbers, and Carthaginians on the other. In this binary, one could possibly see the influence of Henri Pirenne's *Mahomet et Charlemagne,* published just a year before the opening of the play, which posits the thesis that the rise of both the Islamic conquest and the Carolingian Dynasty (France) of the seventh century constituted a break from antiquity and reshaped the Mediterranean world into two major political and cultural forces (Christian and Muslim).[32] This dual vision of the resurfacing of a Mediterranean world in conflict along Christian and Muslim lines, reinforced by the French colonial project, is ever present throughout Sanūsī's fiction. In this way, he defies the French policy of "divide and rule" by strongly asserting the historical and linguistic linkage between Arabs and Berbers through their shared Carthaginian ancestry.

Curiously, it is in the gender constructions of three female characters that most of the political and artistic messages of this text are disseminated, a feature which, incidentally, stands not only in sharp contrast to the rigid, patriarchal, and misogynous colonial pied-noir French novel but also in defiance of the Arab Muslim patriarchal conservatism still operating within much of Arab and Tunisian society of the time. In much the same way, no doubt, that Bertrand was taking a stand against the more liberal faction of his French compatriots toward colonial rule, Sanūsī was staking a position against Tunisians on the religious right. The dialogues between the Arab general (ʿAbdallah Ibn Zubayr) and the story's three female characters were more likely to resonate with contemporary French metropolitan social mores than with Arab Muslim reality, but they nonetheless articulate a contemporary Arab secular, humanist stance toward the East/West, Arab/European, or Muslim/Christian interface. Līlīa, daughter and sole heir to Gregory and the main protagonist of the play, is a strong and independent-minded woman, who resists her father's attempt—in his quest for a political alliance—to marry her off to the son of the Byzantine prince in Carthage. She encounters ʿAbdallah when he visits her father's palace, as part of his mission to devise a truce, and accidentally wanders into the women's quarters. Her lady in waiting (*qahramāna*) Masīna is her go-between and private tutor in matters political and emotional. The third woman, ʿAlīsha, is the concubine-mother of Līlīa, whose true identity as an Arab slave girl from Syria is revealed, along with Lilia's true biological father, all in an attempt to undermine the racial essentialism that has long dominated both Latinist and pan-Arab ideologies. In this regard, the play reads closely to the earlier novels of the Lebanese Jurjī Zaydān (1861–1914), whose mixing of historical facts with romantic modes of writing, especially in his construction of strong, articulate female characters, helped fashion a modern Arabic historical novel.[33]

More to the point, Sanūsī's female characters, in all their blurred and hyphenated identities, allow for an alternative response to a purely essentialist Western

FIGURE 11. *Suzy Vernon au Théâtre Municipal* [Suzy Vernon at the Municipal Theater]. Photograph by Victor Sebag, 1930. From Gérard Sebag, *Tunisie 1910–1960, Victor Sebag, Un photographe dans le siècle* (Tunis: Cérès Editions, 2011). Courtesy of Gérard Sebag.

reading of (or claim to) exclusive Mediterranean sovereignty. In concert with these female characters, Sanūsī uses high theatrical ventriloquism to verbalize a colonial Tunisian view of itself as Mediterranean, by casting ʿAbdallah in two different but complementary lights: as a classical, literary romantic hero and as a benevolent Muslim missionary and conqueror. As commander of the Muslim army, he is portrayed as gentle, articulate, patient, and romantic, encompassing all the shared qualities of the nobleman of high European and Arab chivalry. At the same time, he is the mouthpiece of an Islam that advocates tolerance, inclusiveness, and reason. He preaches to his audience that men are judged by good deeds and noble qualities, not by race or religion—Islam's mission is to liberate not to conquer, to unite people in common fraternity, and to rid the world of divisiveness (*tashattut*) and chaos (*fawḍā*), all of which resonate with secular and religious liberal themes of the reformist debates that permeated the Arab world in the 1930s and 1940s and challenged colonial rulers and their indigene supporters. The play should be understood, as it undoubtedly was by Tunisian nationalists of the time, as a clear response to colonial practices that included widespread censorship and control over most government and civil institutions. In addition to contemplating the recently imposed restrictions on him as a journalist, Sanūsī undoubtedly had in mind the Eucharistic conference held in Carthage in 1930, an internationally staged pageant to showcase the moral, cultural, and political superiority of Christianity at the expense of Arabs and Islam. Its adverse effects smoldered in the Tunisian consciousness throughout the decade.[34] This fusion of Catholicism with the French (and, by extension, Italian) colonial mission to civilize the backward Arab Muslim resonated strongly with the "declensionist narrative" that faulted both Islam and Arabs for the deterioration of North Africa and thus "justified" Europe's right to reclaim its lost history and territory. The widespread reaction to this congress, which several Tunisian government officials attended, was a lightning rod for further Tunisian resistance, and the timing and staging of Sanūsī's *Fatḥ Ifrīqiyā* are best read, once again, as an indigenous response to imperial French attempts to claim exclusive ownership of Mediterranean history.

BINT QAṢR AL-JAMM: A MEDITERRANEAN TUNISIA EPIC

On the first of January 1943, the highly regarded Sanūsī was summoned to the office of the German military commander in Tunis and invited to edit a new journal that would, with generous German financial and political support, help Tunisians in the struggle against their colonial government.[35] This invitation, not the only one of its kind, was part of a broad German campaign to win over Tunisians against the French and the allied powers.[36] Given French interference in and censorship of the Tunisian press, Sanūsī was not against the idea,[37] but he seized the occasion to remind his new benefactor that Tunisians were against all forms of foreign domination, not just French, and that they expected all Europeans to evacuate Tunisia once the war was over. The German official, annoyed by Sanūsī's insolence, nevertheless dispatched him to Italy, very likely with the assignment to cover Habib Bourguiba's meeting with Mussolini. As was the custom of the time, Sanūsī took his thirteen-year-old son, Nūr al-Dīn, with him and set out for Rome, only to be seized, interrogated, and imprisoned by the Italian Fascist government, which had obviously been tipped off by their German allies, who evidently harbored suspicions toward him. Father and son were assigned first to a prison outside Florence and then transferred to a detention center in Naples, where they remained for several months.[38] Back in Tunis, meanwhile, Sanūsī was tried and sentenced to death in absentia by the Tunisian (puppet) government for collaborating with the axis enemy.[39] The severity of the sentence may very well have been a result of increased fear among French authorities of Tunisia's significant Italian population, whose loyalties were suspected to be shifting toward Mussolini's government and its alliance with Germany. Sanūsī's trip to Rome clearly played into these suspicions.

In detention, Sanūsī found himself in the company of American, Serbian, and Albanian prisoners, as well as of a number of Libyan dissidents imprisoned for their resistance to Italian colonialism in their country. Among them was an elderly Libyan, who claimed to be a descendent of the Arabian Banī Hilāl tribe of North Africa. Each night, the *shaykh,* a brother Arab and victim of colonization, narrated an episode of a story about an ancient castle in al-Jamm (Tunisia). Mesmerized, Sanūsī took copious notes that he eventually wove into a novel he completed and published in 1948.

The novel *Bint Qaṣr al-Jamm* (The daughter of jem palace)[40] tells the story of a Hilāli prince, who during a hunting expedition captures a young girl living in the wild among a flock of ostriches. Taken back to the Hilāli campsite, she eventually bears the prince a son and at the same time is discovered to be mute. A physician examines her and discovers lodged under her tongue a leech, which had prevented her from speaking. Once the leech is removed, the young wife regains her speech and gradually reveals her story. However, the more she becomes accepted and honored by the Hilāli inner circle, the more she becomes the victim of jealousy and resentment, especially among the female members of the tribe. Unhappy and estranged, she convinces her husband to accompany her back home. On the way, she reveals her vast knowledge of every inch of the Tunisian terrain, successfully finding her way in the dark of night back to her village and into the family palace. They encounter, by the light of the torches they bear, the luxurious splendor of a wealthy palace and the intact corpses of the wife's father and mother, still clutching the jewel-studded vessels from which they drank poison in an act of joint suicide. In the process of reclaiming and preserving historical memory, she reveals to her husband her father's last words to her and how, facing the catastrophe of a severe draught and the fear of submitting to foreign enemy forces, he had convinced her to flee in order to preserve the memory and survival of the tribe. We are told in the final scenes that she is the sole surviving daughter of the last indigenous Christians of North Africa (*Ifrīqiyā*).

Sanūsī's only full-length novel, and actually one of a very few written in Arabic in Tunisia at this time, draws heavily on the oral tradition of the *Banī Hilāl* epic,[41] illustrating the diversity of sources from which he crafted his fiction. More importantly, his sympathetic portrayal of the Banī Hilāl tribe as positive contributors to

Tunisian history and society contradicts the long-held view, most famously put forth by Ibn Khaldūn (d. 1406) and enthusiastically embraced by proponents of the European colonial "declensionist narrative," that the so-called Hilāli invasions caused massive political, economic, and social devastation to North Africa.[42] Sanūsī's depiction of them as ultimately Arab, Muslim, and Tunisian is yet another example of how he expanded the racial, religious, and national boundaries in order to fashion for a modern Tunisian nation a novel founded on myth but firmly grounded in Mediterranean history and identity.

The locale of the novel shifts between the forests and deserts of central Tunisia and the small towns of the Banī Hilāl settlements wedged between the cities of Kairouan and Mahdiya—the sites of both the first Arab settlements and the capital of the Sanhaja Berber Zīrī ruling family of the eleventh century, the era of the Hilāli invasions. The choice of this area as authentic Tunisian heartland expands the boundaries of the Mediterranean space to include places far away and distinct from the racially and culturally mixed cities that dot the north and east coastlines. It also parallels Bertrand's privileging of Laghouat as the true homeland for Algeria's pied-noir population.

Parallel to the way Bertrand devises a pied-noir population from a variety of peoples, languages, cultures, and provinces along the northern littoral of the Mediterranean, Sanūsī binds together the peoples of the southern Mediterranean rim. In a richly colorful scene of a banquet that tribal leaders organize to celebrate both the passing of a century since the arrival of the Banī Hilāl and the marriage of Prince Makan to the daughter of Jem, we are treated to descriptions of clothing from India, Basra, Morocco, Serbia, and Afghanistan and of flags flying in the colors of Sanhāja red, Shiite green, and Sunni black, the standard colors of the Fatimids and Abbasids. Utensils and food of Phoenician, Coptic, Greek, Roman, Byzantine, Persian, and Turkish origin are evoked, as are guests from Zab, Tripoli, Qafsa, and Gabes, all mixing harmoniously under the patronage and hospitality of an Arabian tribe that brings unity and cohesion into the heart of Tunisia.

The casting of the novel's hero, the captive daughter/wife (with her three names—Aysha, Anīsa, Maryam—that reflect her transformations in identity), bears fertile literary and political significations for the novel. In reworking the oral traditions of the Sīrat Banī Hilāl, Sanūsī taps into literary terrain far beyond the generic boundaries of Western literary import and influence. The novel draws on a highly localized form of storytelling that is deeply rooted in popular history and myth. The novel's male characters bear a stark resemblance to the heroes of the Banī Hilāl, as Makan—his father and his tutor—may be read as a variation of the Hilāli Diyāb, Abū Zayd, and Hasan, while the heroine of *Bint Qaṣr al-Jamm* is clearly modeled on the Hilāli Jāziya, "the most beautiful and wisest of women, capable in battle."[43] Maryam—similar to other female characters in Sanūsī's fictional cosmos, as well as others of early modern Tunisia literature—carries an ambiguous or convertible identity that challenges historical or territorial essentialism. Her lineage to earlier Byzantine, Christian, and Roman roots and her bearing of an Arab Muslim Hilāli son, assumed to be the future leader of the tribe/nation, strongly suggest a Tunisian melting pot of races and cultures as an indigenous component to the wider Mediterranean world running through a long and harmonious, uninterrupted continuum. Her agency as a strong and assertive female casts doubt on French colonial notions of Muslim repression of woman, and her profound knowledge of the native soil, as well as every facet of its history and environment, locks horns with the "declensionist narrative" of Arab Bedouin destruction and Muslim environmental backwardness. Here, the pan-Arab, pan-Muslim, Tunisian nationalist Sanūsī recalls an ancestral memory through an imagined past, in ways similar to Louis Bertrand and other Latin Africanist novelists, to contain a hybrid and indeterminate present and redirect it toward an ideologically coherent future.

"AL-MUHĀJIR": EXPANDING MEDITERRANEAN BOUNDARIES

In contrast to *Fatḥ Ifrīqiyā,* which appropriates Greco-Roman theater to express contemporary North African philosophical and political issues in a medium and idiom of high-European culture, and *Bint Qaṣr al-Jamm,* which adopts a radically different strategy by tapping into the indigenous Arab Banī Hilāl oral epic tradition, Sanūsī's short story "al-Muhājir" (The émigré, 1936) may be read as a hybrid production that draws from both eastern and western literary traditions, a hybridity richly representative of (post)colonial writing.[44] And deviating from Sanūsī's customarily civil and rational voice of resistance to European imperialism found in his fictional work, and in contrast to Bertrand's aggressive, racist, and dismissive "Latinist" argument for sole European supremacy, the tone of "al-Muhājir" projects a direct, confrontational, thinking man's resistance that assumes a face-to-face position for both colonizer and colonized. Here Sanūsī chooses a contemporary time and space for this Sinbad-like tale of a lonely fisherman who drifts away at sea. The story takes place sometime between the death of Aḥmad Bey (r. Tunisia 1837–55) and the beginning of the French protectorate in 1881, with action that shifts from the sailor's hometown on the island of Kerkenna to an unnamed island off the coast of West Africa. The description of the sea, with its dark murky waters and frequent storms, challenges the familiar tranquil blue Mediterranean of idyllic literature. The sailor takes comfort in pleasant memories of his own bravery and skill in dealing with past battles with treacherous waters, until one day a violent storm washes him ashore a deserted island. In the tradition of *Ḥayy Ibn Yaqdhān* and *Robinson Crusoe,* the protagonist is left to his own devices for survival as he waits to be rescued. With an *Arabian Nights* mixture of fantasy and reality, he is suddenly visited by a group of young African women, with whom he cannot communicate. They disappear soon after the initial encounter, but the next day one of them reappears, bearing food and accompanying an elderly man. The characters eventually discover a means to communicate: the older man is a Muslim of the Tījāni Sufi order,[45] who had studied in Morocco in his youth. The sailor, a true son of the Mediterranean, who speaks French, Spanish, Italian, and Greek, finds himself on the shores of Africa, with only the Arabic language and the Islamic faith to communicate. When the sailor loses hope of being rescued, his life continues, as he sires children with the African woman of his first encounter and gradually integrates into the local community. The story whimsically concludes with the arrival of a French vessel, whose crew informs him that Tunisia has now become a protectorate of France. With the pretense of going back to collect his wife and children, the sailor fails to appear the following day at the agreed time, choosing instead to live out his life in exile on the island.

The geographical shift from "classical Mediterranean" to a "Saharan Mediterranean"[46] carries with it political messages that are simple enough to decode. Sanūsī contests the shape of *Ifrīqiyā* as a Roman province and redraws its boundaries to include areas beyond European reach. In ways parallel to Bertrand's project to strengthen and justify Europe's reclamation of mare nostrum, by reaching as far north into the Italian Piedmont to expand the boundaries of a European Mediterranean identity, we see Sanūsī also redrawing the Mediterranean map to include the African interior. He evokes the desert as shared space crisscrossed by trade routes and dotted with Muslim centers of learning in places such as Mauritania and Timbuktu, where the Tījāni Sufis disseminated their teachings. He brings into his mapping the North Atlantic Ocean, to resist, challenge, and best a Latinist claim to Mediterranean history. The protagonist of "al-Muhājir, a "native" citizen of the sea with vast knowledge of its shores, its peoples, and its languages, is compelled in the face of French colonialism to choose sides. All the connectivity that is evoked and celebrated throughout his other works comes to a head in a split moment of fragmentation, when the sailor opts for an Islamic identity that binds and unites the peoples of the southern Mediterranean rim to form a united front against (northern) colonialism.

"Al-Muhājir," the earliest of the three works treated above, nonetheless lays out a broad political statement that is echoed throughout Sanūsī's creative and political writing: that Tunisian, North African, Arab, and Muslim are all equal members of the family of Mediterranean nations, whose history and location are as long and wide as those of any European country. Within the colonial discourse against which his fiction is written and must be read, Sanūsī's "al-Muhājir" recognizes the current reality of a bifurcated Mediterranean in which European hegemony and imperialistic intentions sought to suppress, violate, and deny Arab claims to Mediterranean legitimacy. Like the protagonist sailor adrift at sea, Sanūsī's own Tunisia found itself confronted with European aggression—French, Italian, and German—and sought

FIGURE 12. Photograph of Sanusi and associates. Sanusi is the bareheaded man in the second row, third from the left. Courtesy of Mr. Anas Chebbi, from his private collection of old photographs of the Maghrib.

its strength and security in Islamic identity and unity, not in antiquated notions of turbans and mosques or in any romanticized visions of cultural miscegenation that often appear in the *evolué* francophone literature. It was a strength that was formed on the basis of principles of tolerance and a shared humanity but was uncompromising and had clearly delineated boundaries. Sanūsī's "al-Muhājir" echoes the voices of colonial North African indigenous resistance to European colonialism, which found its most poignant and powerful expression in the idiom and symbols of Islam, the "bête noire of the European settler community," as Dunwoodie so eloquently reminds us.[47] Sanūsī was a product of his times and a voice for an emerging modern nation-state in colonial North Africa, tightly wedged between religious and political conservatives to his right and stubborn secular intellectuals to his left. He labored through both his journalism and creative writing to envision a modern Tunisia at once Arab(ic), Muslim, and Mediterranean—tolerant and humanistic, on the one hand, but defiant in his rejection of colonial Europe's reading of Mediterranean history as its own, on the other.

Toutefois si la culture musulmane en général n'est pas près de s'éteindre, la concurrence que la langue française fait à l'arabe ne permet pas d'augurer pour la littérature proprement dite, à l'exception peut-être du théâtre, un avenir particulièrement brilliant. Les

> *écrivains musulmans se heurtent à un dilemme: l'arabe littéraire est une langue difficile, vétuste, inadaptée aux choses de la ville actuelle et qu'un petit nombre seulement d'indigènes ou d'Européens arabisants est en état de lire couramment; d'autre part l'arabe parlé, qui peut engendrer des chansons populaires, des contes ou des oeuvres dramatiques, est impropre à la rédaction d'ouvrages d'une tenne littéraire plus élevée. Il se peut qu'on parvienne à trouver un compromis, en dépouillant un peu l'arabe littéraire de son allure rébarbative et en étoffant l'arabe vulgaire d'expressions et tournures nouvelles; mais de telles tentatives sont encore dans le devenir.*[48]

The publication of Yves Châtelain's voluminous study of Tunisian literature in 1937 speaks as much about writing French colonial literary history as it does about the politics of cultural hegemony, civilizing missions, and racial essentializing, which were the hallmarks of European imperialism in the so-called age of reason and Enlightenment. The privileging of francophone writing and the scant and dismissive treatment of Arabic writing, as reflected in the quotation above, underscore both the arrogance and ignorance with which French and francophone scholarship pronounced its judgments and flexed its academic and aesthetic muscle over Arabic language, literature, and culture. The literary production, in all its forms of creative and academic writing—penned by Sanūsī, ʿAlī al-Duʿājī, Muḥammad al-ʿArībī,[49] and a host of other Tunisian and North African Arab writers and published in the dozens of journals, magazines, and popular newspapers that saturated the press from the late 1920s until the end of the 1940s—refutes Châtelain's assessments.[50] The idea of an impossibly archaic and difficult literary Arabic, known to but a handful of the turbaned elite, stuck in its static past, and incapable of expressing modern concepts, was contested and successfully put to rest through a consciously aggressive linguistic and literary reform that at once rejuvenated indigenous-Arabic narrative modes and experimented with innovative adaptations of Western models. Its goals were resisting European hegemony and fashioning a modern Arab, Muslim, and Tunisian identity. Châtelain and his like-minded Francophone cohorts—if they were unaware of the radical linguistic innovations in, for example, the widely popular poetry of Muḥammad al-Shādhilī Khaznadār (1881–1954) and Abū al-Qāsim al-Shabbī (1909–34)—needed only to go to any corner kiosk and pick up one of the dozens of periodicals to see what was happening. In fact, al-Shabbī's infamous series of lectures, delivered in the main lecture hall of the Khaldūniyya College in November 1929—the most memorable of which was "al-Khayāl al-shiʿrī ʿinda al-ʿarab" (The poetic imagination of the Arabs)[51]—aggressively derided the lack of poetic creativity and the ignorance of women in much of classical Arabic poetry. This sent shock waves throughout Tunisian intellectual and cultural circles. Al-Shabbī's radical stance against the forces of Arabic literary and cultural conservatism, and his call for a revolution in the Arabic language to express the true feelings and emotions of the modern Arab, resonated loudly with a generation of Arab intellectuals throughout North

Africa—as well as with Arabs as far away as Egypt and Syria—but evidently fell on deaf ears when it came to Châtelain and his like-minded cohort of colonial scholars. The contentious issues in al-Shabbī's lectures that sparked the furious reactions continued to be debated throughout the 1930s and 1940s, resulting in the creation of a new national Arabic literature very much "suited to modern life," dismissing Châtelain's claims.

Sanūsī and other Arab writers of his generation created this new literature by crafting a renovated language denuded of its archaic and overly ornate idiom and coining new words and expressions to promote contemporary ideas of patriotism, civic responsibility, self-determination, national identity, equality for women, education, science, and technology—concepts that were not anathema to Islamic values and were aggressively in tune with modern modes of thought. Sanūsī's fiction, as did that of other writers, tapped into Western culture, including theater, photography, film, and the plastic arts, and embraced much of its philosophical and social values. Its artistry was embellished through imitation, translation, and adaptation of Western models and the reworking of the best themes and narrative techniques from premodern Arabic literature, again with a commitment to creating a modern Arab, Muslim, Tunisian, and Mediterranean national culture. It was an all-embracing literature, accessible and appealing to a rising urban readership, tolerant but resistant to oppression from all sides; it was precisely here that the generation of Sanūsī seized the moral and political high ground from its Latinist francophone counterparts.

From the point of view of local literary history, Sanūsī's fiction lies in a hazy zone between the highly acclaimed radical poetics of Abū al-Qāsim al-Shabbī and the novelistic success of Maḥmūd al-Masʿadī (d. 1986?), which peaked in the late forties and early fifties. For with the possible exception of ʿAlī Duʿājī, widely known for his many highly experimental short stories, Tunisian and Maghribi Arabic fiction of the 1930s and 1940s is little known among the Arab and Western readership beyond the two pillars of early modern Tunisian Arabic literature. This is in good part because of the kind of literary history Châtelain was producing. Sanūsī's fiction, as treated above, nonetheless illustrates graphically that Arabic writing—fiction and nonfiction—was alive and well in the early decades of the twentieth century. Furthermore, his writing is expansive in both historical and geographical scope, giving it, as I have argued, its strong Mediterranean dimension. Arabic writers of the Maghrib were prolific readers of French, of Italian, and to a lesser extent of classical Latin and Greek literatures, as well as of premodern Arabic and contemporary Egyptian and Syrian literatures. This gave them broad exposure and a perspective that matched, if it did not surpass, those of purely French or Francophone writers.[52] Their works interrogate European, Arab Islamic, and Mediterranean histories, as they all connected and intersected with one another; these works embrace the political, religious, and cultural ruptures and continuities that punctuated Mediterranean history.

Above all, theirs is a literature—as opposed to much of francophone literature, which ignores the faceless and voiceless Arab—that opts for a strategy of direct confrontation with the European, colonial "other" to contest European hegemony and assert Arab identity. It is an ideologically loaded literature, like its Latinist counterpart, that is often chauvinistic, careless at times with historical accuracy, and oblivious to generic conventions. It nevertheless espouses contemporary humanistic and democratic ideals.

Finally, Sanūsī's fiction, very much like that of the great Tunisian writers of his time Alī Duʿājī, al-Bashīr Khurayyif, and Maḥmūd al-Masʿadī[53] is Mediterranean in its worldview, in that it rejects a monolithic or unified Mediterranean. Instead, it imagines the Mediterranean World as a shared space, or contact zone, in which different cultures, forced by proximity and overlap, possess a long history that has been punctuated by periods of antagonisms and peaceful coexistence. Because of his lived experiences of French colonialism, German duplicity, and Italian Fascism as negative forces in his own life, Sanūsī's literary project possesses a strong realpolitik dimension. His literary oeuvre, while drawing heavily from a historical consciousness and an artistic sensibility colored by contemporary politics, is still one that very much has one eye on the past and the other eye turned toward the future.

Therefore, in configuring a cartography for his fictional cosmos that extends from ancient to modern historical eras and encompasses various races, ethnicities, languages, religions, and cultures that he deemed constituent parts of an evolved and dynamic Tunisian identity, Sanūsī imagined a mapping of an extended Mediterranean—his own mare nostrum—as a space for the modern (Arab-Islamic) Tunisian nation.

NOTES

1. William Granara, "North African Literature in Arabic" in *Encyclopedia of African Literature,* ed. Simon Gikandi (London: Routledge, 2003), 378–83. I cite links to the Ottoman Empire, contacts with Egyptian and Syrian writers, urbanism, the role of the Zaytuna mosque and other traditional Islamic institutions of learning, and the lack of Berber languages as rival national languages as reasons for the primacy of literary Arabic.

2. Taḥt al-Sūr, literally "below the wall," was the name of the café situated in the old quarter of Bāb Suwayqa in Tunisia, which was frequented by artists, writers, and journalists.

3. Louis Bertrand, *Le Sang des Races* (Paris: Tchou éditeurs, 1978). On the importance of Bertrand in North African writing, see Peter Dunwoodie, *Francophone Writing in Transition: Algeria 1900–1945* (Oxford: Peter Lang, 2005), 75:

> From the late 1980s Algerian writing had been moulded by Louis Bertrand (1866–1941) whose outspoken eurocentric vision of an Algeria wrested from its Islam-induced lethargy by hungry, adventurous European settlers, had inspired a robust self-consciously regionalist aesthetic which defined itself primarily in terms of opposition to what it saw as the excessive refinement and intellectualism of metropolitan trends. Energized by the much-vaunted ethnographic realism of the contemporary colonial novel, (European) Algeria's young writers sought to position themselves not merely as recording, but as shaping a nascent algérianité.

4. Francisco Marshall, "Mediterranean Reception in the Americas," in *Rethinking the Mediterranean,* ed. W. V. Harris (Oxford: Oxford University Press, 2005), 311.

5. For a good summary of Bertrand's views on "Algerian literature," see *Notre Afrique: Anthologie des conteurs algériens, avec un préface de Louis Bertrand* (Paris: Les Editions du Monde Moderne, 1925), 1–22.

6. Diana K. Davis, *Resurrecting the Granary of Rome: Environmental History and French Colonial Expansion in North Africa* (Athens: Ohio University Press, 2007).

7. Davis, *Resurrecting the Granary,* 165–66.

8. Dunwoodie, *Francophone Writing,* 249.

9. Yves Châtelain, *La Vie littéraire et intellectuelle en Tunisie de 1900 à 1937* (Paris: Geuthner, 1937). The author devotes only four pages (268–72) to Arab writers and writing in a four-hundred-page text.

10. Ian Coller, *Arab France: Islam and the Making of Modern Europe, 1798–1831* (Berkeley: University of California Press, 2011), 157.

11. Neil Foxlee, "Mediterranean Humanism or Colonialism with a Human Face?," *Mediterranean Historical Review* 21, no. 1 (2006): 78.

12. Mohamed-Salah Omri makes this point and rightfully reminds us that "French colonies in Algeria and Tunisia were neither homogeneous in their politics nor unanimous in their understanding and use of Mediterranean history. Not all French intellectuals in the colonies glorified Roman history." See Mohamed-Salah Omri, "History, Literature, and Settler Colonialism in North Africa," *Modern Language Quarterly* 66, no. 3 (September 2005): 276.

13. Abdelfattah Kilito, *Les Arabes et l'art du récit* (Paris: Sindbad, 2009), 12. Kilito takes the position that modern Arabic literature is inseparable from European literature.

14. David Prochaska, "History as Literature, Literature as History: Cagayous of Algiers," *American Historical Review* 101, no. 3 (June 1996): 670–711.

15. For a comprehensive study of Maḥmūd Bayram al-Tūnisī's years in exile and of literary production in Tunisia, 1934–37, I refer my Arabic readers to Muḥammad Sāliḥ al-Jābiri, *Maḥmūd Bayram al-Tūnisī fī al-manfā: Hayātuhu wa āthāruhu* (Beirut: Dār al-Gharb al-islāmī, 1987).

16. Bill Ashcroft, Gareth Griffins, and Helen Tiffin, *The Empire Writes Back* (London: Routledge, 1989), 169–70.

17. Peregrine Horden and Nicholas Purcell, *The Corrupting Sea: A Study of Mediterranean History* (Oxford, Blackwell, 2000).

18. For Qāsim Amīn, see *Taḥrīr al-mar'ah* (Cairo: Maktabat al-Taraqqī, 1899) and *The Liberation of Women* and *The New Woman: Two Documents in the History of Egyptian Feminism,* trans. Samiha Sidhom Peterson (Cairo: American University in Cairo Press, 2000). For Al-Ṭāhir al-Ḥaddād, see *Imra'atunā fī al-sharī'a wa-al-mujtama'* (Tunis: al-Maṭba'a al-Fanniyya, 1930) and *Muslim Women in Law and Society,* annotated translation by Ronak Husni and Daniel L. Newman of al-Ṭāhir al-Ḥaddād's Imra'atunā fī al-sharī 'a wa al-mujtama', with an introduction by Husni and Newman (London: New York: Routledge, 2007).

19. Frantz Fanon, "Algeria Unveiled," in *A Dying Colonialism,* trans. Haakon Chevalier, with an introduction by Adolfo Gilly (New York: Grove Weidenfeld, 1965): 35–67.

20. For an excellent overview and analysis of this current round of events, see Joan W. Scott, "Symptomatic Politics: The Banning of Islamic Head Scarves in French Public Schools" in *Postcolonialism and Political Theory,* ed. Nalini Persram (Plymouth, UK: Lexington Books, 2007), 163–91.

21. Bertrand, *Sang des Races,* 198.

22. In addition to the French, Spanish, and Italians, pied-noir peoples included Greeks and Maltese.

23. The irony is reinforced by way of Camus's 1937 lecture "The New Mediterranean Culture," in which he posits a humane and tolerant vision for Algeria, one in stark contrast to that of Bertrand and other advocates of Latinity. However, as has already been noted on numerous occasions, Camus's fic-

tional cosmos does not include Arab characters of any significance. For an excellent article on the complexity of Camus's Algerian stances, see Foxlee, "Mediterranean Humanism," 77–97, 92n11.

24. Mais ce qui le dégoutait plus que tout le reste, c'était ce monde hétéroclite des quais, auquel il était forcé de se mêler. Les indigènes surtout lui répugnaient, à cause de leur malpropreté et de leur platitude. Tous ces déguenillés, qui agitaient autour de lui leur linges sales, lui faisaient l'effet d'une vermine se promenant sur son corps. Leur odeur l'ecoeurait. Leurs cuisines, s'installées dans tous les coins, exhalaient des relents d'huile, de beurre et de graillon. Sur des réchauds enterre, des poêlons fumaient; des morceaux de foie saignants barbouillaient des assiettes; des sardines frites s'empilaient sur des étals; des écorces de pastègne et de figues de Barbarie faisaient autours des vendeurs un tas d'ordures permanent; et ce que Rafael trouvait le plus intolérable c'était la puanteur de ces grands poissons qu'on appelle des "chiens de mer" et don't le bas peuple se nourrit. Il y en avait des piles, tout écorchés et décapités, hideux à voir. à voir. Ces mangeailles se rencontraient avec des tranches de citron, des oranges, des bâtons de chocolat, des quartiers de fromage. Et quel étrange peuple se pressait autour de ces officines! Rafael, qui se rappelait des Arabes du Sud, n'avait que du mépris pour cette caraille. Du milieu de cette tourbe surgissaient quelquefois deux ou trois voyous, Français le plus souvent, ou métis d'"Espagnols,' de Maltais, de Napolitains. Habillés de défrogues, pustuleux et blêmes, ils montraient quelque chose d'encore plus sinistre que le voyou parisien. Aucun n'osait approcher de Rafael, qui les écrasait du regard. Il avait pour eux une horreur insurmontable, qui allait jusqu'à la haine et jusqu'à l'envie de cogner dessus. (Bertrand, *Sang des Races,* 201–2).

25. Bertrand, *Sang des Races,* 135.

26. The entire script of this play was eventually published in Tunis in seventeen installments between June 5, and August 18, 1939. See J-35, Tunisian National Archives (uncatalogued).

27. In the subtext of this plot runs the Qur'anic injunction that the Muslim community must "invite" the enemy to a peaceful treaty before engaging in war.

28. Unity of time stipulates that all the action in a play take place within a twenty-four hour timeframe, unity of place that there must be only one setting for the action, and unity of action that the plot must be centered around a single conflict or problem. See the *Wikipedia* entry on Pierre Corneille, http://en.wikipedia.org/wiki/Pierre_Corneille.

29. Camus wrote *Caligula* in 1938, and Sartre staged his *Les Mouches,* a rewriting of Aeschylus's *Oresteia,* in 1943.

30. It is worth noting here that Sanūsī, like others of his generation, had a curtailed formal education. He graduated from al-Sadiqiyya primary school but completed only one year of secondary school. In 1917, he enrolled at al-Zaytuna University but left in 1920 without a degree. One could say that he was an autodidact, since he was an assiduous reader of history, philosophy, literature (classical and modern), and sociology.

There is no indication that Sanūsī read the texts (Bertrand, Pirenne) or saw the plays I mention in my essay. I assume confidently from his graduation from al-Sadiqiyya that he was fully literate in both classical Arabic and French. His conscious decision to write only in Arabic was a political one, but this does not negate the strong likelihood that he read, read about, or was familiar with Francophone writing at the time. My assumption also rests on the plethora of literary studies and translated texts from European literatures that were published in journals edited by Sanūsī.

31. For a comprehensive study of al-Mas'adī, see Mohamad-Salah Omri, *Nationalism, Islam and World Literature: Sites of Confluence in the Writings of Maḥmūd al-Mas'adī,* Routledge Studies in Middle Eastern Literatures (London: Routledge, 2006).

32. The Belgian historian Henri Pirenne (1826–1935) first presented this "thesis" in article form in 1922. It was completed in book form and posthumously published in 1937, and his work had a strong impact on the later Annales school of French historiography. See Henri Pirenne, *Mahomet et Charlemagne,* 2nd ed. (Paris: Quadrige, 2005). For an English translation, see *Mohammed and Charlemagne,* trans. Bernard Miall (New York: Barnes and Noble, 1992).

33. See Jurjī Zaydān, *Sharl wa ʿAbd al-Raḥmān* (Beirut: Dār maktabat al-ḥayāt, n.d.). In this novel, the characters of Mariam and her mother Salma bear uncanny resemblances to Sanūsī's Lilīa and ʿAlīsha.

34. For a history and analysis, see Ali Mahjoubi, "Le Congrès Eucharastique de Carthage et le mouvement national tunisien," *Les Cahiers de Tunisie* 26, no. 101–2 (1978): 109–32.

35. Tunisia fell briefly under German occupation, from November 10, 1942, until May 7, 1943. For a fairly detailed account of Sanūsī's "German" experience, see Muḥammad Ṣāliḥ al-Mahīdī, "Man huwwa al-ustādh Zīn al-ʿAbidīn al-Sanūsī," *al-Ṣabāḥ*, pt. 1, May 20, 1965, 4–5; pt. 2, May 27, 1965, 4–5; and pt. 3, June 3, 1965.

36. Under German pressure, the French authorities at this same time released leaders of the neo-Destour resistance party, to whom the Germans made similar offers. See Christine Levisse-Touzé, *L'Afrique du Nord dans la guerre 1939–45* (Paris: Albin Michel, 1998), 361.

37. Muḥammad Ṣāliḥ al-Mahīdī (cited above) suggests that what the Germans had in mind was actually a takeover of a Tunisian Francophone periodical called *Le Petit Matin*, which had been edited by a prominent Tunisian Jewish journalist, who was expelled when the Vichy government restricted Jewish activity. "The first Jewish Statute [by the Vichy government] was promulgated on 3 October 1940. Jews were excluded from holding most sorts of public office, including teaching in schools, and from running newspapers or cinema companies." Richard Vinen, *The Unfree French: Life under the Occupation* (London: Penguin, 2007), 135.

38. Aḥmad al-Ṭawīlī, *Zīn al-ʿAbidīn al-Sanūsī* (Tunis: al-Kāhia, 1997), 14.

39. It was after he was released from the detention center that Sanūsī learned from British diplomats that he had been sentenced in Tunisia. Unable to return, he remained in Italy until July 7, 1945. Arriving at the Tunisian port of Binzart, he was arrested by the French and imprisoned until February 26, 1947. See al-Mahīdī, "Man huwwa," pt. 2, March 27, 1965.

40. The novel, first published in serial form between January 4, and May 2, 1948, has now been edited and published. See Zīn al-ʿAbidīn al-Sanūsī, *Bint Qaṣr al-Jamm*, edited and introduced by Muḥammad al-Hādī Bin Ṣāliḥ (Tunis: al-Aṭlasiyya, 1999).

41. Dwight Reynolds, "Sirat Banī Hilāl," in *The Cambridge History of Arabic Literature: Arabic Literature in the Post-classical Period*, ed. Roger Allen (Cambridge: Cambridge University Press, 2006), 307–18.

42. This point is well emphasized by Muḥammad al-Hādī Bin Ṣāliḥ in his introduction to the novel.

43. Reynolds, "Sirat Banī Hilāl," 310.

44. Zīn al-ʿAbidīn al-Sanūsī, "al-Muhājir," ed. Muḥammad al-Hādī Bin Ṣāliḥ (Tunis: al-Markaz al-waṭanī li-l-ittiṣal al-thaqāfī, 2008), 111–27.

45. The Tījāni Sufi order was a late eighteenth-century North African mystical movement that spread to West Africa, especially in the middle of the nineteenth century. See Jamil Abun-Nasr, "Tidjāniyya," in *Encyclopaedia of Islam*, ed. P. Bearman, Th. Bianquis, C. E. Bosworth, E. van Donzel, and W. P. Heinrichs, 2nd ed. (Brill, 2010), www.brillonline.nl.ezp-prod1.hul.harvard.edu/subscriber/uid = 1478/entry?entry = islam_SIM-7537.

46. See David Abulafia, "Mediterraneans," in *Rethinking the Mediterranean*, ed. W. V. Harris (Oxford: Oxford University Press, 2005), 75.

47. "Islam . . . *bête noire* of the European settler community became the backbone of the indigenous resistance in colonial Algeria—less because it had been a consciously dominant factor in indigenous auto-representation before the French invasion than because it was quickly demonized by the European occupiers as the essential difference/obstacle separating coloniser and colonised." Dunwoodie, *Francophone Writing*, 113.

48. Translation of the epigraph: Even though Muslim culture in general has hardly faded away, the competition that the French language has imposed on Arabic impedes it from anticipating a brilliant

future in the sphere of literature, with the possible sole exception of theater (dramatic arts). Muslim writers face a dilemma: on the one hand, literary (classical) Arabic is a difficult language, is obsolete, is poorly suited to modern life, and can be read fluently by only a small number of natives and European Arabists; on the other hand, spoken (colloquial) Arabic can be used to produce popular songs, stories, or plays but cannot be the vehicle of expression for works of a high-literary quality. Perhaps they could come to a compromise, by paring down some of (literary Arabic's) cumbersome style and by padding colloquial Arabic with new expressions and phrases. However, such attempts as these are yet to materialize. Yves Châtelain, *La Vie Littéraire,* 272.

49. For the life and work of al-Du'ājī, see William Granara, "'Alī al-Du'ājī" in *Essays in Arabic Literary Biography 1850–1950*, ed. Roger Allen (Weisbaden: Harrassowitz Verlag, 2010), 79–85. Muḥammad al-'Arībī was a poet, journalist, and short story writer, on whom very little has been written. He committed suicide in a Paris hotel on Christmas Day, 1946, and al-Sanūsī wrote a short piece commemorating his death two years later. See Zīn al-'Abidīn al-Sanūsī, "Min ḍaḥāyā al-nubūgh al-bakīr: Muḥammad al-'Arībī," *al-'Alam al-adabī* (n.d.).

50. Sanūsī himself expressed the goals of these periodicals: "For four years, since the very first edition of this periodical, we've been working towards publishing a series of Tunisian stories which illustrate Tunisian life in all its various social (*al-sha'biyya*) aspects, and which present to its readers various aspects of daily life's problems in these difficult times we're experiencing." Zīn al-'Abidīn al-Sanūsī, "al-Adab al-qawmī," *al-'Alam al-adabī* (September 7, 1930): 2.

51. Abū al-Qāsim al-Shabbī, *al-Khayāl al-shi'rī 'inda al-'arab* (Susa: Dār al-Ma'ārif, 1998).

52. From December 1945 through 1946, the influential Tunisian periodical *al-Mabāhith* published a series of articles. They ranged from translations of world literature, to a series of critical studies on Aeschylus's *Prometheus Bound,* to a series of articles on Arabic literature in medieval Spain *(al-Andalus),* and included various pieces on the *Arabian Nights,* translations of Brazilian short stories, and articles on contemporary Polish and Czech writers, to name several examples that illustrate the range and scope of literary interest in the Tunisian Arabic media.

53. All three of these Tunisian writers situated fictional works in the Mediterranean. As mentioned above, al-Mas'adī wrote *al-Sudd* [The dam], which takes the form of classical Greek mythology and draws on contemporary French existentialism; 'Alī al-Du'ājī composed a 1933 travelogue novella, *al-Jawla bayna ḥānāt al-baḥr al-mutawssiṭ* [Bar-hopping along the Mediterranean], about his journey around the Mediterranean Basin; and al-Bashīr al-Khurayyif authored a historical novel, *Barq al-layl* [Night lightning], published in 1961, which deals with Tunisia during the Hafsid dynasty and its ongoing rivalries in the context of the post-1492 Christian Mediterranean World.

CONTRIBUTORS

OSAMA ABI-MERSHED is associate professor of history and former director of the Center for Contemporary Arab Studies at Georgetown University. His research focuses on the ideologies and practices of colonialism in nineteenth-century Algeria and on processes of state and nation-making in France and North Africa. His most recent publications include the edited volume *Social Currents in North Africa: Culture and Governance after the Arab Spring;* "A History of the Conflict in Western Sahara," in *Perspectives on Western Sahara: Myths, Nationalisms, and Geopolitics,* edited by Anouar Boukhars and Jacques Roussellie; and *Apostles of Modernity: Saint-Simonians and the Civilizing Mission in Algeria.*

EDMUND BURKE III is professor emeritus of history at the University of California, Santa Cruz. The founder of the Center for World History, he taught world history; French, Middle East, and North African history; and Mediterranean history. Burke is the author of numerous books and articles. His recent publications include *Islam and World History: The Ventures of Marshall Hodgson* and *The Ethnographic State: France, Morocco and Islam 1890–1925.* He also cowrote (with Kenneth Pomeranz) *The Environment and World History, 1500–2000.* He is currently completing *France and the Sociology of Islam, 1798–1962.*

JULIA CLANCY-SMITH is Regents Professor of History at the University of Arizona. She was recently awarded a Guggenheim Fellowship to research a scholarly monograph devoted to women, gender, and education/schooling in colonial North Africa. Clancy-Smith is the author of, among other works, *Tunisian Revolutions: Reflections on Seas, Coasts, and Interiors; Mediterraneans: North Africa and Europe in an Age of Migration, c. 1800–1900;* and *Rebel and Saint: Muslim Notables, Populist Protest, Colonial Encounters (Algeria and Tunisia, 1800–1904).* She coedited *Domesticating the Empire: Languages of Gender, Race, and Family Life in French and Dutch Colonialism, 1830–1962* and *Walls of Algiers: Narratives of the City in Text and Image.*

WILLIAM GRANARA is Gordan Gray Professor of Arabic and Comparative Literature at Harvard University. He specializes in Arabic literature in both the medieval and modern periods. He writes extensively on Muslim Sicily, especially the poetry of Ibn Hamdis, as well as on Muslim Christian cross-cultural encounters. His work on modern Arabic literature is anchored in postcolonialism. He has published translations in English of several Arabic novels, and his *Narrating Muslim Sicily: War and Peace in the Medieval Mediterranean World* is forthcoming in 2019.

NABIL MATAR is professor of English and Samuel Russell Chair in the Humanities at the University of Minnesota. He has written numerous articles, book chapters, and encyclopedia entries, as well as the trilogy *Islam in Britain, 1558–1685; Turks, Moors and Englishmen in the Age of Discovery;* and *Britain and Barbary, 1589–1689*. He has completed a second trilogy on Arabs and Europeans in the early modern world: *In the Lands of the Christians; Europe through Arab Eyes, 1578–1727;* and *An Arab Ambassador in the Mediterranean World* (1779–1787). He also has edited, introduced, and annotated *Henry Stubbe and the Beginnings of Islam:* The Originall & Progress of Mahometanism and written *British Captives in the Mediterranean and the Atlantic, 1563–1760*.

JUDITH E. TUCKER is professor of history at Georgetown University, president of the Middle East Studies Association (2017–19), and former editor of the *International Journal of Middle East Studies* (2004–9). She is the author of *Women in 19th Century Egypt; In the House of the Law: Gender and Islamic Law in Ottoman Syria and Palestine;* and *Women, Family, and Gender in Islamic Law*. She is the coauthor of *Women in the Middle East and North Africa: Restoring Women to History*. Her research interests include women and gender in Middle East history; Islamic law and gender; and more, recently, the Arab world, the Mediterranean, and global connections in the eighteenth century.

JOSHUA M. WHITE is associate professor of history at the University of Virginia. He received his PhD from the University of Michigan in 2012. He is the author of *Piracy and Law in the Ottoman Mediterranean*. His research, which focuses on the social, legal, and diplomatic history of the early modern Ottoman Empire and Mediterranean World, has been supported by fellowships and grants from the American Council of Learned Societies, the American Research Institute in Turkey, the Council of American Overseas Research Centers, the Fulbright-Hays Program, and the National Endowment for the Humanities.

SELECTED READINGS

INTRODUCTION

Abulafia, David. *The Great Sea: A Human History of the Mediterranean*. London: Penguin Books, 2011.

Braudel, Fernand. *The Mediterranean and the Mediterranean World in the Age of Philip II*. Translated by Siân Reynolds. 2 vols. New York: Harper and Row, 1972.

Clancy-Smith, Julia A. *Mediterraneans: North Africa and Europe in an Age of Migration, c. 1800–1900*. Berkeley: University of California Press, 2011.

Dursteler, Eric. "Bazaars and Battlefields: Recent Scholarship on Mediterranean Cultural Contacts." *Journal of Early Modern History* 15, no. 5 (2011): 413–34.

Greene, Molly. *A Shared World: Christians and Muslims in the Early Modern Mediterranean*. Princeton, NJ: Princeton University Press, 2000.

Horden, Peregrine, and Nicholas Purcell. *The Corrupting Sea: A Study of Mediterranean History*. Oxford: Blackwell, 2000.

O'Connell, Monique, and Eric R. Dursteler. *The Mediterranean World: From the Fall of Rome to the Rise of Napoleon*. Baltimore: John Hopkins University Press, 2016.

CHAPTER 1. THE "MEDITERRANEAN" THROUGH ARAB EYES IN THE EARLY MODERN PERIOD

Esposito, Claudia. *The Narrative Mediterranean: Beyond France and the Maghreb*. Lanham, MD: Lexington Books, 2014.

Fusaro, Maria, Colin Heywood, and Mohamed-Salah Omri, eds. *Trade and Cultural Exchange in the Early Modern Mediterranean: Braudel's Maritime Legacy*. London: I. B. Tauris, 2010.

Greene, Molly. "Beyond the Northern Invasion: The Mediterranean in the Seventeenth Century." *Past and Present* 174, no. 1 (2002): 42–71.

Kahlaoui, Tarek. "The Depiction of the Mediterranean in Islamic Cartography (11th–16th Centuries): The Suras (Images) of the Mediterranean from the Bureaucrats to the Sea Captains." PhD diss., University of Pennsylvania, 2008.

Lorcin, Patricia M. E., and Todd Shepard, eds. *French Mediterraneans: Transnational and Imperial Histories.* Lincoln: University of Nebraska Press, 2016.

Matar, Nabil. *Europe through Arab Eyes, 1578–1727.* New York: Columbia University Press, 2009.

CHAPTER 2. THE MEDITERRANEAN OF THE BARBARY COAST

Brummett, Palmira. *Mapping the Ottomans: Sovereignty, Territory, and Identity in the Early Modern Mediterranean.* Cambridge: Cambridge University Press, 2015.

Clancy-Smith, Julia. "A View from the Water's Edge: Greater Tunisia, France, and the Mediterranean before Colonialism, c. 1700–1840s." In "France and the Mediterranean in the Early Modern World," edited by Gillian Weiss and Megan Armstrong. Special issue, *French History* 1, no. 29 (2015): 24–30.

Isabella, Maurizio, and Konstantina Zanou, eds. *Mediterranean Diasporas: Politics and Ideas in the Long 19th Century.* London: Bloomsbury, 2016.

Kinoshita, Sharon, and Brian A. Catlos, eds. *Can We Talk Mediterranean? Conversations on an Emerging Field.* London: Palgrave Macmillan, 2017

Ortega, Stephen. *Negotiating Transcultural Relations in the Early Modern Mediterranean: Ottoman-Venetian Encounters.* Transculturalisms, 1400–1700. Farnham: Ashgate, 2014.

Talbayev, Edwige Tamalet, and Yasser Elhariry, eds. *Critically Mediterranean: Temporalities, Aesthetics, and Deployments of a Sea in Crisis.* London: Palgrave, 2018.

Trivellato, Francesca. *The Familiarity of Strangers: The Sephardic Diaspora, Livorno, and Cross-Cultural Trade in the Early Modern Period.* New Haven, CT: Yale University Press, 2010.

CHAPTER 3. THE MEDITERRANEAN OF MODERNITY

Bourguet, Marie-Noelle, Daniel Nordman, Vassilis Panayotopoulos, and Maroula Sinarellis, eds. *L'Invention scientifique de la Mediterrannée: Egypte, Morée, Algérie.* Paris: École des hautes études en sciences socials, 1998.

Burke, Edmund III. "Changing Patterns of Peasant Protest in the Middle East, 1750–1950." In *Peasants and Politics in the Modern Middle East,* edited by Farhad Kazemi and John Waterbury, 24–37. Gainesville: University of Florida Press, 1991.

Burke, Edmund III, and Kenneth L. Pomeranz, eds. *The Environment and World History.* Berkeley: University of California Press, 2009.

Khater, Akram. *Inventing Home, Emigration, Gender, and the Middle Class in Lebanon, 1870–1920.* Berkeley: University of California Press, 2001.

Raveux, Olivier, Gérard Chastagnaret, and Paul Aubert, *Construire des mondes: Elites et espaces en Méditerranée, XVIe–XXe siècle.* Aix-en-Provence: Publications de l'Université de Provence, 2005.

Tabak, Faruk. *The Waning of the Mediterranean, 1550–1870: A Geohistorical Approach.* Baltimore: Johns Hopkins University Press, 2008.

CHAPTER 4. PIRACY OF THE OTTOMAN MEDITERRANEAN

Earle, Peter. *Corsairs of Malta and Barbary.* London: Sidgwick and Jackson, 1970.

Fontenay, Michel. *La Méditerranée entre la croix et le croissant: Navigation, commerce, course et piraterie, XVIe–XIXe siècle.* Paris: Classiques Garnier, 2010.

Greene, Molly. *Catholic Pirates and Greek Merchants: A Maritime History of the Mediterranean.* Princeton, NJ: Princeton University Press, 2010.

Vatin, Nicolas. "Une affaire interne: Le sort et la libération des personnes de condition libre illégalement retenues en esclavage sur le territoire Ottoman (XVIe siècle)." *Turcica* 33 (2001): 149–90.

Weiss, Gillian. *Captives and Corsairs: France and Slavery in the Early Modern Mediterranean.* Stanford, CA: Stanford University Press, 2011.

White, Joshua M. "Fetva Diplomacy: The Ottoman Şeyhülislam as Trans-imperial Intermediary." *Journal of Early Modern History* 19, nos. 2–3 (2015): 199–221.

———. *Piracy and Law in the Ottoman Mediterranean.* Stanford, CA: Stanford University Press, 2017.

CHAPTER 5. PIRACY OF THE EIGHTEENTH-CENTURY MEDITERRANEAN

Benton, Lauren. *A Search for Sovereignty: Law and Geography in European Empires, 1400–1900.* Cambridge: Cambridge University Press, 2010.

Bono, Salvatore. *Les corsairs en méditerranée.* Translated by Ahmed Somaï. Paris: Éditions Paris-Méditerranée, 1998.

Heller-Roazen, Daniel. *The Enemy of All: Piracy and the Law of Nations.* New York: Zone Books, 2009.

Khalilieh, Hassan Salih. *Admiralty and Maritime Laws in the Mediterranean Sea (ca. 800–1050): The Kitāb Akriyat al-Sufun vis-à-vis the Nomos Rhodion Nautikos.* Leiden: Brill, 2006.

———. *Islamic Maritime Law: An Introduction.* Leiden: Brill, 1998.

Panzac, Daniel. *Barbary Corsairs: The End of a Legend.* Leiden: Brill, 2005.

Rubin, Alfred P. *The Law of Piracy.* Newport, RI: Naval War College Press, 1988.

CHAPTER 6. THE MEDITERRANEAN IN SAINT-SIMONIAN IMAGINATION

Abi-Mershed, Osama. *Apostles of Modernity: Saint-Simonians and the Civilizing Mission in Algeria.* Palo Alto, CA: Stanford University Press, 2010.

Coilly, Nathalie, and Philippe Régnier. *Le Siècle des Saint-Simoniens: Du Nouveau Christianisme au canal de Suez.* Paris: Bibliothèque Nationale de France, 2007.

El Shakry, Omnia. *The Great Social Laboratory: Subjects of Knowledge in Colonial and Postcolonial Egypt.* Palo Alto, CA: Stanford University Press, 2018.

Emerit, Marcel. *Les Saint-Simoniens en Algérie.* Alger: Les Belles Lettres, 1941.

Laurens, Henry. *Le royaume impossible: La France et la genèse du monde arabe, 1990.* Paris: Armand Colin, 1990.

Morsy, Magali, ed. *Les Saint-simoniens et l'orient: Vers la modernité.* Aix-en-Provence: Édisud, 1989.

CHAPTER 7. THE MEDITERRANEAN IN COLONIAL NORTH AFRICAN LITERATURE

Al-Jābiri, Muḥammad Sāliḥ. *Maḥmūd Bayram al-Tūnisī fī al-manfā: Hayātuhu wa āthāruhu.* Beirut: Dār al-gharb al-islāmī, 1987.

Ashcroft, Bill, Gareth Griffins, and Helen Tiffin. *The Empire Writes Back.* London: Routledge, 1989.

Coller, Ian. *Arab France: Islam and the Making of Modern Europe, 1798–1831.* Berkeley: University of California Press, 2011.

Dunwoodie, Peter. *Francophone Writing in Transition: Algeria 1900–1945.* Oxford: Peter Lang, 2005.

Granara, William. "North African Literature in Arabic." In *Encyclopedia of African Literature,* edited by Simon Gikandi, 378–83. London: Routledge, 2003.

Omri, Mohamed-Salah. "History, Literature, and Settler Colonialism in North Africa." *Modern Language Quarterly* 66, no. 3 (September 2005): 273–98.

———. *Nationalism, Islam and World Literature: Sites of Confluence in the Writings of Maḥmūd al-Mas'adī.* Routledge Studies in Middle Eastern Literatures. London: Routledge, 2006.

INDEX

Note: Page numbers in italics indicate illustrative material.